GLOBALISATION AND
LABOUR STRUGGLE IN ASIA

Dedicated to my families:
the Moores, the Carters, and the van Somerens

GLOBALISATION AND LABOUR STRUGGLE IN ASIA

A Neo-Gramscian Critique of
South Korea's Political Economy

PHOEBE V. MOORE

Tauris Academic Series
LONDON ³ NEW YORK

Published in 2007 by Tauris Academic Studies, an imprint of I.B.Tauris & Co Ltd
6 Salem Road, London W2 4BU
175 Fifth Avenue, New York NY 10010
www.ibtauris.com

ISBN 10: 1 84511 378 0
ISBN 13: 978 1 84511 378 0

A full CIP record for this book is available from the British Library A full CIP record is
available from the Library of Congress

Library of Congress Catalog Card Number: available

CONTENTS

LIST OF FIGURES AND TABLES

ACKNOWLEDGEMENTS

I would like to thank several people for their ongoing support over the years in the composition of this study. After studying and working in South Korea at various intervals throughout the years 1997–2000, I realised that my experience living in this former 'hermit kingdom' merited a good old fashioned Gramscian analysis of the international political economy. I would like to thank the publishers at I.B.Tauris including Elizabeth Munns and Nadine El-Hadi. For the development of my research agenda, I have Joo Hee Lee of Ehwa Women's University to thank for her ongoing assistance and friendship over the years, as well as David Kim of Yonsei University, Yoon Yong Mo of the Korean Confederation of Trade Unions, and Andreas Bieler, for their ongoing support and guidance. Finally, without my family, Dr and Mrs Moore, my husband Daniel Carter and brothers, none of this would have been possible.

INTRODUCTION

Adaptation to the new methods of production and work cannot take
place simply through social compulsion.[1]

South Korea's history of economic development and corresponding
political struggle is usually told from the perspective of speculators whose
intellectual investment in this nation is rooted in pursuits toward capital
accumulation.[2] But Korea's ongoing melee of labour unrest has transformed the face of development domestically throughout several stages of
what Antonio Gramsci called 'passive revolution', which I relate to global
political economic struggles for the creation and control of ideas about
how to best compete and survive in the rapidly globalising world without
complete destruction of national accord.

In South Korea, workers' battle for their rights within accelerated
development plans of several authoritarian governments throughout time
has been a prominent antagonism preventing synchronicity of development goals between the controllers of means of production, or management and state agencies, and the producers themselves. To add to the
mayhem, political strategies to downplay nearly constant labour conflict
since the division between South and North in 1948 have been influenced
by a transnational capitalist network (TCN) of business owners, globalising politicians and educators who generally aim to protect the status of
capitalism as a globally dominant, but not 'hegemonic', political economic
model. The neo-Gramscian perception of the consolidation of hegemony
requires coercion plus consent, and the logic of this kind of hegemonic
struggle is ideal for an account of Korean development in this context of
class struggle because it emphasises the importance of knowledge and
ideas for a complete understanding of power relations. Neo-Gramscian
concepts of power, discussed below and also in chapter 1, are conducive
to a study of the way in which economic development and the
restructuring of Korea over time looks suspiciously like an elite-led
strategy aiming to prepare the Korean labour force to compete within a

capitalist global system of continuously rearticulated and constructed historical blocs of the ideas that make capitalism successful.

But the growth of capitalism as an ideology and a guideline for nations' development, in particular after the collapse of the Berlin Wall in 1989, do not stem from an immutable force as the orthodoxy of positivism assumes. Instead, patterns of capitalism are based in a historical trajectory which has been both historically and contemporarily directed by elites. Capitalism is not an irreversible or 'natural' force that cannot be challenged. It is, then, also not a hegemonic ideology, but is dependent on a recognisable historical journey led by a global network of capitalists that is gradually incorporated by nations under what are most often non-hegemonic forms of state.

Furthermore, revolutions are not exclusive to grassroots movements as they are normally associated, but are also a function of unstable elites who seek to consolidate and perpetuate hierarchies that capitalism requires. In response to worker resistance to capitalist development, Korean governments have put up a fight against workers throughout this semi-peripheral nation's modern history via a political strategy that occurs during a crisis of hegemony, or when previously powerful social forces recognise the weakness of their control over the economy and society. There are two distinct conditions that reveal a case of passive revolution to do with production relations and political strategies for hegemonic leadership. The first condition requires elite-led economic development, involving exploitative worker/state production relations. Secondly, passive revolution requires institutions and elite-generated activities that facilitate the political strategy Gramsci names *trasformismo*, which rhetorically helps workers adapt to capitalist norms through limited concessions and appeals to sentiment and common sense as a resource for workers' subjectivity, which in effect, acts to re-articulate this powerful social group's needs, and ultimately prevents labour from instigating complete revolution.

Economic development and prosperity of South Korea has typically been measured by the rapid growth of its GDP, and the government's development strategies have only recently been questioned regarding inclusion of a range of voices. But what forms of state and political strategies have been necessary for this 'hermit kingdom' to adapt to capitalist norms at several levels of activity? Is it possible for semi-peripheral states to integrate to capitalist norms and achieve nationally consolidated consensus and hegemony? I would argue that this has not been possible within Korea, and demonstrate this by revealing that the conditions for passive revolution have been achieved over time and in turn, I claim that international struggles surrounding the 'best' production methods and their substantiating ideology have never permitted Korea to achieve the consent crucial for Gramscian hegemony within its own borders. A clear question here is whether it is accurate to delineate a portrait of international 'hegemony' that Robert W. Cox claims to locate in a number of historical periods, when nations themselves have not consistently or universally incorporated internationally expansive modes of production via nationally hegemonic forms of state. This conceptual challenge has not been resolved within Cox's extremely influential work (1981, 1983, 1987, 1989, 1996, 1999, 2000, 2001, 2002).

Whilst elite groups in Korea have been involved in increasingly transnational hegemonic projects that herald a particular form of knowledge defining economic development over time, workers, without whom production would be impossible, are far more sceptical. In the context of several decades of authoritarian forms of state and elite-led accumulation strategies, intense and often brutal struggles between social forces have continued to prevent Korea from becoming internally hegemonic. Nonetheless, Korea's status as a semi-peripheral state means that it has played a supportive role to global capitalist expansion.

In response to a globalising world, relatively new pressures toward conformity and convergence of particular norms are worded in such a way as to help less developed nations 'catch up' with the developed. Powerful economic international organisations such as the International Monetary Fund (IMF) have become increasingly involved with helping nations identify strategies of 'good governance' rather than simply providing technical assistance (Morton and Bøås 2003: 50), presenting leaders with a choice between the 'good' form of governance and all other forms of governance. Knowledge defining the goodness of governance has expanded to include sustainability of development and ideally includes participation of a wider range of groups toward policy making. But this knowledge is still underwritten by a confidence in the value of modernisation and growth. Agenda changes at the upper tiers of the global system of capitalism have created layers of crises within developing nations, who feel pressured to sign up for access to the 'best' knowledge for development which has been transformed within stages of development from Industrialisation to the era of Information and Knowledge.

The pressure to follow IMF and Asian Development Bank formulas for development has caused unrest within affected nations. Governments increasingly defend their decisions to agnostic populations who are not convinced of the merit of development projects based on an itinerary of experts whose advice for the best forms of governance are usually steeped in Washington Consensus goals of deregulation of trade and investment and privatisation of national sectors. In other words, leaders are convinced that they must accommodate a global system of neoliberal capitalism to survive in the global political economy regardless of the opinions or experiences of populations, even within democracies! This powerful conviction must be supplemented with a political strategy, therefore, to circumvent significant resistance from groups most subordinated by capitalism.

Resistance emerges from both camps in a battle for hegemony: both from the elite and from subordinated groups involved in struggles for leadership, or at the very least, representation. The following story of Korean development looks at two related patterns of development: the global or international convergence strategies relating to production and response, including resistance at the national level. Within nations, this process has occurred through various vocational educative channels along a network of transnational capitalists that is composed of government leaders and ministries, international organisations and agencies, and nationally and transnationally located management. Transformation of vocational education and training for the workplace, for example, has a significant affect on developing nations' workforce, particularly as transnational agencies have assumed the role of educator. In fact, as a response to workers' discontent, the provision of training for market led changes to the workplace is a form of elite 'passive' revolution, managed by the tools Gramsci calls *trasformismo*. International forces including the IMF and the UN provide organic intellectual insight of development norms to inform peripheral and semi-peripheral nations of the 'right ways' to revolutionise their work forces in preparation for neoliberal capitalism.

Ultimately, the way in which development occurs is determined by the work skills of labour forces. Knowledge and skills are becoming increasingly regulated by government-designed and transnationally directed training programmes such as the UNESCO's Project on Technical and Vocational Education (UNEVOC). The process involves the creation of partner institutions such as the Korea Research Institute for Vocational Education and Training (KRIVET), whose production of knowledge is intended to disseminate particular ideas surrounding skills, knowledge, and employability.

Using the Gramscian concept of passive revolution to understand Korean development is as yet an atypical pursuit,[3] and the orthodox International Political Economics (IPE) literature desperately needs to see more qualitative research on production relations and restructuring in relation to the global political economy. Nationally based power struggles between particular social forces can either substantiate or negate the assumptions often made by international analysts.

Why Gramsci?

Much of the Gramscian literature analyses global historical movement such as John Agnew and Stuart Corbridge (1995); Robert W. Cox and James Mittelman (1997); Enrico Augelli and Craig Murphy (1988; 1993); Craig Murphy (1994); Stephen Gill (1990, 1993a); Barry Gills (1993); and Giovanni Arrighi (1993). Mark Rupert's work (1995, 2000) represents another field within the Gramscian-inspired literature, written by a group of scholars who utilise Gramscian ideas to tackle debates within IPE about the causes and workings of global hegemony between Neorealism and Liberal Institutionalism. This literature however suffers a gap in research on semi-peripheral states (Farrands 2002: 23), like South Korea.

A handful of authors have applied Gramscian theory to cases of nationally engineered methods of incorporation of, and accommodation to, contemporary international pressures. Case studies within the 'neo-Gramscian school' or Gramscian-inspired authors include Mark Rupert's analysis of the Ford Motor Company in relation to American hegemony (1995: 59–78); Adam Morton's analysis of neoliberal structural change in Mexico (2000, 2003); Kees Van der Pijl's work on Russian transformation and passive revolution (2003); Dominic Kelly's analysis of Japan's regional passive revolution (2002); Andreas Bieler's analysis of Austrian and Swedish integration into the EU (2000a); Owen Worth's study of Russian passive revolution (2003); and John Girling's research on the con-solidation of bureaucratic power in Thailand (1984). This collection of research looks at either peripheral or core nations' experiences with globalisation. Whereas, my story of Korean development shows how a nation can become a relatively successful player in the global political economy but maintain authoritarian forms of governance for such pro-longed periods of time, even in the guise of democratic transformation.

A study of production relations, bearing in mind that I have emphasised power struggle, must involve a study of political strategies for overthrow and revolution sought by the groups involved. Production relations involve first, property relations, i.e. power relations between owners and non-owners or the employed and the unemployed; and second, work relations, referring to the ways in which workers are organised in the process of production. My aim is to focus on the power relations between forces that have amassed during various stages of economic development within one semi-peripheral nation.

These relations have facilitated Korea's accelerated development, and in the rapidly changing face of this nation's global economic identity, the production structure and production norms have been quick to change. I ask, what production relations have emerged from the restructuring of institutions and material capabilities? I observe that changing production structures have historically not involved the representation of workers' voice despite a prominent and ongoing labour struggle against neoliberal capitalist development in South Korea.

In Korea, worker strikes and student protests are the principal forms of resistance and have occurred regularly since Japanese occupation began in 1910, and these have continued into the present despite the government's attempts to quell uprisings and workers' resistance to neoliberal globalisation. Typically, studies of non-hegemonic or politically unstable societies assume that resistance only emerges from subordinated groups like those seen in the uprisings of 'global civil society' depicted by the 2003 London School of Economics yearbook. I argue that less directly obvious forms of resistance emerge from both sides of struggle, i.e. subordinated and elite social forces resist each other's pursuit of hegemonic authority. At some points, resistance itself is not obvious or physically manifest, and subordinate groups are constantly in danger of being co-opted into elite-directed rhetoric. In fact, when a government resorts to the use of *trasformismo* it shows evidence of the state's knowledge of the very real possibility of effective resistance and overthrow, and therefore works to set up a counter-resistance to these possibilities which will absorb subordinated groups' resistance into the elite's development and accumulation strategies. The elite resistance strategy of passive revolution is a 'last resort' government tactic that shows failure to achieve consensus, an important facet of consolidated, Gramscian hegemony.

Much of the literature on Korean development is written from a liberal perspective and does not speak about ground level circumstances or the effects that development and rapid economic change has had on workers. In fact, much of the literature heralds Korea's developmentalist growth as a radical alternative to democratic economic development such as that of Western Europe. Alice Amsden (1989), for example, writes of Korea as 'Asia's Next Giant', describing a formula for late industrialisation that Korea followed, with its own particular recipe of 'getting the prices wrong' (1989: 139–55). She understands Korea's phenomenal growth of the 1960s onward according to a formula originally fashioned by Western countries that have been in control of the ideas contributing to capitalism since the 19th century.

In England, industrialisation was based on invention. In the US, it was based on innovation, and later, late industrialisers (or what Amsden calls 'backward' countries), had to industrialise by 'learning' (1989: 4). Her work is part of a number of writings from the late 1980s and through the mid-90s that marvelled over the rapid growth of the Asian Tigers. These nations' development was based on a) a highly educated (and subservient) labour force, b) intimate corporate relations between governments and states, and c) the implementation of liberal institutions. Korean late development - development that took Korea from one of the poorest economies in the world to the 11th largest in the world - was dependent on the 'formation' (Kim and Moon 2000: 54) of human capital, export promotion, Confucian culture, and geopolitics. Stephen Haggard and others (1994) worked in conjunction with the Harvard Institute for International Development and the Korea Development Institute (KDI) to analyse Korean development via macroeconomic strategies. These documents praise the rapid economic development Korea experienced between 1960 and late 1990 and assess the phenomenon with admiration.

After the Asian economic crisis of 1997, several authors began to criticise flaws to Korea's market liberalisation and seemed to forget the hope and praise they had held for this nation's rapid development in previous years. Xiaoke Zang and Geoffrey Underhill (2003) chastise Korea for its failure to liberalise rationally but policy-making usually reflected private interests of 'parties carrying historical and institutional baggage' (2003: 244). These authors maintain that integrated liberalisation requires more than economic adjustment, but involves facilitative political and institutional reform. Donald Kirk (2001) looks at political scandals during Korea's economic miracle and the strength of the *chaebol* in Korea to explain events that led up to the crisis. He reports on Korea's tensions between political history and international demands for reform, but his recovery recommendations are directed toward Korean institutions and business. Timothy Lane, Atish Ghosh, Javier Hamann, Steven Phillips,

Marianne Schulze-Ghattas, and Tsidi Tsikata (Lane 1999) provide a review of the design of IMF restructuring programmes in Indonesia, Korea and Thailand. This IMF report looks at financial vulnerabilities, crisis background, programme finance and market reactions, macroeconomic environments after the crisis, and monetary, exchange rate and fiscal policies that would need to be made for fully integrated reform of these nations. The authors of this report do not propose any alternatives to the stipulations of IMF reforms but are committed to full reform of these countries' markets, institutions and policies. So a certain calibre of literature emerged after the 1997 crisis in Korea that represents the power of knowledge: a specific knowledge that is supposed to be the most beneficial and helpful for all nations of the world.

Following democratisation of South Korea, research typically brings to light the growth of 'civil society', seen from an orthodox liberal perspective that condones immutable development conditions but nonetheless imagines that democracy has provided a space for the rise of civil society groups. This literature in particular positions civil society as a positive arena for involvement in Korean democratic reform (Seong 2000; S. H. Kim 1996, 1997, 2000; Song 1994; Sin 1995; Diamond 1994). Workers are not given such a celebrated role, however, and labour activism is seen as a negative symptom of economic change. Jong-Ryn Mo (1999) outlines Korean democratic reform but notes that the relative liberties granted to workers have not been positive for the economy, and Mo is consistently uncritical of the government's efforts to 'rein in the labour movement' (1999: 110).

On the other hand, from the left of the political spectrum, writers such as Nancy Abelmann (1996), Frederic Deyo (1989), Hagen Koo (1987, 1993, 2000, 2001, 2002), Jang-Jip Choi (1987, 1989), and Barry and Dong Sook Gills (2000) throw light on the ongoing oppression of workers that has been, and is, a large part of the reason for Korean economic 'success'. However, these authors still do not fully explore the impact of attempts to integrate Korean workers into the accumulation strategies of the government and continuous attempts to facilitate a passive revolution. As is described in 2.4, a passive revolution has been 'legitimised' by co-operation with a growing global network of the Transnational Capitalist Class (TCC) (Sklair 1997, 1995, 2001a, 2001b; Van der Pijl 1984, 1997, 1998). This account of Korean development fills a cleft in the literature by addressing questions of actual elite political strategies used to apply tenets of neoliberal capitalist global integration.

There is a substantial amount of literature written to describe and understand developed nations' industrialisation and resultant frictions (i.e. McEachern 1990; Barlett and Steele 1996; Paton 2000). Less literature in the English language has been written about the impact that internationally-driven state and business-led economic development in the East Asian NICs has had upon populations. Much of the literature on topics of East Asian development has been written by Western authors in a prescriptive tone with detailed recommendations for economic and political development to developing countries such as South Korea (i.e. Yusuf and Evenett 2002; Park 1980; Kang 2002; Haggard et al. 1994). The described literature comes out of a liberal tradition that accepts the inevitability of globalization and recommends increased liberalisation of markets, deregulation of trade and investment barriers, privatisation of local services, and flexibility of labour markets.

When countries are faced with challenges to develop according to the international political economic standards put forward by the IMF and the World Bank, there is an inevitable impact on workers, but very few case studies have been conducted to address this. Dominic Kelly (2002: 130–1) points out that very little research has been done on local restructuring of material capabilities, institutions and knowledge structures and local changes are made in direct response to global hegemonic struggles and pressures. Furthermore, analyses of passive revolution are not in abundance, but include Robert W. Cox (1983: 165–7); Robert Fatton (1993); Dominic Kelly (2002); Adam Morton (2003); Anne Showstack-Sassoon (1982, 1987); and Kees Van der Pijl (1993; 1997: 128–32). I aim to build upon this literature by looking empirically at the historical and contemporary struggles between social forces at the national level in Korea throughout a series of elite-led hegemonic projects, and the conditions under which struggles have occurred. If the circumstances and social forces in analysed historic periods strongly demonstrate characteristics of passive revolution, then it can be claimed that Korea lacks hegemonic integration of international neoliberal 'norms'. Perhaps most importantly, a nation state that lacks hegemonic ideological ownership within the conditions of passive revolution harbours potential avenues for emancipatory dissent.

Analytical Framework

This section looks at a methodological tool that Cox envisaged (1981: 136, 138), and Andreas Bieler and Adam Morton expand (2004) to understand how forces interact during hegemonic struggles (see Figure1, Matrices). Cox's matrices give a framework to illuminate historical structures with reference to ideas, material capabilities, and institutions within nations, and how those are related to forms of production and engendered social forces, forms of state, and finally, theorised world orders. Both configurations of forces are important for the logic of my argument.

Cox's frameworks are composed as historical structures derived from Gramsci's concept of hegemonic historic blocs, and they are intended to provide tools for understanding possibilities for resistance from a critical theoretical perspective. Cox's depiction of historical blocs or structures as 'frameworks for action' (1981: 135) allows for a wider area of analysis in the sense that they are arranged in terms of international hegemony rather than the focus on national politics, which was the chosen context for Gramsci himself. From a 'political economy perspective, we move from identifying the structural characteristics of world orders as configurations of material capabilities, ideas and institutions [matrix 1] to explaining their origins, growth and demise in terms of their interrelationships of the three levels of structures [matrix 2]' (1981: 141). Furthermore, if this process is understood, there is a potential for social forces to create an alternative structure that parallels the hegemonic structure, in other words within similar methods but with emancipatory inclinations.

Relationships between the levels within Cox's matrices perpetuate ideal-type historical models: levels that are not fundamentally hierarchical or deterministic, and provide a 'gateway' for an analysis in deeper diachronic (dynamic) terms. Sinclair (1996: 10) argues that 'the task of the analyst (is) to specify the forces that interact in a structure, through the delineation of ideal types, and determine the 'lines of force' between these different poles, which is 'always an historical question to be answered by a study of the particular case'.[4] While matrices cannot possibly represent all of life, they are useful tools to analyse, contextually place, and link situations and events, and provide the means to follow the progression and expansion of hegemony, as well as to aid in a depiction of circumstances that provide limitations and possibilities for resistance.

Cox does not seek to construct a theory that can be tested with positivist meta-theoretical assumptions but rather aims to 'delimit the balance between the conditions that constrain what is possible and the opportunities for action' (Mittelman 1998: 74). As a form of historicism, Cox's application of the matrices he has developed is to 'validate an interpretation [of] coherence and plausibility—that is, whether it accounts satisfactorily for the available evidence' (74). Thus, I propose to include 'evidences' of the Korean case study within the first matrix, to perceive how Korean forces have worked in conjunction to manage international pressures, which is discussed with recognition of the second matrix of forces.

Matrix 1: National Manifestation of Struggles for Hegemony

The first of Cox's matrices designates three categories of forces that constitute a structure in a relatively synchronic light; those forces not yet understood in the context of hegemonic historic blocs. The relations between these categories have a direct impact on the status of 'hegemony' in the global scenario. Institutions, material capabilities, and ideas are linked within the first framework of analysis. The relationships between each level are not statically delineated, but 'the question of which way the lines of force run is always a historical question to be answered by a study of a particular case' (Cox 1981: 136).

The case study of Chapter 4 looks at the 'lines of force' in South Korea in the historical period of crisis recovery from the 1997 economic shocks that would lead to mass changes to several aspects of the Korean economy. Groups in Korea positioned themselves during the period of crisis recovery preparing for the probable 'battle' for hegemony that the unrest of restructuring could trigger. Korean IMF/state-led restructuring of the economy resulting from the economic crisis between 1997 and 1999 is specified here as a period within which a war of position can be observed. Conditionalities, in the standard IMF-form, targeted material and institutional aspects of Korea's economy. Here, I go beyond standard analyses that concentrate on material and institutional factors in the restructuring, by claiming that ideational factors must be recognised as a vital component for understanding the impact of restructuring.

Material capabilities are technological and organisational, and are also defined in terms of natural resources that are transformed by technologies and regulated by organisations and refer to society's infrastructure and thus hold the potential for reinforcing a particular economic model. Material capabilities emerge from the institutions themselves such as corporations and business itself. This category also includes institutions in charge of corporate reform and restructuring.

Figure 1. Matrices: Configurations of Forces (Cox 1981: 136, 138)

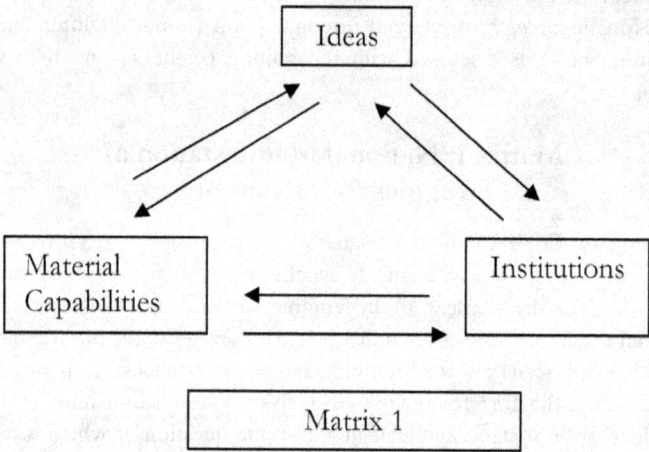

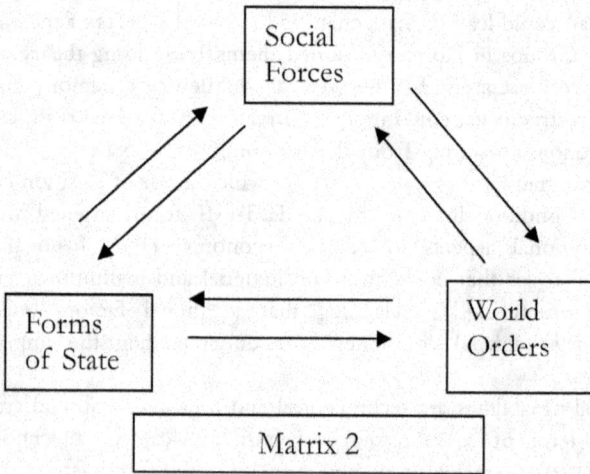

The provision for material capabilities that support a particular type of shared meaning, in the institutional context, reduces the risk of hegemonic instability or resistance from exploited groups. What can also occur during a crisis of hegemony is that the elite attempts to shape forces and to create a passive revolution. In Korea, I claim that this appeared to be happening within the state's crisis recovery initiative in the period following 1997, which indicates a crisis of hegemony at the national level.

The institutional category of forces is understood as the conglomeration of ideas and material power. This category constitutes the organisation of society; the adhesion of which requires ideological accord between members. Institutions are intimately involved in the reproduction of knowledge, and institutionalisation involves the creation of groups occurring in what appears to be a compulsory relationship of forces, which is a method of curtailing of the other forces, of maintaining order. Representation of an image of reality presented to or conceived by an institution must be either strictly shared by all members, or perceived by all members, including the 'weak', as beneficial for the common good, whether or not it is advantageous for the majority. Institutions and institutionalisation minimise the need for the use of force or power existing within a society's material capabilities, and their function is to merge ideas to the extent possible within groups, and on a larger scale, across groups. Within the case study of Korean restructuring, I look at the reform of institutions for social dialogue, including the formation of a tripartite commission, and the creation of a government funded research institution, KRIVET, that has taken charge of restructured curricula of VET programmes. VET is designed to aid workers who have lost jobs due to IMF restructuring to become re-employable, and its function is the reproduction of knowledge, which is a characteristic of production relations in the broader sense (Cox 1989: 39).

The third category of the configuration of forces within the first matrix is the ideational. This area of analysis is often overlooked in International Relations (IR) / International Political Economics (IPE) literature (Bieler 2001: 93) but I argue that it is the most important element for the construction and prolongation of a hegemonic historic bloc, if an economic system is to remain stable via transnational networks and national production relations. Ideas are defined in two categories. In the first instance, ideas are historically conditioned perceptions by members of populations of social systems and their operations, thus what can be expected of actors within those systems. In the second instance, because ideas are not universally shared across populations, there may be rivalries across 'collective images' (Cox 1981: 136). Neo-Gramscian writers have highlighted the role of ideas and intersubjectivity: 'Ideas can neither be simply reduced to interests nor (as in Idealism) be reified as existing prior to practice. It is only in human activity that ideas are generated' (van Apeldoorn 2002: 14). Rupert (2000: 26–7) writes that ideologies are the 'cement' for hegemonic historic blocs. Ideologies start with ideas – ideology is 'in the 'right sense of the word referred to the world view of a class, i.e. to a class ideology expressing a collective consciousness' (van Apeldoorn 2002: 19). Bieler (2001) aims to overcome the limitations of constructivist and cognitive approaches to the study of ideas by advocating a neo-Gramscian approach, which transcends the limitations of other attempts to investigate the role of ideas in policy making and a search for causal relationships. The neo-Gramscian advantage is that this method enables a clear definition for the creation and acceptance of the 'material structure of ideas' (2001: 94). In a period of structural change and unrest, ideas that appear to be universally accepted may be challenged which become 'the heuristic for strategies of action in the emerging … order' (Cox 1992/1996: 147). Ideas are the starting point for the power relations involved in ideological formations and expansion at transnational levels, have a direct affect on nationally observed material and institutional restructuring, and are the arena within which resistance to hegemonic leadership from both sides of a struggle is most crucial.

As stated, it is within the realm of ideas that hegemony is most vulnerable and most fought for. A group or network of groups that seeks power will apply a strategy to build a common worldview among various social classes and forces and to increase class alliances via the education of organic intellectuals of hegemonic knowledge, often through the positioning of *trasformismo*. Institutions are formulated to propagate particular ideas; a manifestation of the struggle for ideological leadership. Institutions such as KRIVET are a breeding ground for organic intellectuals, who are the leaders of society; the 'dominant group's 'deputies'' (Gramsci 1929-35/1971, hereafter named *PN*: 12); and act as both the instigators of histories and representatives of national ideologies through the application of *trasformismo*. *Trasformismo* is a political strategy to appeal to people's common sense or to provide a sense of belonging and/or empowerment that ultimately prevents workers from meaningful participation in production. It is a method to incorporate the expression of workers' needs into a discourse that keeps them in a subordinated position. It is an elite strategy to keep workers from effective revolt.

Gramsci did not restrict the intellectual to those located within the academy but states that 'all men are intellectuals … but not all men have in society the function of intellectuals' (9) and not all men fill the category that is historically and socially set for that role. Thus, to approach consensus across groups, intellectuals are the middlemen for society and the state, and any information that is representative of that society; whether its history or contemporary ideology, will:

> ... undergo more extensive and complex elaboration in connection with the dominant social group. One of the most important charac- teristics of any group that is developing towards dominance is its struggle to assimilate and to conquer 'ideologically' the traditional intellectuals, but this assimilation and conquest is made quicker and more efficacious the more the group in question succeeds in simul- taneously elaborating its own organic intellectuals.
>
> (Gramsci, 1916-35/1988: 304)

Gramsci (*PN*: 6-22) separates intellectuals into two categories: traditional, and organic, to distinguish their relations with the state. Traditional intellectuals are those who have traditionally behaved as co-operative entities with the state, i.e. lawyers, notaries and so on, those men with a 'politico-social function, since professional mediation is difficult to separate from political' (14), or court historians and obliging labour leaders. Due to the historical identities of organic and traditional intellectuals, a dominant class may find it more difficult to convince organic intellectuals of the legitimacy or their leadership than to appropriate consensus of traditional intellectuals. Nonetheless, organic intellectuals are those who are in a leadership position regarding the knowledge that is necessary for the 'best' governance of economic development, and thus are in charge of educating workers on ways to adapt to supposedly immutable and unchangeable employment scenarios.

The following section outlines Cox's second matrix. It is the setting, i.e. the historical background for the configurations of forces occurring in the national context, which the first matrix demonstrates. Dynamics between categories in the second matrix compose theorised hegemonic historic blocs.

Matrix 2: Historic Blocs, the International Configuration of Forces

The second matrix is like the first in that it is not intended to represent a totality of history; in this way they avoid the trap of determinism that orthodox forms of historicity offer. 'Like ideal types they provide, in a logically coherent form, a simplified representation of a complex reality and an expression of tendencies, limited in their applicability in time and space, rather than fully realised developments' (Cox 1981: 137). Thus, the second matrix represents global historical structures within which spheres of activity at the national level occur, represented in the first matrix. These spheres consist of:

- Organisation of production, more particularly with regard to the social forces engendered by the production process,
- Forms of state as derived from a study of state/society complexes, and
- World orders, that is, the particular configurations of forces which successively define the problematic of war or peace for the ensemble of states (1981: 137–8).

At each level, this second matrix represents a series of competing and mutually influential structures existent within a period of time. Chapter 2 outlines a history of world orders, viewing particular forms of state and social forces that emerged throughout a succession of what Cox portrays to be hegemonic or alternatively, non-hegemonic periods.

Cox refers to E. H. Carr's argument (1945) about the involvement of the social forces of industrial workers in effecting a new form of state of economic nationalism and imperialism. Simultaneously this indicated a fragmenting world economy, and led to conflicts in international relations and ultimately world order. However, relations between levels are not exclusively unilinear, but must be approached with flexibility in research. For example, forms of state may affect the type of social forces that emerge through 'the kinds of domination they exert, for example, by advancing one class interest and thwarting others' (Cox 1981: 138).

A hegemonic historical bloc is formed by the dialectic between the structure and superstructure indicating that social forces play a role in the potential solidification, or alternatively, transformation of a historical bloc (1981: 366). Cox uses the term social forces to refer to groups that participate in the formation or challenge historical bloc(s). Here, I map a history of world orders and forms of state throughout hegemonic and non-hegemonic periods to observe the way in which social forces are engendered throughout this process.

Figure 2. Economic Growth and Political Hegemony (Lewis 1984:15)

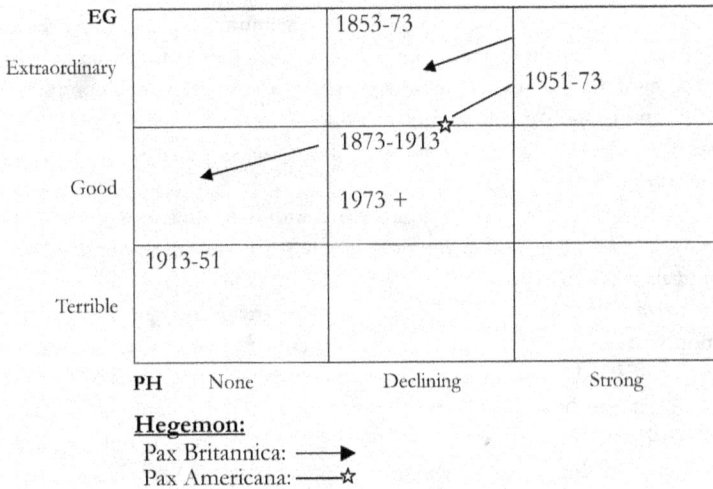

Hegemon:
Pax Britannica: ⟶
Pax Americana: ⟶☆

Social forces at the national level emerge from groups who aim to consolidate organic intellectuals around their goals for economic development. Analysis of the formation of organic intellectuals – or workers' education that intends to compose a workforce that facilitates the elite's accumulation strategies – is important because this ideologically-driven education provides a basis for the capabilities (or lack thereof) which they possess for enacting revolution and resistance. Workers play a direct role in the formation or fragmentation of hegemony, and organic intellectuals are both educators who train workers into a sympathetic position for particular accumulation strategies, and the workers who are 'successful' along the measures set forth by educators, and who embody the forms of knowledge that formulate hegemonic global systems.

A look at forms of state at the national level 'implies that during certain periods of history some states are based on comparable configurations of social forces and animated by a similar raison d'etat' (Cox 1987: 105). The establishment of forms of state also explains certain aspects of how nations respond to global hegemonic struggles. Gramsci's formula for consolidation of hegemony intimately involves the identification of forms of state, or state/society relations (*PN*: 238). The locus of transformation from traditional norms and practices of governments and civil societies, to international competition and internationalism occurs throughout the development process within particular forms of state and power relations that emerge therefrom. This is seen in the changing role of the state as an agent of global economic and political hegemony, and the changes in relations of production. The Korean labour movement can be represented by the evolution of various forms of trade unions, activities conducted, and relations with governments (both co-operative and uncooperative) over time. These relations demonstrate both areas of analysis of forms of state and production relations.

Cox's matrices analyse struggles surrounding an upset of 'balance of forces' which 'only culminate in the sphere of hegemony and ethico-political relations' (*PN*: 167), and the establishment of historical structures (Cox 1981: 136; 138). Cox's matrices are frameworks for action which are 'development of his synchronic tool kit, incorporating a series of ideal types, as dictated by the particular circumstances under consideration. They are a gateway to diachronic understanding within this method' (Sinclair 1996: 10). The matrices can thus, if fully applied/developed within a particular case study reveal potential arenas for action that can be taken against hegemony if placed in the context of history (Cox 1981: 135). Essentially, the framework is important for the understanding of transnational historic blocs, and the lines of force within nations likewise, who are not immune to international hegemonic struggles.

Interviews and Data Collection

To give depth to my claims, I took advantage of the time I spent in South Korea from 1997–2005 at intervals of work, study and research and made several contacts with people whose knowledge was immensely valuable for my work. I was invited to a particularly interesting Korean Confederation of Trade Unions (KCTU) meeting in 1999 that hosted an ILO representative, who told leaders of this militant union that they should consider the European 'service' union style of labour market management. This message fell on incredulous ears, since that very day, the KCTU President had been thrown in jail and several protestors carted off to the hospital after a labour conflict in the city centre. Union leaders were surprised to hear the ILO diplomat's words, which, while kind and encouraging, were also quite out of proportion to the travesties of the day to day lives of Union leaders and members in the post-crisis Korea. Workers and leaders told me that rapid economic and social transitions over time have perpetuated continued labour/government/ management conflict, and interviews provided first hand accounts of experiences.

I also was privileged to meet and interview several 'elites', including a Minister of Labour who authored an initiative aimed to redesign the Korean 'Labour Culture', which I discuss in Chapter 4. There are a number of issues in interviewing foreign elites and in particular when conducting elites abroad when access to institutions and organisational structures require a different set of rules and codes. Herod writes about his own experiences:

> ... to contact officials of the Central de Trabajadores de Cuba prior to visiting the island a few years ago to arrange an interview [which] was greatly complicated by the poor state of the telephone system in Cuba and the fact that one of the US operators from whom I was trying to get telephone numbers either or would not or could not give them to me.
>
> (Herod 1999: 315)

I did not encounter those difficulties specifically, probably because I had lived in the area and was relatively familiar with ways to gain information about the organisations I visited. At some points, the location of an interview was difficult to decipher but taxi drivers and receptionists were very helpful in most cases.

An advantage of conducting elite interviews is that members of the upper echelons often have access to institutional resources that would not become available otherwise (1999: 315). Public and private research institutes alike gave me full use of their institutions' libraries but also gave me several pieces of literature on the topics of labour, restructuring after the economic crisis of 1997, and vocational training. Pieces had been organised and written by Korean elites so this was an invaluable resource. Merriam (1998) writes that the provision of literature authored by interviewees themselves is part of a 'triangulation strategy' to verify interview statements, which is not as commonly provided by non-elite interviewees.

Research institutes' brochures and blueprints of government strategies such as the Labour Culture were very useful in formulating a view of Korean forms of state over time, because that material shows the way in which elite researchers, in co-operation with the government have worked very hard to create a systematic view of the process of Korean development. I visited the Korea Labour Institute's 'Labour Library' several times and gathered information particularly about Korea's labour history and experiences with restructuring. The series 'Korea Labour News', published by the Korea International Labour Federation (KOILAF) was a good resource for English language news stories of corporate upheaval and restructuring as well as workers' strikes and uprisings. Both the KLI and KOILAF were very helpful to me over the years and I am in their intrinsic debt.

Silverman describes three 'versions' of interview data: positivism, emotionalism, and constructionism (2001: 86–98). Each version answers the questions above in specific ways according to the data they seek to locate and the questions they believe are most important in order to do so. Positivism searches for the 'truth' and for facts about the world (87), and positivists aim to identify data that can 'hold independently of both the research setting and the research of interviewer' (88). Maseide criticises this approach to interview-based data analysis by pointing out the assumptions of positivists:

- The aim of social science is to discover unknown but actual social facts or essentials.
- Reality is supposed to be 'out there'. Thus it is a matter of finding the most effective and unbiased methods that, as precisely and objectively as possible, could bring out information about this reality.
- The existence of typical respondents is explicitly presupposed. These respondents are implicitly supplied with standardised mental structures that match the analyst's reasoning and use of language.
- Methodological problems are more technical than theoretical or interpretive (adapted from Maseide 1990: 4, in Silverman 2001: 90).

My choice to conduct interviews was not to find the 'truth' about Korean development, but for example, to gather information about how KRIVET researchers and other people within society view government-led development plans that include the reform of VET, during the post-crisis restructuring period. Chapter 1 critiques the epistemology, which is a term that means 'way we know what we know' that underpins positivism.

Emotionalism, the second interviewing method Silverman introduces, places emphasis on a similar aspect in locating 'facts' about the world, but is sympathetic to subjectivity and interviewees' interpretation of what may or may not be 'facts' as well. An interviewer should seek 'undistorted communication' (Holstein and Gubrium 1997: 116), and build a rapport with interviewees through story sharing and informal conversation. Emotionalist interviewers hunt for authentic information that can only be located within the interviewee's subjectivity, which Silverman critiques for being a 'stubbornly persistent romantic impulse in contemporary social science' (2001: 94). I did not use this version of interviewing.

A constructionist perspective is more appropriate for a critical theoretical research project, because it ascribes agency to both interviewer and interviewee within the interviewing process. There is no 'right' way to conduct an interview, but all interviewers are interested in the 'synchronisation of meaning' (Cicourel 1964: 100). Importantly, constructionists note not just what interviewees say, but 'how they get to say it' (Silverman 2001: 97). The constructionist interviewer therefore does not rule out historical experiences, social expectations, or speakers' limitations that could skew discussions. Before interviewing subjects, I took into account the extent to which interviewees felt they were able and free to speak their minds. At some points, interviewees shared their personal opinions of the circumstances they had experienced, whereas at other times they were not willing to share such matters.

Silverman (2001: 84–6) presents an example of some of Michael Moerman's ethnographic work. Moerman entered a research project with a particular question in mind, which he proceeded to change after learning enough information about the circumstances that he had originally aimed to investigate. He realised that as a researcher, his own assumptions must be recognised. I began the interview process in Seoul recognising that I would be perceived as a white, young, American girl, and I took into account ongoing social dissatisfaction with American presence in South Korea. I knew this from speaking to Korean people and from reading accounts in the English language newspaper, the *Korea Herald*. While simply 'recognising' these factors did not automatically enable me to act as a completely objective researcher, which indeed was not my intention, it helped me to see the potential limitations to responses. In terms of 'problematising positionality', Herod claims that 'personal physical or social characteristics of the interviewer (class, race, gender, nationality, age, etc.)' are most often problematised by social researchers in considering their own positionality as an interviewer, but he claims that these classifications are not enough (1999: 320). He stresses that one should avoid making 'essentialist' assumptions regarding categories, for example, racial or national categories and the attitudes and interpretation of these can become blurred depending on location. Furthermore, a researcher from a university of high social status may be viewed differently than other researchers, and this could affect the results of research as well as the process itself. Herod stresses that a researcher should remain aware of the following:

- The ability to consciously manipulate one's own positionality
- The fact that how others view one's positionality may be different from how one views one's own positionality, and
- That a researcher's positionality may change over time (1999: 21).

From a post-positivist, historical materialist perspective, it makes sense to claim that interview subjects are involved in the creation of meaning and of history itself. Thus I conducted semi-structured interviews with a number of elite individuals as well as non-elite members of the public, in order to gain a more complete understanding of the way in which Korean people understand rapid and often externally imposed economic restructuring and transitions within their nation. Although interviews are not the only data used to support my claims, they have aided claims about a series of particular historical moments in South Korea. Those moments are contingent and my own subjectivity is contingent, but the claims I make are meaningful perhaps because there is something at stake: the position of workers in the making of their own history.

Chapters

So Korean economic development and the historical restructuring of production have resulted in spectacular domestic power struggles that are particular to the case studied, but are evidence of a more complicated scenario and network at the global level. The struggle between social forces represents a process of organisation and production of the global reconfigurations of capitalism and resistance. In applying a transnational historical materialist methodology, several aspects must be covered to analyse the impact of global hegemonic struggles on Korean development.

The first couple of chapters of this volume introduce the rather abstract ideas of passive revolution and what it involves. Chapter 1 offers a history of IR theory in conjunction with historical events, to show that theory is not just an academic experiment, but results from people's trials and tribulations, wars, and times of jubilation. As this book intends to add to the IR and IPE, I note that this literature is often written with a prescriptive tone that makes assumptions about the inevitability of neoliberal capitalist development models, but the epistemology of 'post-positivism' challenges these ideas. The chapter expands on the neo-Gramscian terms I use to explain Korean economic and social development, which are hegemony, the transnational capitalist network (TCN), and passive revolution. I apply an unconventional range of terms to the Korean case study to demonstrate an innovative claim to a non-hegemonic status of this nation.

Chapter 2 then provides a global history of historic blocs for the analysis of expansion of world order. Applying elements of the second of Cox's two matrices, Chapter 2 looks at a history of world orders, forms of state, elite activities and the formation of powerful ideas that have fed into the establishment of specifically delineated modes of production.

In Chapter 3, I identify how Korea has been affected by global struggles and how production was restructured by elite-led passive revolutions throughout each form of state, from the Japanese colonialist government to the more recent 'democratic' knowledge economy. I link Korea's stages of development to the historical periods Cox (1987) names Mixed Imperialisms, Pax Americana, and Neoliberalism. Because Korean modern history begins after the period of Pax Britannica, I contextualise development from Japanese occupation which occurred during the period of globally Mixed Imperialisms, a period that overlaps with Pax Americana. Pax Americana is then divided into two phases of effects upon South Korea. The first is a period of American occupation, and the second is the period of Korean developmental dictatorships. Establishing the conditions for passive revolution, the chapter identifies whether these have been in place within South Korea. The chapter is a portrayal of the lack of consolidated hegemony in this semi-peripheral nation.

Along this historical timeline, I discuss both elite-led production restructuring and *trasformismo*, because these factors are indicative of governments' efforts to force accumulation strategies forward via passive revolution. Labour relations over time show that workers have never been completely pacified or consensual to state-led economic development initiatives despite elite projects of *trasformismo*, which include appeals to workers' 'common sense' of how development should occur in their nation. Elites within Korea have attempted over time to rearticulate workers' needs for such things as job stability and the legality of union status by using the technique of *trasformismo*, which has gradually given workers an increased responsibility for their own employability. *Trasformismo* is noted by the molecular changes imposed upon workers' lives and work environment. For this, I look at training programmes as one form of *trasformismo* that corresponds with elite groups' interest in hegemonic control through the articulation of skills norms to workers. Other forms of *trasformismo* can occur in an appeal for nationalism, a celebration of a work ethic, sympathetic policy-making, and other forms of concessions that rearticulate workers' needs for a tolerable work environment and protection throughout the accelerated development trajectory that Korea has experienced. In particular, the need has been emphasised for workers to prepare themselves to be employable after the economic crisis eliminated millions of jobs. *Trasformismo* is consistently observed throughout Korean history in various guises, but the overarching goal of the elite initiative is the same: to keep workers from a complete revolution that could overthrow the capitalist system of development Korean elites so rapidly and effectively embraced.

Finally, the fourth chapter is constructed around the first configuration of forces (see Figure 1), which I call 'matrices' for action, or 'reciprocal relationships' (Cox 1981: 138). Matrices offer a rigorous conceptual tool for the analysis of national responses to international hegemonic pressures and increasingly transnational relations in the battle for hegemony in the period of neoliberalism. Chapter 4 is a contemporary case study of post-1997 crisis recovery and looks at the material, institutional and ideational restructuring occurring with IMF guidance. The chapter continues the discussion of passive revolution and gauges whether, despite democratisation, Korea is yet a nation in the siege of passive revolution. Korean elites have established increased relationships with international organisations for the restructuring of the Korean economy, during this time period, expanding the role of the TCN for Korean development. The chapter looks at the impact that the government's choice to build Korea's compatibility as a knowledge economy has had on VET and expectations placed on workers during reformist restructuring. Relations at this level require a process of incorporation at the superstructural level: ideologies at this level require subjectivity of participants who 'should' become complete benefactors of those values that support a hegemonic system in order for the stabilisation of hegemony.

Here, Korea is seen as a participant to a certain extent in a global hegemonic project of neoliberalism, in that it has absorbed much of the ideologies of neoliberal capitalism and is accelerating this process in the era of restructuring following the economic crisis. Restructuring has involved deregulation of inward foreign direct investment (FDI), and financial, corporate and other institutional restructuring at the suggestion of the IMF that demands restructuring of the labour force itself. It has also involved the introduction of a new variety of skills within VET programmes simultaneous to the launch of KRIVET, a government-funded and directed research institute that manages VET curricula and qualification programmes. Looking at the three categories within Cox's matrix gives a systematic portrayal of one nation's response to the expansion of global capitalism.

In 1997 the 'great labour struggle' embodied its nickname and several attempts were made to bring labour into agreement with the accelerated reform initiatives taken on by the government, in cooperation with transnational agents. Chapter 4 does not neglect the subject of resistance to economic restructuring via an analysis of the boycott of President Kim Dae Jung's Tripartite Commission, ongoing strikes and worker resistance to vocational training, which were introduced as part of the restructuring package at that time. The 'common sense' of decisions made to execute those plans in cooperation with international surveillance mechanisms must be convincing for their facilitation. However, restructuring has not been 'hegemonically' incorporated, because the government has applied tactics of *trasformismo* to counteract worker uprisings. Chapter 4 therefore unravels this process with empirical research on these initiatives. Ultimately, my story of Korean development aims to paint a picture of a nation's responses and the incorporation of new norms and the state's requirements of the Korean population, for the incorporation into the global neoliberal hegemony, which has been conducted within non-hegemonic national circumstances of passive revolution. This analysis aims to throw light on a relatively untouched area of analysis within the Gramscian and the IPE literature alike.

The fifth chapter then concludes that the ascendance of liberal expansion of particular norms in a global context is in line with the second of Cox's matrices. Cox's matrices represent the configurations of forces in the positioning of groups in a struggle for hegemonic power. Matrices are useful as an analytical tool toward understanding of how ideology is propagated through the various levels of material capabilities and institutions, and thus how historical blocs are formed. Activities that are represented by first matrix, including institution-building, the development of powerful ideas affecting the day-to-day, and the emergence and development of material capabilities can be seen as influential upon as well as reflective of historic structures that are represented by the second matrix. The first matrix clarifies to what extent hegemony 'is' an incontestable concept in the contemporary age.

Workers' sacrifice to production in the semi-periphery is an oft told story, but production is usually viewed within very limited parameters. Cox claims that:

> Production ... is to be understood in the broadest sense. It is not confined to the production of physical goods used or consumed. It covers the production and reproduction of physical goods used or consumed. It covers the production and reproduction of knowledge and of the social relations, morals and institutions that are pre-requisites to the production of physical goods.
>
> (Cox 1989: 39)

So the innovations of the following chapters do not restrict analyses to one aspect of production, but look at power relationships as the first stage of the process of production. Passive revolution is an ongoing struggle for control over production of goods and services, and requires production and re-production of particular ideologies and forms of knowledge for its own longevity. To prevent the oppressed from enacting a complete revolution, elites have led their own revolution, which over time in Korea has guided production and economic development.

1

WHY 'IR'?
WHY GRAMSCIAN 'IPE'?

Introduction

Positivism is rooted in a way of thinking that is committed to an enlightenment rationale that is committed to a scientifically measurable and predictable reality, but 'post-positivist' theories have challenged traditional ways of thinking about international relations and the movement of history. In this chapter, I critique the increasingly popular discipline International Relations (IR) for its positivist underpinnings, and then look to the 'post-positivist' literature to establish a foundation for the case of South Korean development in the context of international hegemonic struggles.

So first, I outline IR theories from the year 1919 when this discipline was founded at the University of Aberystwyth, and then I look at the way in which post-positivist theorists have become increasingly influential in conjunction with contemporary events to the extent that positivist thinking is increasingly seen as inadequate for a full understanding of political/economic development and restructuring in the age of neoliberalism. The chapter then turns to a discussion of the specific Gramscian ideas chosen for the Korean case study of labour relations and development within the international context of hegemonic struggle that follows.

International Relations: Questioning Change

IR theory began as a commentary on the global status quo, and was based in people's questioning of, and thinking about, global circumstances and changes. Because the establishment of dominant academic theories is never completely separate from global politics and economics that inspire and effect their formation, debates between IR theorists must be seen in relation to historical circumstances. This section outlines the emergence of IR theories and the debates between authors to understand states' and other actors' interactions in relation to history, and in light of their epistemological assumptions.

The Orthodoxy

The memories of First World War atrocities in the early part of the twentieth century inspired scholars, diplomats, and government leaders to form an international organisation which was intended to prevent future wars: the League of Nations. The idealism of the League made an impact on the nascent academic discipline of IR. Idealism, or what E. H. Carr (1946) termed utopianism, emerged from the optimistic mentality at that time. However, the outbreak of World War II challenged the idealist concepts that supported the League of Nations when this innovative organisation rapidly dissolved. With it, theories in the IR school took a turn toward more seemingly *realistic* ideas that could follow the norms of natural, rational science, and a positivist epistemology was ignited. Influentially, Steve Smith (1995) referred to this pivotal moment in the nascent discipline of IR as a first 'Great Debate' held between idealists and realists, which had a lasting impact on the way scholars have discussed the origins of the discipline. Breaking IR theorists' discussions into a series of Debates has been critiqued for authors' lack of accurate historical contextualisation (Ashworth 2002, Wilson 1998), and Vigneswaran and Quirk have warned that advocates of this type of categorisation have never 'formally presented [an] argument about ideational change' (2004: 3). In response to these criticisms, I have chosen to look at the ontological and epistemological roots of early IR theory for a deeper understanding of the emergence of a relatively new discipline.

On the realist side, philosophies of Machiavelli and Morgenthau, whose writings attribute humankind with power-seeking, objective, and rational characteristics became accepted after the outbreak of WWII, and optimistic ideals surrounding the ideas of international harmony waned. IR Realism is the theoretical viewpoint that a) prioritises states' behaviours toward one another, b) assumes that power is sought at the state level, and c) believes that these phenomena drive all international relations. Along similar lines to Morgenthau's conviction of the rational nature of individuals which claimed rational and power-seeking *states* are the most important actors, theorists expected states to behave as 'unitary-rational agents' (Waltz 1986: 331); and expected a type of anarchy at the international level to shape states' motives for action, even when faced with a situation wherein potential cooperation would meet all participants' best interests. These ideas flourished during a time when the system of international relations seemed to be anarchic, with no overarching rules of global governance or regulation of states.

Morgenthau's *Politics Among Nations* (1948) is what Burchill calls a 'realist textbook', written just after the end of the Second World War (Burchill 2001: 77). This text influenced the US academic community greatly, as methodologies and assumptions of natural science simultaneously entered the forefront of scholarly pursuit, and relied on the language of 'laws and principle, objectivity, and science' which is embedded in a positivist epistemology. Morgenthau authored the 'six principles of political realism' (adapted here from ibid.: 79–80):

1. Politics is governed by objective laws, rooted in human nature.
2. The key to international politics is power.
3. The form and nature of state power will vary contextually but will remain consistent overall.
4. States are NOT moral agents, despite some state behaviour being linked to moral/ethical implications.
5. No universal set of moral principles – language of morality used by states for pursuit of power.
6. Political sphere is ultimately autonomous from other human concerns.

These core principles of realism pervaded IR theory during the early stages of the discipline and not surprisingly, hopes for mutually supportive international and/or intergovernmental organisational networks that the League had promoted simultaneously ebbed. In fact, all transnational channels for cooperation were radically blocked by the time the Second World War began (Van der Pijl 1997: 130). IR became a kind of science based in a predominantly positivist epistemology.

The positivism of orthodox methodology restricted and still restricts IR researchers amongst the orthodoxy from more pervasive examinations of sources of power and change in international relations, and does not permit extensive normative analysis of world order in historical context. Critics have pointed out that realism does not account for social activity beyond structurally determined behaviour (Bieler 2000). According to Cox, positivism assumes that the 'universality of ... basic attributes of the social system comes to be perceived as standing outside of and prior to history' (Cox 1985/1996: 53). While idealists aimed to portray a world as they 'might like it to operate, realists strive to show how the world really operates' (Ferguson and Little 2004: 3) in a pessimistic way, and this debate continued throughout the 1940s and 50s. Soon, realists' methodologies were called into question, because despite Waltz's 'scientific' requirement of IR studies for parsimony, very few studies were based on anything but broad generalisations in international relations.

The 1960s and 70s

The 1960s and 1970s saw an emergence of a range of voices in IR theory, and increasingly, the realist agenda and previous epistemological assumptions were evaluated in the light of emerging global inter-dependence and an influential set of transnational actors which could not be categorised as 'states' in the traditional sense. The increase in interdependence of economic trade and investment and the neoliberal policies of American President Reagan and British Prime Minister Margaret Thatcher prompted theorists to reassess the global spectrum, and adapt the claims of realism accordingly. Kuhn's work (1996) influenced the way that we describe this 'interparadigm debate'.

Liberalism and a series of neo-Marxist writers began to influence IR theory with a strong reminder toward a range of voices in international society that were not represented in the state-centric theoretical paradigm of realism. The third debate within IR occurred between the traditional school of realism, the liberal paradigm that focused on interdependence and sought the influence of liberal internationalism, and a school that sought to include neo-Marxist, postpositivist ideas into the discourse.

The three schools of thought within the interparadigm debate were not themselves unprecedented entities, but events and politics at the international level influenced a repositioning of theories within each school. This debate began to widen the realist perspective to observe the power of multilateral institutions, but still presumes that state power is the ultimate driving force for international relations. Neorealism analyses structural totalities that determine politics. It is a theoretical school that 'claims to surpass its predecessors by offering a "truly scientific" rendering of its subject matter—an objective, theoretical rendering, which breaks radically with its predecessors' allegedly commonsensical, subjectivist, atomistic, and empiricist understandings' (Ashley 1986: 257). As a subtle move away from the traditional realism, neorealism incorporates ideas regarding the hierarchy of relations between influential actors in the global arena who struggle to sophisticate and possess hegemony in the global arena. Neorealism takes from realism the idea that states are primarily interested in power. But neorealism utilises predominantly the explanatory variable of capabilities between states rather than power politics alone. Nonetheless, it still treats the given world as a kind of natural order and does not consider history and historical change.

Neorealists, including Kenneth Waltz (1979), Paul Hirst and Graeme Thompson (1996), and Robert Keohane and Helen Milner (1996) continued the positivist tradition initiated by realists, but the atmosphere of Cold War détente, along with increasing interaction between non-state actors, challenged the realist unitary state focus. Waltz's 1979 work on international politics defends the concept of balance of power, as was evident in the Cold War, and claims that this global situation is a *natural* and *self-perpetuating* international state of affairs. Neorealism established the orthodox theory as a theory within social *science*. These overtones of positivist epistemology are part of the development of orthodox realist theory to neorealism. One important theory of this school is that of the hegemonic stability theory, which maintains that 'for maintaining freer trade and a liberal flow of capital and aid ... leadership is necessary in the absence of delegated authority' (Kindleberger 1973: 307). The theory advocates a single-country control of international regimes whose relations are regulated by agreed rules. In this understanding of hegemony, states accept leadership of a singular hegemon because their leaders believe that a world system of this nature is the best option and will perpetuate world stability. The most powerful state is granted legitimacy by other states.

Peter Burnham states that hegemonic stability theory is insufficient for research on economic behaviour and decline, and collective action (1991: 73). He references Strange (1987), Snidal (1985), and Guerrieri (1988) whose works show that the hegemonic stability theory is 'dead' outside of a cosseted group of American realists. Before these authors engaged with the concept, Lenin, Russian Marxists, and Gramsci had pondered the idea of hegemony, divulging more complete theories than realist attempts had offered, i.e. of *how* and *where* hegemony is consolidated. Gramsci's theory of hegemony contributed to postpositivist critical IPE theory which transcends the determinist and incomplete realist and neorealist configurations, and fills in some gaps left by the Russian Marxists likewise.

Ashley (1986: 290–3) critiques classical realism and neorealism for their neglect to perceive objects of analysis as *historical* constructions, and comments on the constraints of neorealism by stating that it does not account for the limits and possibilities for action in different places and times. Furthermore, the neorealist actor is not ascribed agency, consciousness or the capability of effecting or affecting their social environment. The role of the actor is simply to support the system within which s/he lives; her role does not fall within the construction or maintenance of the world.

Orthodox IR theories do not account for historical change, sources of change, or in studies of hegemony the '*rise* of hegemons in the first place' (Keohane 1986: 179). Neorealism, like realism, focuses on power as the primary motivation for state action, and does not question the origins, basis or limits of power. The historicism of neorealism is such that politics are not seen as important or relevant for the economic behaviour of states that occurs within economic constraints. Realism and neorealism adopt a positivist assumption of static truths, which can be located only in the external object. Realism does not account for morality in the political sphere, since state activity is seen to be carried out for very clear reasons of self-help and survival that are not concerned with normative considerations of, for example, citizen welfare. Neorealism stresses material forces enabled by state activity, nor address the importance of how social forces work in the establishment of world orders. Neorealism, in fact, does not recognise forms of state or the normative and institutional factors that contribute to their prolongation, as later theorists did.

Also in the 1970s, a group of 'post-positivist' theorists began to challenge the orthodoxy of these schools' epistemological assumptions. The post-positivist, third paradigm of thought within the debate brought neo-Marxist ideas to the table, and *dependencia* (dependency) and world systems theories (WST) served to address some of the missing elements for analyses of contemporary global affairs left by realism and liberalism. *Dependencia* theory emerged after World War II in protest to classical economic theories that ignored the plight of less advanced and developing nations. Raul Prebisch, former head of the Central Bank of Argentina, was involved in the formulation of a new way of thinking about international political economics, which he hoped could acknowledge different social norms and behaviours within an increased variety of nations. Prebisch was head of the United Nations Economic Commission for Latin America (ECLA) that hoped to locate an organic Latin American voice regarding development. Several South American populist regimes applied the ECLA strategy in the 1950s to adopt an import substitution model, only to begin the 1960s with severe unemployment and economic downturns.

The ECLA was soon critiqued for following a parallel line for analysis to orthodox economic theories, and a series of *dependencia* theorists, led by Andre Gunder Frank (1970, 1971, 1978), began to call for a return to Marxist and neo-Marxist thought to understand the exploitations within the increasingly international system of economics. Theorists noted that underdevelopment of the periphery was a result of loss of economic surplus to the centre. These thoughts challenged the liberal ideals of the ECLA, and theorists Furtado (1963), Sunkel (1972), Dos Santos (1970), and Cardoso and Faletto (1970) critiqued the modernisation strategies that the Commission promoted, for the dependent relationships it began to build between developing and developed nations.

The 'basic hypothesis' of *dependencia* theories is that 'development and underdevelopment are interdependent structures within the global economic system' (Peet 1991: 45). This hypothesis challenged the classical economic theories of comparative advantage that assume exchange of industrial products from core states for peripheral nations' primary goods can benefit every nation, and that these exchanges will result in an ongoing, natural course of countries' evenly paced economic development. Modernisation theories were also greatly challenged by *dependencia* analysis; the latter of which is reliant on the understanding that capitalist development of the core requires the blocking of peripheral nations' development.

However, in the late 1970s, Immanuel Wallerstein led a group of radical scholars at the Fernand Braudel Center for the Study of Economies, Historical Systems, and Civilization at the State University of New York (Binghamton). This was a concerted response to a range of international activities that they claimed could not be researched and explained by the *dependencia* school (So 1990: 168–9). WST incorporates several of its theoretical contributions of *dependencia* but questioned this school's inability to account for development of the semi-periphery. Furthermore, WST re-located the focus of analysis to historical time and space, and identified the contemporary global status quo as having emerged from power relations and the construction of three layers of transhistorical interrelations during the European industrial revolution. WST shows that the economic organisation of a world economy is a 'single, worldwide division of labour that unifies the multiple cultural systems of the world's people into a single, integrated economic system' (Thompson 1992: 24; see Wallerstein 1979: 5). Wallerstein pointed out that economic and political *colonisers* are at the pinnacle, or core, of world systems of exploitation. Economically operative but not expansive countries are semi-periphery units; and the exploited 'periphery' nations exist at the lowest rung of the system. In his analysis, Wallerstein views European countries as the core during early industrialisation and in the contemporary environment; the USA has become an influential core.

Now, the Asian Tigers can be classified as semi-peripheral states: states that have consciously accelerated development to achieve international norms of production, finance and trade. Semi-peripheral nations are sites for industry and production used by core nations for the labour cost benefit. In this way, semi-peripheral nations support the global system but do not ultimately dictate their own development. They also demonstrate characteristics from both the core and the peripheral categories, and act as an intermediary between their power struggles. Semi-peripheral states usually require state intervention to implement expected courses of development and to provide some protection from core competition. Because these states are stronger than peripheral states but are unable to develop to the complete standard of a core state, political instability is often rife within these nations. South Korea has demonstrated both elements of semi-peripheral nation status, but while WST seeks to analyse inequalities and exploitation within development to some extent, theorists do not identify the way in which nations, in practice, incorporate development expectations such as those outlined by the IMF or other transnational actors. World systems analyses often make assumptions about systemic laws that determine the status of countries according to stages of economic development with a deterministic lens of positivism.

What was needed, therefore, was a theoretical backbone for research that could look at the influence and impact of international structures on national settings and vice versa, but would not view either international systems or the negotiation between national and international as based on inevitable circumstances or events. In the next section, I continue the critique the meta-theoretical limitations of positivist epistemology, and look at a group of critical post-positivist theorists who became influential in the 1980s and seemed to have the key for the future of IR. Neo-Gramscian analysis allows the analysis of nations' interplay of social forces and the understanding of how global hegemonic production structures have been translated and incorporated into national settings through specific political strategies of passive revolution. This school of thought also recognises that global hegemony is dependent upon not just the direct domination of one state over other states. Metaphorically, the Gramscian view of consent and coercion is applied to the international within neo-Gramscian literature.

The Critical Turn

In the era of globalisation and transnational economic and political relations, there is a need for an epistemology that empowers social actors, rather than the confinement of events and action to inevitable positivist 'universalities' of the global status quo. There is a need for increased analysis of political and social involvement of international, historical changes that transcend the pursuits within the orthodox IR camps. The missing 'link' within positivism has led to a significant shift to a post-positivist pursuit within IR and IPE theory to explore the avenues of critical theory, and Robert Cox's work represents this shift. His writings challenge the status quo and open a space for critique of the orthodoxy, and to locate theory that 'is at the service of the weak rather than the strong' (Cox 1992/1996: 504). The following section outlines the shifts to contemporary theories of IR, demonstrating that there are alternatives to the previously dominant position of positivism.

Neo-Gramscian IPE

Antonio Gramsci was the General Secretary of the Communist party from the autumn of 1924–1926 during the period of Mussolini's rule in the Italian State of the early twentieth century. Gramsci was not spared when the fascist Mussolini dictatorship decided to cleanse parliament and society of wayward thinkers, and the hunchbacked activist was incarcerated with a 20-year sentence beginning in 1927. While his body was kept prisoner, his mind clearly did not stagnate and in prison, Gramsci wrote 2,848 pages of notes by hand, gripped by the question of why Italian civil society had not risen to overthrow the oppressive state. His conclusion was that Italian leaders had achieved a specific form of hegemony that requires coercion of societies, as well as consent, that can only be achieved through a penetration of the core of institutions and consciousness that compose civil society itself.

In the *Prison Notebooks* Gramsci refers to Marx's work as 'philosophy of praxis', which is one of a number of coded terms he used to refer to potentially incriminating ideas under the conditions of imprisonment. Marx had written that:

> Men make their own history, but they do not make it as they please; they do not make it under self-selected circumstances, but under circumstances existing already, given and transmitted from the past. The tradition of all dead generations weighs like an Alp on the brains of the living.
>
> (Marx 1852)

Gramsci's understanding of historicism to a large extent was an adaptation of Marx's impressions and encouraged a 'revolutionary perspective ... [whose] practical function is the modification of social existence and existing social arrangements' (*PN*: 219). So people and their behaviour are not simply determined by their circumstances as is suggested in structural Marxism and idealism, but people are the creators of history.

Robert Cox introduced Gramsci's concept of hegemony to IR theory with his seminal article 'Social forces, states and world orders: beyond international relations theory' (1981), which cleared a space for invaluable critical theoretical research on ideas of hegemony, passive revolution, and the impact of social forces on history and theory. Scholars of the neo-Gramscian and what Burnham (1991) calls the 'Amsterdam School' (Van der Pijl 1984; Overbeek 1990) use Gramsci's particular understanding of the relations that perpetuate hegemony to analyse *international* expansion of world order rather than Gramsci's predominantly nationally focused writings. The incorporation of these ideas demonstrates a clear shift from positivist theorising inherent to the orthodox IR and into the critical arena of IR theory.

Gramscian-inspired work explores questions of power and social relations of production which provides a framework to analyse hegemonic processes, with the allusion that a national expression of world hegemonic transformations is the ultimate evidence of a hypothetical progression of world history and theory itself. Rupert has called the historical global phenomenon capitalism and the historic periods identified over a contemporary trajectory of political economic activity a case of 'liberal globalization' (Rupert 2000: 45–9), while Cox (1987: 111–50) has discussed the 'emergence' and 'consolidation' of the 'liberal world order'.

What distinguishes Gramsci from other Marxist writers is the analysis of a diverse range of social forces that participate in the formations of historical blocs. This analysis has inspired research by Gramscian neophytes, but these writers do not restrict their analyses to the economic sphere alone. Neo-Gramscians recognise that sustainability of economic practices in a nation requires more than forced change. Ideological consent is the gateway for complete consolidation and thus requires extensive analysis for the understanding of how the elite class actually works to achieve control in this area. 'Elites lead historic [hegemonic] blocs understood in the Gramscian sense as coalitions of social forces bound by consent and coercion' (Sinclair 1996: 9).

'New Gramscians', by exploiting Gramsci's interventions and applying them to a contemporary scenario:

> ... adopt a broad historicist or historical materialist framework to examine the structural organisation of world order, and focus upon the emerging terrain of global civil society as the principal battle-ground over which the struggle for world hegemony is now occurring.
>
> (Germain and Kenny 1998: 71)

My analysis of Korea's subjection to the global surveillance and structuring organisations of the IMF and the UN through UNESCO agencies in the following chapters demonstrate that these entities have directly played a role in Korean economic, political and social development. The struggle against externally generated, but internally affective phenomena is seen at the level of workers and unions, groups that compose a fraction of civil society. The arenas of Korean civil society who question IMF restructuring that occurred in response to economic crisis tend to reassess the depth of a material environment of capitalism in South Korea. Therefore, contemporary Gramscian-inspired work aids in my contextualisation of Gramscian theories about the state, civil society, social forces, and historicism to bring to light a contemporary global hegemonic struggle surrounding neoliberal capitalism.

What differentiates the neo-Gramscian/Coxian methodology from other methodologies is its analysis of social relations of production. Contrasting perspectives and resulting relations between institutions within the superstructure of Korean society represent the tensions within the social relations of production. The struggle for hegemony over production in Korea has resulted in class formations and divisions that are evident among the corporate, intellectual, and political arenas. Within the first category, corporate forces are represented by business formations over time and the expansion of transnational capital. The second category of intellectualism encompasses workers, research institute personnel and think-tanks within the research sector. Within the third category (political), trade unions and states and the relations between these institutions over time, play a role.

A neo-Gramscian perspective therefore views not just production processes, but emphasises a more inclusive view: the 'social relations of production'. Cox writes that the consolidation and sustenance of hegemony are dependent on the social relations of production.

> Production ... is to be understood in the broadest sense. It is not confined to the production of physical goods used or consumed. It covers the production and reproduction of physical goods used or consumed. It covers the production and reproduction of knowledge and of the social relations, morals and institutions that are pre-requisites to the production of physical goods.
>
> (Cox 1989: 39)

Tooze (1990) writes that:

> ... a Gramscian analysis ... denies the very possibility of 'objective' theory which is the epistemological bedrock of orthodoxy and explains, in a non-determinist frame, its own emergence as well as explaining the emergence of other perspectives as part of the global political economy itself ... a Gramscian political economy is inherently reflexive.

Thus the epistemology of Gramscian-inspired writers strays from the orthodoxy, or the positivist notion that objective understanding of events is possible. The above quote indicates further the shift from the logical, empiricist positivism that dominated IR thought since the 1960s, to a strain of critical IPE. The shift is shown by the gradual recognition of distinctions between subject and object, the decrease of distinction made by both realists and idealists between morality and politics, the notion of agency, the reopening of history as a resource for understanding, the inclusion of politics and political economics in analysis of IR topics – generally, the reassessment altogether of what is important within international relations.

This shift in the discipline has emerged as international politics and economics have become more and more intertwined due to business, government, and class networks that increasingly develop across the globe. Ultimately, the burgeoning global struggle for ideological hegemony and ownership of ideas in the contemporary world order is seen by conducting a case study of South Korea's passive revolution, a project intended to advance Korea's international competitiveness as well as to incorporate workers into internationalisation measures.

Hegemony

Hegemony is the prolongation of certain systems within which economics and politics interact, and social forces move, but there are quite distinct differences among theories of hegemony. Whilst the theory of hegemony can be traced back to the ancient Greeks, the modern concept of hegemony originates from ideas within the Third International regarding strategies of the creation of the Soviet state and the Bolshevik Revolution, and Machiavelli's ideas of consent and coercion. The idea of the Third International was that the working class would formulate partnerships and ally with other subordinated groups, aiding in revolutionary goals. This is similar to Lenin's work inspired by the Russian Labour movement that emerged to contest Tsarism. Lenin's, and the Russian Marxists' under-standing of hegemony is thus revolutionary in essence, and requires solidarity across groups of the working class with other groups.

Gramsci responded to Lenin's ideas on alliances between classes with the claim that hegemony cannot be fully achieved if the class in some role of coercion does not address national-popular interests rather than its own interests alone. Gramsci wrote in the 1920s, but his ideas were not revived until 60 years later. In the meantime, realist and neorealist conceptions of hegemony allow this form of state power to be evident in a unipolar sense alone, and can only account for political power supported by military capability. Orthodox ideas of hegemony maintain that one nation has superior economic strength over other nations that retain control over the globally important technological sector. The attractiveness of Gramsci's ideas is that they apply to a wider range of cases and a more complex range of analyses than orthodox theories of hegemony.

Gramsci's understanding of hegemony requires more than dominance or leadership, and necessitates more than Lewis's determinist framework of hegemonic leadership as related to economic growth (see Figure 2). Gramscian hegemony is not simply a material condition of power and economic strength, as neorealism imagines, but its 'decisive' elements are cultural and ideological. The General Secretary's work was preceded by Lenin's revolutionary conceptions of hegemony from the Russian Labour Movement in the late 19th century and the Third International regarding strategies of the creation of the Soviet state and the Bolshevik Revolution, and by Machiavelli's ideas of consent and coercion. Gramsci's innovation was not just an unprecedented concept of hegemony, but also the analysis of elite behaviour that occurs during crises of hegemony, such as passive revolution, as elites aim to recapture hegemonic power. Whereas subordinated groups are most often considered to contain 'revolutionary' motives, Gramsci considered that dominant classes enact revolutions with power-seeking motives. Passive revolution creates an ambiguity between resistance and rule by merging ideologies of both in a manner less obviously coercive but coercive all the same, through the use of *trasformismo*. In the case of fascist Italy, hegemonic leadership applied to situations such as the capitalism of northern Europe in which the petty bourgeoisie and workers were absorbed into state strategies through concessions and allowed them leadership roles that were intended to provide an overall harmony. While Italian leaders may have achieved hegemonic status, I aim to identify power relations and strategies in the semi-peripheral nation of Korea that have occurred in the absence or struggles for hegemony.

In Gramsci's notes on the Prince, or the political party, he envisages a metaphor of the Greek centaur, half animal and half human, which is a symbol of a 'dual perspective' (*PN*: 169–70) of how representatives of a class enforce coercion as well as enhance consent over and with subordinate classes. The hegemony referred to by this metaphor is not a direct domination in the realist sense of authority over the ruled, but involves ideological leadership. Gramsci's use of the words *direzione intellettuale e morale* (leadership, direction) can be equated with his use of *egemonia* (hegemony) as they are applied interchangeably, while *dom inaione* (domination) clearly diverges in his work in the *Prison Notebooks*. Gramsci acknowledges that leadership within an effective hegemony requires not just military rule but involves more complex direction and even incorporation and integration of classes into the state, to the extent that they are no longer distinguishable.

Gramsci thus weighed Lenin's idea of hegemony with the idea that the capitalist class or its representative's actions may ultimately gain state power, and maintain that power. Gramsci questioned why Lenin's and

Marx's prophecies for overthrow of oppressive governments had not occurred, and reasoned that civil society must have some say in the workings of hegemony. So hegemony within a particular bloc of history involves consent as well as some amount of coercion: ideological leadership and consolidation is the cohesion that maintains hegemonies. The analysis of historical blocs is an instrument for the 'creation of conscious history' (Salamini 1981: 28–9) that is seen in the ideological consolidation of interests. Hegemony can become consolidated from the revolution of the oppressed classes, but also emerge from the formation of new classes via one class's strategic activity. A class becomes hegemonic when it effectively transcends its corporate phase of solely representing its own interests but succeeds in representing universally, at least in rhetoric, the main social forces that form a nation. Gramsci (*PN*: 180–95) noted that there are three levels of consciousness in the trajectory toward hegemony. The first level is *economico*-corporative, wherein only one group's interests are represented. The second level is that of solidarity and class-consciousness of a social class in its entirety which remains at the economic level. The third level is hegemonic because the interests of subordinate classes are incorporated into a universally accepted ideology.

Gramsci came to his conception of hegemony and historical blocs from the knowledge of hierarchical structures *within* a state and was interested in national struggles for leadership. So is Gramsci's hegemony valuable for contemporary research, during which time *international* forces struggle for hegemonic leadership, a battle that divides national groups in unprecedented ways? The neo-Gramscian school has incorporated Gramsci's ideas to accommodate for contemporary phenomena in ways that will be delineated.

Neo-Gramscian writers utilise the concept of historical blocs but expand its application to look at contemporary struggles for *international* hegemony, building on earlier conceptual developments envisioned by WST for a broad division of labour. Cox has been the most prolific in his writings on the formation of historical blocs over time. He writes that historical blocs are formed around ideas, institutions and material capabilities (see Introduction, Figure 1), and the relations between these forces are both a reflection of, and the creators of international historical blocs. The manifestation of struggles for international hegemony emerges with a discussion of world orders, forms of state, and social forces (see Introduction, Figure 2). Cox discusses a trajectory of power relations that have constructed what he reasons holds the potential for being a contemporary historical bloc of global neoliberal capitalism, a description that applies to both the national and the international progression of events. Cox (1987: 106) writes that powers of principal states and forms of state have changed the global distribution of production, and that this transformation has further altered the structures of power relations and productive powers within states that are affected by the new global configuration. Cox (1987: 111–271) places these relatively abstract concepts into empirical context with an analysis of hegemonic struggles that occurred via the expansion of particular forms of state and production relations that have resulted in a contemporary hegemonic struggle around neoliberal capitalism.

Because I aim to identify conditions for a series of non-hegemonic passive revolutions in Korea that have forced capitalist development forward, for the sake of comparison, the question of what hegemony 'looks like' is crucial. Femia outlines three phases of hegemony from a Gramscian perspective (1981: 47). First, 'integral' hegemony means that at social and ethical levels of society, the relationship between rulers and ruled is devoid of contradictions or antagonisms. An integral hegemony does not know opposition because the leading group has integrated all potential opposing ideas into its own leadership rhetoric. A less austere phase is 'decadent' hegemony. In this form, a bourgeois economy and the ideas that once lent legitimacy to the leading group appear outdated and outmoded. A decadent historical bloc shows signs of decay, meaning that 'the potential for social disintegration is ever present: conflict lurks just beneath the surface' (1981: 47). It is at this stage that the disjuncture between once-integrated social units begins to surface. Thus ideological fray begins when the 'dominant group has lost its function' (Gramsci 1949: 72).

The lowest form of hegemony is 'minimal' (Femia 1981: 47). This form shows domination but not leadership: any intervention of popular masses is stalled or deemed illegitimate by the dominant classes. But hegemony will not endure without consensus of ideology that incorporates 'concern' for the welfare of all members. Therefore the group who wishes to maintain hegemony should ensure that it is 'developing a critical self-understanding, making alliances, and capturing the ideological realm and, if it intends to extend its hegemony to a larger public, assuring economic development' (Augelli and Murphy 1993: 132). Overall, hegemony is an ongoing struggle and therefore, cannot be definitively 'complete', however it knows a series of increments that make it more or less likely to become integrated or consolidated.

It is a 'constant struggle against a multitude of resistances to ideological domination; any balance of forces that it achieves is always precarious, always in need of re-achievement' (Fiske 1987: 41). In fact, Gramsci's ultimate vision was a scenario wherein the hegemony of knowledge could be wielded by the democratic socialist classes, and he struggled to identify how this ideal could become reality. So under what conditions is hegemony not integrated, despite groups' or classes' efforts to achieve this end? Very little work has been done to answer these questions, much less in the context of East Asian social, political and economic development. Dominic Kelly adopts an 'eclectic' Gramscian approach (2002: 7), showing that for a period of time, Japan behaved as a hegemon for the region during a particular historic bloc throughout the 1960s and early 1970s. Kelly considers the role of Japan in the East Asian region, looking at forces for social change in the Japanese state-society complex and concludes that political and economic circumstances within the territorial boundaries of Japan directly affected the region as a whole. This occurred particularly when it began to lose hegemonic status after the Nixon and oil shocks and various domestic political events began to affect foreign policy.

Kelly notes social change in conjunction with the negotiation between forces as depicted by Cox (material capabilities, ideas and institutions). Interrelations between forces and hegemonic struggles within Japan imposed pressures on groups and individuals both nationally and regionally. In marked contrast to the story of following chapters, Kelly does not explore in full the space between hegemony and its absence.

Transnational Capitalist Network

With a commitment to recognising the impact of the international on the national, I should discuss exactly who or what drives capitalism. Within developing societies, particular units of socialisation and new class formations emerge, or more specifically in the process of groups' socialisation to capitalist norms and leadership is necessary for the prolongation and maintenance of class struggle. The leaders of the development of capital are people of a sub-category of cadres who play a guiding role for the subdivisions of class (Van der Pijl 1998: 139–40). The international expansion of the ideologically informed work norms of neoliberal capitalism creates friction and the foundation for class fractions. Bieler and Morton (2003) reiterate that:

> ... an analysis of global restructuring has to ... account for class
> struggle that takes place at the transnational level not only in sub-
> stance, but also in form involving national and transnational class
> fractions, which operate from within and through national forms of
> state.

So, as the name suggests, the transnational capitalist class is a class specific
to capitalism, whose members are generally people who would have been,
or were, members of the petty bourgeoisie in original communities, and
who are agents of the expansion of capitalism. While these cadres do not
necessarily *experience* class identity, they retain some aspects of the identity
of preceding social units i.e. class solidarity and sensitivity to social status.
Coherence of the cadre arrangement develops historically and involves
several responsibilities that are ultimately meant to integrate 'the various
moments of alienation into an integral world of rules and norms' (Van der
Pijl 1998: 138). These class members are typically individuals who have
become managers or major stakeholders in business. Cadres within states
are involved in the facilitation of the development of capital and the
world-wide network, or what I call the transnational capitalist class
network (TCCN) because this class has become rearticulated in the
present stage of capitalism a la 'Network Society' (Castells 2004) and
provides the rules of standardisation and regulation of subordinate classes.
   In a nation like Korea, 'class' is not a particularly rigid concept due to
its lack of historical ideological embeddedness. Korea does not have a
history of class-based social organisations in the same way that nineteenth
century Europe has, and so it is anachronistic to discuss class expansion
without noting that Korea's class formations and divisions themselves are
relatively new manifestations. Korea has seen the rise of working class
consciousness occurring during rapid industrialisation (Koo 2001: 8); and
like industrialisation in Europe, the environment within which class-
consciousness transpired was, in Korea, 'extremely unfavourable'
culturally and politically (11). The emergence of a working class
consciousness has been paired with a growth of a separate class formation
at the corporate managerial level (see Cox 1987: 360–1). A neo-Gramscian
discussion of class permits the focus on struggles between various social
forces for the establishment of a hegemonic production structure at the
national level. What is seen in the Korean case is an ascendance of groups
who have taken the initiative to operate within the criteria of transnational
norms, and the co-operation of the state, to attempt to incorporate

subordinate classes of workers into this paradigm. Government involvement and *trasformismo*, discussed in Chapters 3 and 4, have led to increasing divisions between groups and perhaps 'classes' within the working force: workers who are employable because they can keep up with international norms, and those who cannot.

Embong (2001: 93) writes that class analysis has often been restricted to national analyses and must now take on transnational dimensions, particularly with the predatory nature of transnational corporations who challenge the traditionally local identity of capital and its social dimensions. The concept of a transnational 'class' has been authored by Leslie Sklair (1995, 1997, 2001a, 2001b, 2002) and Kees Van der Pijl (1984, 1997, 1998, 2001–2), and could be perceived as a hegemonic notion that makes assumptions about the way that groups are divided regardless of historical differences. But 'class' is a definition specifically and ultimately designated by 'men as they live their own history' (Thompson 1963: 11). Gramsci understood the idea of class as an historical artefact of Western European societies, and most class theories themselves have been conceptualised by American or European authors. Neo-Gramscian analysis can transcend the determinist leanings of Open Marxism for its understanding of class composition, by looking at class identity as one of the factors emerging from economic exploitation in an historical context. The TCC is depicted as the final synthesis of a dominant class and its members are in charge of cultivating globalization via a network of elites.

Van der Pijl (1998: 15, 138) writes on ideas originating in Marx's early work, particularly on the process of socialisation (*Vergesellscahftung*): a term not to be confused with 'socialisation' in sociology, or transmission of culture in a limited sense. The use of the theory of socialisation in critical IPE refers to 'the planned or otherwise normatively unified interdependence of functionally divided social activity'. National manifestations and agencies of the 'beast' of capitalism often reveal themselves as class struggles in production and in the labour process as related to historical and contemporary hegemonies. Van der Pijl is influenced by Marx extensively but is generally neo-Gramscian in his analysis of Marxist and Gramscian theses, both in their original forms and in the international and transnational locators. Van der Pijl notes, in the spirit of Marx, that 'the penetration of the commodity form into the labour process itself' (1998: 20) is the starting point for consolidation of capital. Marx (1887/ 1999: 385) analyses the labour process as an observation of the discipline of capital.

Socialisation and commodification are two stages of the consolidation of capital. Polanyi writes that commodification is restricted from three vital areas: land, labour, and money, but

> In the labour process considered in itself, the worker was the means of production; in the labour process which is at the same time the capitalist process of production, the means of production employ the worker in such a way that the labour is no more than a means by which a given sum of values, or a determinate mass of objectified labour, absorbs living labour in order to conserve and increase itself.

Van der Pijl (1984) maintains that the state/civil society relationship is the primary driving force of history and it is from this relation that the TCCN has emerged, and looks at class expansion in historical context through the observation of the earliest process of formation of a transatlantic ruling class in the first half of the twentieth century. The bourgeoisie have been able to, in partnerships with state and civil society in this time period, 'reinforce its hegemonic position both nationally and … internationally' (1984: xiii).

The following section looks at techniques that elite groups of the transnational class have assumed for increased expansion of transnational production practices, within the ethico-political strategy Gramsci called 'passive revolution'. While Gramsci wrote about the following political strategies in a national case with less comment on international affairs, I re-interpret concepts to incorporate the influence of transnational forces who struggle themselves to manage crises of hegemony. Class formations and divisions themselves are a modern phenomenon and in Korea are a result of internationalisation which started after the Second World War, and in this country, members of the TCCN are politicians throughout time who have facilitated semi-peripheral development; *chaebol* and other business management; and elite educators of ever-changing skills expectations throughout capitalist development. These agents have been consistently involved in the process of passive revolution for economic development.

Passive Revolution

Here, I review the definition of passive revolution as a political strategy of elites, and then identify the conditions that are necessary for a passive revolution to occur. Passive revolution is a 'revolution without a revolution', or an 'elite-engineered social and political reform … attractive when a regime possessed domination but lacked hegemony and needed to curb a progressive force, preferably [but not necessarily] without any resort to violence, or at least without a protracted struggle' (Adamson 1980: 186). This section discusses the way that passive revolution is observable when two conditions exist within relations between states and civil society as well as workers. The first condition is a case of elite-led accumulation strategy; and the second is passive revolution which involves the practice of *trasformismo*.

A power-seeking class applies a strategy to build a common world-view among various social classes and forces, and seeks to increase class alliances via the education of organic intellectuals who have hegemonic knowledge and are involved in the final integration thereof. The strategy is used at two points in history: during a war of position, and during a war of movement. However, passive revolution is applied during the *war of position*. Gramsci (*PN*: 120) depicts the *war of position* as the period within which economic preparation and the ideological and thus class alliances are organised for consolidation of hegemony during the class and ideological struggle. A *war of movement* is the arena within which consolidation or resistance actually occurs. During the war of position, control of the existing hegemonic class is enforced through the re-articulation of the subordinate groups' 'needs', via reformist rhetoric that counteracts revolutionary stances. Violent overthrow is the frontal assault mechanism seen in Bolshevik strategy, which is possible within the war of movement. This can only occur in the case of a weak civil society; one that is incapable of buffering an elite programme.

Passive revolution occurs during a war of position, during which time ideological alliances are organised for attempted consolidation of hegemony (*PN*: 120; Showstack-Sassoon 1987: 210). During the war of position, there is no embedded social ideology, so groups that seek power affect various strategies in a power-seeking game. A group that seeks hegemonic power builds a common worldview among various social classes and forces, and frames this worldview to subordinate groups as beneficial and necessary, which is a tactic of *trasformismo*. I argue that this has been attempted in South Korea via educational tactics such as VET. Educational materials are used to enforce a potentially dominant worldview wherein elite groups use 'the tools of the war of position, the various ideological apparatuses … to pre-empt the creation of an hegemony by the working class' (Showstack-Sassoon 1987: 210).

So without hegemonic status, a dominant group may utilise the strategy of *trasformismo* in order to put into motion a 'passive revolution' (*PN*: 59). Empirical analyses of passive revolution include Matt Davies (1999), Richard Fatton (1993), Phoebe Moore (2005), Adam Morton (2003), Anne Showstack-Sassoon (1982, 1987), Kees Van der Pijl (1993,1997: 128–32), and Owen Worth (2004). Cox also discusses passive revolution and *trasformismo* in various sections of his work (i.e. 1983: 165–7).

Gramsci wrote about passive revolution and *trasformismo* occurring at the time of the Italian *Risorgimento* (Resurrection). Italy was a torn country after the Roman Empire fell and was divided into city and Papal States. The movement's aim was to join sections into one political whole, toward a final unification of Italy. During *Risorgimento*, revolutionary, clandestine organisations emerged from the middle classes and nobility (Trevelyan 1935), and peasant classes were not considered in the movement. Thus eventual unification in 1861 was enacted without an inclusive public voice and without uprising from the marginalised classes: a passive revolution. In the period of passive revolution, Gramsci maintains, 'relatively far-reaching modifications are … introduced into the country's economic structure in order to accentuate the "plan of production" element' (*PN*: 120). This 'negative strategy' of *trasformismo* occurs when 'the dominant group takes the initiative in making limited concessions … to subordinate classes, hoping to co-opt their leading elements and forestall more comprehensive counter-hegemonic challenges' (Rupert 1995: 30).

First, a case of passive revolution can be noted wherein governments' accumulation strategies are elite-engineered and do not succeed in garnering consensus from the wider society. Passive revolution involves 'socio-economic modernisation so that changes in production relations are accommodated within existing social and institutional forms but without fundamentally challenging the established political order' (Morton 2003: 632). Thus elements of production relations that protect a capitalist regime are not eliminated but are reformed and restructured, giving an appearance of integrating workers' needs into the regime of accumulation but ultimately stabilising power over workers' lives. For the state to sustain social order, potential resistance forces must be somehow co-opted into the dominant classes.

Van der Pijl (1993) discusses the historical formation and transformations in socialist Russia, and succinctly refers to formations of class that have occurred in consecutive 'waves' under the conditions of passive revolution.

> Passive revolution combines the notions of (a) a 'revolution from above' without massive participation ... and (b) a creeping, 'molecular' social transformation in which the progressive class finds itself compelled to advance in a more or less surreptitious, compromised fashion.
>
> (Gramsci *PN*: 108)

Van der Pijl's case study (1993: 244) notes molecular changes within Russia, which he calls the 'organic social compromise' that occurs under the conditions of passive revolution.

Lack of consensus from society is an element of the conditions for passive revolution, because the Gramscian concept of hegemony involves coercion *and* consent. The nature of 'passivity' within passive revolutions 'refers to the way challenges may be thwarted so that changes in production relations are accommodated within the current social formation' (Morton 2003: 634). Thus passivity is not 'passive' in the commonly understood sense, but indicates a state's attempts to initiate a form of revolution or change that occurs either by intervention, or by gradual incorporation of 'new social groups within the hegemony of a political order' (634–5). In this sense, the government maintains leadership but does not require consent for its own revolutionary strategies. A 'revolution' is represented by the state's chosen accumulation strategy, whether it is export-led development or neoliberal deregulation and so on. The non-hegemonic conditions for passive revolution are evident in the case of elite-led accumulation strategies. Fatton comments that '... passive revolutions institutionalise ... power. They enhance the stability and authority of the ruling class as they integrate subordinate classes into political and economic structures that protect and serve the fundamental interests of the ruling class itself' (1990: 468).

Morton (2003: 636) emphasises that 'hegemonic projects are typically oriented to broader issues grounded not only in the economy but the whole sphere of state-civil society relations'. Hegemonic projects are, in effect, elite-organised and managed passive revolutions that are designed and propagated in progressive terms. A hegemonic project is not the same thing as hegemony; it is a struggle between social forces for leadership. If the circumstances and social forces within the analysed historic blocs strongly demonstrate those characteristics or even some of the characteristics that comprise a passive revolution, then Korea can be claimed to have lacked hegemonic integration both nationally and internationally. I discuss VET programmes in the realm of hegemonic projects because workers' abilities are a very important part of state-led accumulation strategies and aid in my final claims regarding the nature of hegemony in Korea.

The second category of 'conditions' over a historical trajectory of Korean economic development involves *trasformismo*. A government that is capable of convincing its population of the merits of elite-authored economic development strategies increases its chances of consolidating hegemony and superficially involves the nation via the efforts of *trasformismo*. This method can be observed within a number of activities emerging from *chaebol* management, politicians, and educators, and in the case of the present work, are often advocates and members of transnational capitalist networks. For example, *trasformismo* is seen in management's or government's appeal to nationalism and work ethic as is noted throughout Korea's political and economic history. A strong national identity can indicate complicit support for elite-led decisions regarding development and production. Furthermore, the offer of training programmes is framed in such a way as to provide tools for workers' survival in an increasingly uncertain world. Programmes that appear to offer worker empowerment or authority, such as limited management of worker associations are ultimately managed by pre-existing power structures, or ineffective, formalised discussion forums such as the Tripartite Commission. These provisions have been designed to tackle the needs of workers to remain or to become newly employable, but perhaps do not meet fundamental needs which include basic humane working conditions during accelerated development of Korea, and involve the need for secure employment in the more recent years.

Hegemony represents the ruling totality, but leadership cannot exist unless the totality saturates society to such an extent that it 'constitutes the limits of common sense for most people under its sway' (Williams 1980), and *trasformismo* is one method to control 'common sense'. In late capitalist societies, common sense has become fragmented and distorted and emerges from both public and private discourses, so its saturation requires the infiltration into three areas, which are power, ideas, and institutions. Ideological consent is the gateway for complete consolidation and thus requires extensive analysis to understand how the elite class actually works to achieve control in this area. 'Elites lead historic [hegemonic] blocs understood in the Gramscian sense as coalitions of social forces bound by consent and coercion' (Sinclair 1996: 9).

Transformations of production relations are fundamental within a case of hegemonic struggle. Production relations have the most direct effect on people's lives and represent an integrative aspect of the way in which hegemony is consolidated. Beginning in the early 19th century, the increase of the adoption of similar processes of production relations at the national level of a liberal state and the liberal world order have transpired via British- and later American-inspired global hegemony. However, the adoption of expansive production relations in Korea has required more than a 'natural' evolution of norms, and has required top-down strategies within passive revolutionary conditions. The process requires restructuring of the national consciousness through ideational training as well as material restructuring, which has occurred in Korea through VET for workers. The social safety net provided by training programmes was presented as a means to alleviate layoffs that were a direct result of the crisis, or a form of *trasformismo*.

The state, whether or not it exists in a hegemonic society, provides the economic framework for the norms of production. This framework creates the rules for social relations of production. In the process of *trasformismo*, organic intellectuals provide a set of guidelines or a legal-institutional framework (Bieler 2001: 99; Cox 1983: 172–3) for the economically dominant class that advocates its own version of appropriate economic practices. This is a reaffirmation of the leading groups' ideological alignment and sets the precedent for the development of production relations. There are particular requirements and expectations to ensure the durability of a dominant mode of social relations of production and in the process of *trasformismo*, all other modes are inferior and discredited. The integration of a dominant framework of legal institutions is often dependent on the disruption and reconstruction of production norms and labour markets. The process of adoption of standardised norms of production occurs via the elite's articulation and enactment of the strategy of *trasformismo*. Within each phase of Korean history covered in chapter 3, I identify conditions for passive revolution in South Korea, looking at powerful forms of *trasformismo*. The latter political strategy has appeared in different forms across historical periods, but the objective is the same: to provide limited concessions or empowerment campaigns designed to keep workers from enacting complete revolution, through the guided articulation of their needs, and an appeal to common sense.

So, the leading class, to resist the ascendance of the subordinate classes' potential gain of hegemony may enact passive revolution, or the reassertion of the dominant class's rhetoric, applied with minimal or no violence. Workers are explicitly co-opted via *trasformismo*. Socio-economic modernisation of production relations can occur via passive revolution, which means that the two conditions discussed here have been affected with some 'success' according to development schemata of TCCN elites. The established political order of top-down relations will be maintained, with a sufficient programme of concessions provided to subordinate groups.

Conclusion

The chapter has thus outlined the development of IR theory, claiming that its positivist epistemological roots are insufficient for an analysis of the contemporary world scenario and case studies into the impact that global struggles have on nations and states. Gramscian perspectives are preferable to reveal activity that occurs for the consolidation and perpetuation of historically dynamic social, political, and economic global hegemonic struggles. To illuminate contemporary struggles, neo-Gramscian writers have written about the struggle for control over the relations of production in a context of increasingly transnational hegemonic inclinations that consolidate particular patterns, and thus relations, of production. But these works do not explore forms of state and political strategies such as passive revolution that appear at the national level in response to increasingly globalised requirements for development, so the neo-Gramscian literature has been explored for a foundation for the following case study.

While different scholars understand hegemony differently, Gramsci resurrected the idea through a deeper analysis of how hegemony is sought by various actors from a number of social classes. Gramsci's concept of hegemony makes it clear that historical periods are not always hegemonic, i.e. the link between the base and superstructure is not inherently consensual. The abstract concepts of passive revolution and *trasformismo* give a clear case of *non-hegemonic* elite behaviour, because these activities can only occur via top-down, dominant class relations. In a case of internationally inspired passive revolution, elite groups from business, politics and education are involved in a network of the transnational capitalist groups or TCC, but cannot effortlessly gain consent from its own population. The state may enact forced development plans and carry this further to force restructuring of national institutions such as education to acquire popular consent. The next chapter deconstructs elements of Cox's matrices of forces, looking at world orders over time to provide an international setting for the analysis of increasing pressures upon political and economic development of South Korea under a series of passive revolutions.

2

HISTORY OF WORLD ORDERS: INTERNATIONAL STRUGGLES FOR HEGEMONY

Introduction

While the previous chapter discusses terminology to build a foundation for the relatively abstract ideas I use to look at Korean development in the context of international hegemonic struggles, this chapter provides an historical analysis of power relations and social change at the global level. I highlight forms of state and social forces engendered by production relations within 'world orders', or historical periods of capitalist expansion, to understand conditions for global hegemonic leadership and to provide a background for the case study of nationally located hegemonic struggles in South Korea.

An historical bloc is a 'coherent historical structure' (Morton 2006: 65) composed of forms of state and relations of production seen to contribute to a world order, supported and expressed by a powerful worldview that becomes evident in the way production is managed and carried out during a specific period. I argue that the formation of *hegemonic* historical blocs requires national alignment to international elites' expansive ideologies and a kind of convergence of relations of production that are supportive of a 'global' mode of production. This can be seen by the formation and consent of organic intellectuals who begin to manage international and national responses to what we can now identify as 'globalisation' through educational projects. The function of intellectuals is 'sustaining the mental images, technologies and organisations which bind together the members of a class and of an historic bloc into a common identity' (Cox 1981: 168). 'What is "politics" to the productive class becomes "rationality" to the intellectual class' (Gramsci 1975: 134). Traditionally, intellectuals take charge of the management of national common sense and order the understanding of reality. The role of intellectuals is to sustain or to fight for hegemonic leadership, fully aligned with the government and responsible for spreading the ideology of the dominant classes to the subaltern. Leaders at the helm of capitalist expansion work to ensure 'the promotion and expansion of a mode of production' (Bieler and Morton 2004: 95) via elite-directed estimations of 'proper' economic development and supportive modes of production that have become increasingly shared internationally. For effective expansion of decided modes of development, the formation and enlargement of groups of organic intellectuals in the workplace and across civil society who are sympathetic to development strategies becomes increasingly important.

So here, I look at a historical background of the struggles for con-solidation of global hegemony via the consolidation and development of those groups who are linked to the impact of struggles upon South Korea, covered in the following chapter. Gills reminds us that 'the domestic and the international are … as inseparable as the political and economic as aspects of social power' (Gills 2001: 234).

Several authors have written about the historical patterns of capitalist proliferation and world accumulation, including Fieldhouse (1982), Frank and Gills (1993), Wallerstein (1996), Amin (2000), and Beaud (1983). Discussions of inequalities and exploitation inherent to the global capitalist system constitute the bedrock for these authors' work. I am indebted to these writers for their commitment to disclosing a more complete picture of histories than many standard history textbooks offer, and in this chapter I will focus on the historical expansion of capitalism as led by elites, whose forms of state promulgated this process.

Facilitated by organic intellectuals, who ultimately manage the expansion of ideologies of historically specific modes of production, capitalism has enjoyed various hegemonic and less hegemonic phases (Cox 1987). Cox (1983, 1987) writes about modes of production and forms of state relevant to four historic periods with the purpose of making a claim regarding whether or not historical blocs can be named 'hegemonic', according to conditions for Gramscian hegemony of consent and coercion. Within Cox's matrices of forces, a 'world order' is similar to Gramsci's concerns of 'historical blocs' (Cox 1981: 139, 152 fn14). Cox breaks down world orders into four historical periods: 1845–1875, 1875–1945, 1945–1965, and 1965–present (1981: 170) and looks at directed changes throughout each period (1987) to pinpoint prevalent modes and relations of production. Cox reasons that some world orders have been more hegemonic than others, but for the present analysis, I have not focused on distinguishing a global hegemony from a non-hegemonic historic bloc. Instead, I look at the way in which elites have struggled to accumulate power through the expansion of a progression of forms of state and production relations that were intended to become and remain expansive across the world. This differs from the way the next chapter treats 'forms of state', which are nationally located, and claimed to exist within an ongoing case of passive revolution.

In this chapter I identify expansive forms of state throughout each historical period tailored toward dissemination of production relations in South Korea. Elites throughout Korea's history have typically aimed to consolidate groups of nationally-based organic intellectuals or workers who are sympathetic to development plans and become members of elite groups themselves. Intellectuals of this nature involve foreign experts, who come from domestic institutes of research and government agencies. These outsiders work with local management to train workers to become organically attuned to market-led forces, and as such, these intellectuals have sophisticated and perpetuated the myth of the immutability of the expansion of capitalism into many layers of social life. The previous chapter discussed the various interpretations of the concept of 'hegemony' at length, and specified that I will not rely on realist interpretations of single-state power. Rather, the profundity of Gramscian hegemony is acknowledged, and at the global level, 'hegemony' refers to:

> ... dominance of a particular kind where the dominant state creates an order based *ideologically* on a broad measure of consent, functioning according to general principles that in fact ensure the continuing supremacy of the leading state or states and leading social classes but at the same time offer some measure or prospect of satisfaction to the less powerful.
>
> (Cox 1987: 7)

The struggle for hegemonic leadership is therefore heavily ideological. At the national level, elite, state-operated groups aim to educate workers to adapt to capitalist ideology through the implementation of directed norms of production, which 'unif[ies] secondary groups into an historical bloc with a fundamentally capitalist world view, while it enters the consciousness of the masses as part of their confounded and fragmentary "common sense"' (Rupert 1987: 30). A hegemonic worldview of capitalism thus serves to protect elite interests and to steer social forces away from the articulation of alternative world views. Organic intellectuals form the most important group in this process, as they either actively incorporate, or alternatively resist norms that hegemony-seeking groups attempt to propagate. During Pax Britannica in the mid-nineteenth century and Pax Americana in the mid-twentieth century, the formation and success of particular knowledge for development that resulted in consolidated hegemonic projects (Cox 1983: 170) universalised certain economic doctrines. My analysis underscores the way in which this has been achieved, because it provides a background for analysing these social forces at the national level in times of international hegemonic struggle.

In order for the expansion of ideas that contribute to production practices seen in the skills required of workers to be fully hegemonic, consent as well as coercion of workers is required. Workers are most affected by changing expectations but without accompanying concession mechanisms, production norms are unlikely to become established. Cox does not emphasise the role of workers and how they are integrated into hegemonic projects and I aim to resolve this deficiency by looking at a specific case study of the management of workers in one semi-peripheral state, in the following chapter. Cox's work (1987) begins this type of exploration by making suppositions regarding emerging social forces and forms of state that grew up emerged during the expansion of modes of production in each historical bloc from the late nineteenth century to the present.

This chapter takes Cox's work into account by identifying relations between leading nations' elites to understand forms of state prevalent within each period, and also observes characteristics of production relations specific to historic periods. Cox's work lacks analyses of specific nations' experiences with the incorporation of certain expansive norms, based around supposedly hegemonic modes of production, so in this chapter I assess Cox's analysis over four periods, showing his and other authors' ways of describing hegemonic and non-hegemonic periods of history.

So, reflecting upon Cox's second matrix, Chapter 2 conducts an analysis of configurations of forces through a discussion of the forms of state and social forces emerging from the expansion of certain forms of production relations throughout four periods of world orders. This analysis is important as a background for the following chapter, which clarifies how the societal 'need' for particular types of human capital at various points in history is grappled with at the national level, in conjunction with the restructuring of capitalism.

Pax Britannica

The roots of liberal capitalism are found within British history during the period of Pax Britannica from 1845 to 1875. Cox claims this era to be hegemonic because economic doctrines of free trade, the gold standard, and comparative advantage were coercively 'universalised' across dependent nations who took on these norms despite the unequal relations that their promotion and prolongation required.

Pax Britannica: Forms of State

The principles of liberalism guided capitalist expansion, and were rooted in the early Mercantilist period between 1500 and 1800. During this period, Atlantic centres of power dictated the accumulation of capital to the peripheral Americas. After these introductory centuries of the establishment of trade between nations, starting in the early nineteenth century, liberal principles were openly institutionalised in Great Britain and began to expand to neighbouring countries during the 1840s to the 1870s. The 'Irresistible Rise of Industrial Capitalism' (Beaud 1983: 74) introduced a 'classical model' for liberal economics called the 'basic forms of capitalism' (Amin 2000: 1). This classical model emerged from the industrial revolution and continued until the end of the Second World War during which time a world division of labour and production facilitated capital expansion, based on the agricultural and mineral industries.

The liberal world order of Pax Britannica enforced the classically capitalist commitment to the separation of economics from politics, a distinction that isolated groups' roles accordingly. Liberal ideology relies on free trade and open markets to set nations on a path to prosperity. The role of economic actors and political leaders should be separate according to these assumptions, but the latter is expected to reinforce the former. Cox discusses the social roles of groups in Britain (1987: 129) during this historical bloc, which led to a bourgeois form of state. The bourgeoisie directed economic affairs, whilst the aristocracy managed politics and foreign policy. Nonetheless, the British aristocracy's political decisions became inherently committed to the support and beneficence of the economic system of liberalism. Pax Britannica was thus a bourgeois hegemony, led by the aristocracy.

During this period, the aristocracy managed the drastic improvement of transportation between and within countries, and facilitated trade and unprecedented resource imports/exports as well as the export of ideas and influence. Gold mining was on the increase, paper currencies were circulated more frequently, and techniques for credit were introduced, meaning that the mobilisation of capital also accelerated significantly. Britain in particular extended its external relationships through emigration, trade and capital investment, and countries with peripheral status were the centres of production for these industries while the 'bourgeois' states flourished. 'Catching up' became the tune of modernisation and a goal for peripheral states. Any resulting social unrest was seen as a scientific necessity for development and eventual prosperity. Ricardo (1951) and Say (1953) promoted this lassez-faire, free enterprise, free market notion of the 'liberal utopia'. For a liberal utopia to become established, these philosophers took for granted that some social groups would have to suffer. The poor would have to support the idea of riches despite poverty-stricken groups' obvious exclusion. 'Lacking wealth oneself, one must wish wealth for others: an indigent has infinitely greater possibilities for earning his living and becoming well off if he lives among a rich population, than if he is surrounded by poor people like himself' (Say 1953: 195).

The hegemonic liberal world order of Pax Britannica thus came to fruition via British-led establishment of mechanised industry and via the expansion of trade in the 1800s and early 1900s. Perhaps the best known theorist to have conceptualised how this might occur is the Scottish economist Adam Smith. His work *The Wealth of Nations* (1776) opposed any government intervention in economies, advocated no restrictions on manufacturing, no barriers on commerce, and no tariffs. 'Free' trade is the predominant characteristic of liberal capitalism. Thus the role of the state during the hegemonic liberal world order was increasingly geared toward the reduction of controls and diminishing state regulation for this purpose. Likewise 'free' enterprise and 'free' competition were two complimenting ideals for this economic order. In countries where Britain or America established some form of tangible relations of trade or investment, the 'core' nation was not necessarily directly in command of the internal activities, but relied on local governments to enforce the 'rules' of open markets and liberal practice.

Britain maintained positive relations by way of favourable trade agreements with countries who were most compliant with liberal trade practices. Cox shows that this early liberal expansion project was spherically hierarchical, that the world of liberal states in the 1840s to 1870s was constructed with Britain at the heart, and a secondary interior circle (Figure 3) included consenting (and in various ways, coerced) nations. 'Inner circle' countries were the participants in industrial growth and trade expansion, countries who were originally protectionist but who were quickly converted to the principle of free trade, and until 1914, to the reception of the gold standard.

Figure 3. Hierarchy of Liberal States 1840s–1870s (Cox 1987: 144–5)

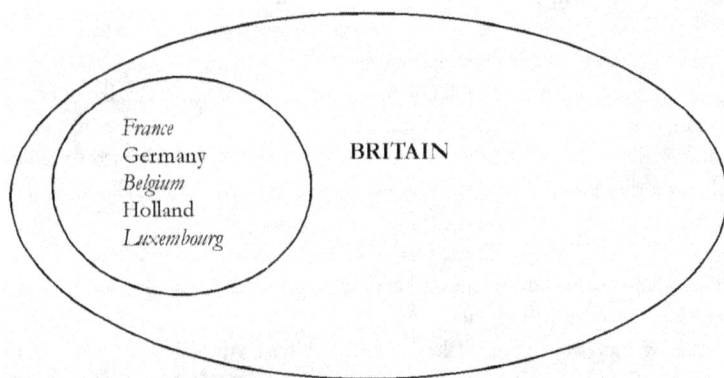

Pax Britannica: Social Forces Engendered by Production Relations
Both forms of state and production relations were affected during this time period in what Cox calls 'penetrated' areas, as a result of the political/economic influence and leadership of expansive nations (1987: 144, 146). In penetrated areas, or those areas at the periphery of expansive nations, traditional institutions were uprooted and replaced, or otherwise adapted to British and European industry requirements. During Pax Britannica, vocational education became increasingly separated from 'classical' education. States rebuilt infrastructures of society in order to integrate previously 'unnecessary' functions that in sum protected growth of the liberal economy. British and European expansive states thus

directed coercion abroad through requiring unprecedented tax policies, restructuring property laws, and the elites prioritised financing and investing in communications facilities and transport. This state leadership was accompanied in Asia, Latin America and the Mediterranean by the agency of local bourgeoisies, who functioned as organic intellectuals to the hegemonic economic doctrines, and who were the intermediaries of capital between the penetrated areas and expansive countries.

Production relations remained static in this time period only in areas of traditionally local tributary or peasant-lord production methods, where pressure was applied to increase surplus of goods to be traded for other goods. In several areas, production relations began to resemble those of the expansive countries, an enterprise-labour-market process. Cox points out evidence of this transformation in for example the United States, where after the Civil War, slave production was replaced by the enterprise-labour-market plantation production of cotton. Egypt saw the destruction of the peasant agriculture as British and European factories demanded cotton at rates exceeding the traditional production rates, and land holdings were redistributed accordingly. Since India was actually ruled by Britain, its traditional production methods and land ownership were dramatically changed. The Indian artisan was ruined; British cotton textiles led to sudden unemployment of masses of labourers. And finally in Africa, mining enclaves owned by expansive countries were placed in various units, enclaves that required an organically directed labour force. Organic intellectuals were thus needed within penetrated areas to enforce introduced modes of production.

The works of Irving Fisher (1906), Alfred Marshall (1890), Adam Smith (1776), and Johann Heinrich von Thunen (1875) each maintain a particular view of the role that people play in the capitalist system. These elite, ideologically Western intellectuals perceived human beings themselves as capital. For Smith, the aggregation of abilities and skills of residents were as much a factor of capital determining a nations' prosperity as trade relations. T. Paul Schultz (1971: 26, 27) of the Chicago School of Economics writes that if labour is a 'produced means of production', then workers are *not* equal in their abilities and skills and must compete to become capitalists through

> ... the acquisition of knowledge and skill that have economic value. This knowledge and skill are in great part the product of investment and, combined with other human investment, predominantly

account for the productive superiority of the technically advanced countries.

This portrayal of workers originated with intellectuals of Pax Britannica who marvelled at Britain's rapid expansion, but their ideas have not disappeared and are evident in neoliberal economic theory.

Despite the 'hegemonic' nature of the time period, workers were originally excluded from 'access to ... power in the state' and were not represented by the state. This lack of representation occurred at several levels of the employment stratum. I would ask, how, then, could workers be portrayed as a 'consenting' force to Cox's vision of global hegemony? At this time, workers were ostracised from government involvement in the same way that manufacturers and agricultural workers were excluded from decision making. Uprisings against this oppression included the 1830 Swing Riots, which were violently countered by the government. However the government finally permitted some extent of involvement of middle class workers in state affairs via the Whig reforms. The working class remained alienated from decision making and subordinate to supposed market forces, and the peril of workers' uprising posed an increasing threat to the bourgeois hegemony. Tory member Sir Robert Peel intervened at a strategically intelligent moment and provided a 'solution' to the potential for ongoing uprisings. He made a proposal for concessions and worker appeasement, and introduced a bill to reduce working hours. Peel downplayed class divisions by avoiding the direct association of the propertied class to the state (50–1). This ingenuity led to the minimisation of uprisings and a hegemonic consensus across groups in Britain. Cox (1987: 147) writes that 'class conflict in the expansive centre was not polarised—the bourgeoisie had ceased to be a revolutionary force since the old-regime aristocracies had learned to rule in their interests, and the workers had not yet become a coherent challenge' (147).

Across Europe and the wider world, British troops, intellectuals and bureaucrats aided the development of organic intellectuals who would sustain production relations and social norms during the world order of Pax Britannica. 'British-ness' had become the desired form for fashion, work ethics, and sports. British 'domination' spread across five continents. Sterling enjoyed international currency status. But Cox's theorised 'hegemony' could not last forever, and colonial uprisings began to emerge in Algeria, Egypt, and India, where the supposed consent to ultimately coercive trade relations and national requirements made of workers and the formation of organic intellectuals were not fully established. British leadership came to an end at the turn of the century, and the period of 'mixed imperialisms' began.

Period of Mixed Imperialisms

During this second period (1875–1945), states finally challenged British power and the Great Depression and two World Wars occurred, resulting in the dispersal and fragmentation of the previous 'hegemonic' world order, into economic blocs. The peak of the liberal era faded and entered a phase of novel regeneration. Economic depression hit in 1873 and this shocked the world order significantly: it was the 'threshold between competitive and monopoly capitalism' (Cox 1987:158). This period involved 'development of a second generation of industrial techniques and industries … concentration of capital and the emergence of finance capital, and a new wave of colonisation and expansion on a world-wide scale, leading to the dividing up of the world and the Great War' (1983: 117).

Mixed Imperialisms: Forms of State

Germany's political power rose steadily after the unification of Germany in 1871, which challenged the previous Pax Britannica. Despite the following claim, ruptures in the previous world order were soon to emerge.

> And may God grant that we and our successors on the imperial throne may at all times increase the wealth of the German Empire, not by military conquests, but by the blessings and the gifts of peace, in the realm of national prosperity, liberty, and morality.
> (Wilhelm I, Kaiser und König, The Imperial Proclamation,
> 18 January 1871)

Protectionism was revived in Germany, Italy and France during 1880s and 1890s. Political and economic weakening marked Britain's decline in world power. In 1890 the USA was in the lead for steel and industrial production, which severely affected Britain's previous status of global power. The Great Depression is the second era of capitalism, what Beaud calls the 'period of imperialism' (1983: 117), but Cox calls it the period of 'rival imperialisms' (1987: 151) indicating the struggles between powerful nations to gain hegemony of global production.

Urbanisation was a major phenomenon of the final decades of the nineteenth century. Population numbers rose rapidly in European cities. Modernisation was fuelled by the expanding labour markets. The growth and density of urban populations created new possibilities for joint collaboration during a war of position that can occur during non-hegemonic times in history. Penetrated countries of the earlier phase of liberal expansion recognised their subordination in the capitalist world order and began to react. Elite relations at this time were not hegemonic in the Gramscian sense, because expansive nations took on a directive leadership role over the peripheral nations. Globally, colonisation, such as Japan's colonisation of Korea, and expansion of struggles for industrialis-ation proliferated with unprecedented vigour, perhaps leading to a crisis of capitalism resulting in what has become known as the Great Depression.

Beaud (1983: 117) characterises the crisis leading to the Great Depression in this way. There are four contradictions of capital which cause crisis situations:

- Contradiction between capitalist companies and working classes.
- Contradiction between capitalists in same sector or between sectors.
- Contradiction between national capitalisms.
- Contradiction between dominant capitalisms and dominated peoples, countries, or regions (117).

The Great Depression occurred predominantly as a result of the first and third contradictions. First, the working classes were placed in a position of extreme oppression during depressed economic circumstances resulting from the expansion of capitalist norms. In the third category, German and North American capitalism rose to challenge British capitalism. While Britain managed ¼ of the world's overall trade in the year 1880, this proportion fell to ⅐ by 1913, to ⅛ in 1948. North American, Japanese, and German trade accelerated. While Britain had surpassed the world of steel and coal production in the 1870s and 1880s, American production in these industries surpassed Britain's drastically by 1913.

Mixed Imperialisms: Production Relations and Social Forces
From the 1870s–90s, a change in the nature of work was evident that occurred as a result of the change in the point of production. Work no longer occurred in workshops but was transferred to the assembly line.

This led to changing qualifications required for employment, new modes of organisation of labour and unprecedented methods of control over labour. States were faced with the 'labour problem' for the first time. The labour force was weakened through unprecedented divisions between skilled and less skilled arenas of work required in large industrial organisations. Social forces emerged out of changing relations of production in the form of trade unions and co-operatives, but labour-led political parties also emerged from the skilled worker units, while other areas of labour struggled for a voice. Only skilled workers were permitted Union involvement. In the US, two major unions emerged at this time, both of which were ideologically intertwined with the Cold War-influenced foreign policy. Both anti-Communist, the American Federation of Labour (AFL) and the Congress of Industrial Organisations (CIO) were established. The AFL emphasised 'voluntarism', which is an 'ideology of self-help emphasising an economically oriented brand of "pure and simple" trade unionism for skilled workers organised along craft lines' (Rupert 1995: 47). Any other forms of unionism were discouraged and given Communist-leaning status.

The formation of organic intellectuals became an issue for a hegemony-seeking state and education began to reflect this urgency. Jarvis writes that adult vocational education of the nineteenth century in Britain was directed by an 'enlightened bourgeoisie for the mass of people … who were expected to receive rather than participate, and to be passive recipients of the bourgeoisie's well-intentioned offering' (1993: 12). The bourgeois were thus in charge of directing production relations and they changed the very nature of work during the era of mixed imperialisms. Beginning in the 1880s and 90s in the advanced industrial countries, production was transformed. A fundamental aspect of this change is that workers were quite suddenly expected to carry out work in an assembly line environment rather than in the workshop environment. Qualifications were increasingly required for employment, and new modes of control over the process of work simultaneously changed the nature of work. As a result, workers began to organise differently and to behave differently politically. This completely changed the way labour was carried out and perceived. Henry Ford (1863–1947) is known for his role in this transformation of the social forces of labour. The first moving assembly line opened in 1913: Ford's Highland Park in Michigan. Craft based work was soon to become a thing of the past. The industrial division of labour in such assembly line production processes was designed by Frederick

Winslow Taylor around the idea of scientific management which defined tasks in detail and essentially rejected the creative process of production altogether. Workers in this way were alienated from the mode of production and were subordinated to management control in the workplace.

This new model for production was adopted across the USA and in industrialising countries, including Korea during Japanese colonisation. Over time however, there was a backlash from labour. Governments responded to the threat of the labour problem in Europe by invoking nationalism and revamping society's state loyalty by kindling national support for foreign policy. This steered the sights of labour to another direction to some extent, but did not prevent the increasing tendency toward the welfare state of the early twentieth century. Until the Great War, social policy was increasingly 'from below' rather than completely elite led.

In Britain in 1906, the Liberal Party enacted several social reforms for labour. In the United States, the Progressive Party saw increased success in elections, and in Germany the Social Democrats in 1912 were victorious in elections. Militant labour unions emerged in the 1930s and it was only when those unions were de-radicalised and incorporated into the social infrastructure of economies that labour relations stabilised. Despite a history absent of socialism or welfarism, even the US showed signs of social protection through the legalisation of such unions. During the early years of the Cold War, the CIO in the spirit of anti-Communism eliminated any 'Communist' labour unions; an action that complemented the emerging powerful role of the USA in the global context (Rupert 1995). The Pax Americana era of history was in bloom.

Pax Americana: Post-war Mixed Economic Consensus

Cox states that the post-war period (1945–1965) was hegemonically influenced by American ideologies that appeared to be more suited to the increasingly widening world economy than British hegemonic ideals of the first period. Following the Second World War, the United States, having endured the Great Depression and recovered substantially, soon became a kind of global relief worker. The US organised several loan programmes by way of the Marshall Plan and after the Korean War, provided extensive aid to South Korea. The global 'benefactor' however, carried with it new ideologies of the market, emerging with changing forms of state and production relations.

From the 40s–70s, the global economy can be defined according to a more or less Keynesian market ideology of state regulation of the economy and intervention at some points, and a maintained welfare function likewise. In the early 1970s there was a crisis of the legitimacy of this system, but during its primacy, the ideology behind Pax Americana was consolidated via new forms of states, whose roles as participants in the consolidation of hegemony were to activate adjustment of economic policies at national levels. Two forms of states represent the most active participants in this world economy after the Wars, named by Cox as the *neoliberal* and *neomercantilistic developmentalist* forms (1987: 219+; 230+). Events such as the Truman doctrine in the United States, and the Attlee settlement, which nationalised coal and steel in Britain, launched the new identity of welfare nationalist states in their adjustment to mixed economic forms of state. Welfare nationalist states with the most developed productive forces transformed into the new *mixed economic* form of state, and took on a new role in world politics as a 'hegemonic' leader.

Pax Americana: Forms of State

During the early phase of Pax Americana, market models of free trade and less state intervention were the norm. This meant that states became increasingly busy regulating economies, but only to the extent that they felt was necessary to harmonise with a global economy. Inequalities became increasingly prevalent - labour welfare was not prioritised in most cases and in particular in the developmentalist states i.e. South Korea. Peripheral states industrialised during this third period. States with newly recovered political autonomy worked to modernise and became an integral part of the world production system, for better or worse. This occurred particularly in Latin America and Asia.

Rupert describes the post world war neoliberal ideological hegemony constructed by the USA (1995). He notes the tirade of anti-Communism in the international labour organisations implemented by US powers, painting a picture of Democracy Vs Communism. During this period, elite groups restructured liberal superpower objectives and prioritised international trade. This led to a perpetuation of a growth- and productivity-centred labour strategy, and the soporific quality of prosperity led governments to gloss over policies concerning social welfare. So, for world orders to become established in the 'post feudal era,' a separation into distinct spheres of politics and economics has been crucial and more noticeable. The delineation between these categories potentially masks exploitation of workers through placing responsibility for what happens to workers within the 'economic' field.

The variation between the ideal type of a welfare nationalist state and the mixed-economy state has, firstly, to do with the common objectives seen across categories of these forms of state. While the forms of state are nearly identical in terms of the tripartite relations inherent to corporatism, what marks the mixed-economy state are the 'goals pursued, in the uses to which the structure was put' (Cox 1987: 221). The first type retained the objectives to a) protect national economies from external affects, and to b) enhance national power in contrast to enemies or rivals. However, the goal of the mixed economy state was to achieve economic growth nationally, and to participate unflinchingly in a free and open world economy internationally.

Perhaps the most significant event during 'Pax Americana' was the depiction of 'best' practices for forms of state in the global economy, conveniently organised by the American government. The US intended both to provide a new institutional planning mechanism for national economies and also design a blueprint for international economic relations based on the tenets of currency stabilisation and liberalisation of international trade. A very important meeting was held in 1944 in Bretton Woods, New Hampshire. 44 delegates of the United and Associated Nations met essentially to design a system that would organise the financial and economic requirements and norms for the post-war world. Delegates decided on a type of gold standard: the value of the American dollar would be fixed to the value of gold. This system would be called the Bretton Woods System.

A British economist named John Maynard Keynes and his American colleague Harry White participated in this architecture for the post-war world by way of a Bretton Woods system. White was most influential in the creation of the IMF, a fund that was originally intended to reach the size of half of the world's imports. This would be a reasonable size to garner significant influence on the global monetary system. The IMF did not reach this size in practice and, in the early 1990s, when more than USD 1 trillion crossed international boundaries every 24 hours, the IMF controlled liquidity at an amount equal to only two percent of total global imports. However, at its inception it was intended to act as recourse for potential instabilities that could occur in the global economic system (Power 1995).

Keynes's vision for the global economy was based on different ideals which contrasted with those of many of the delegates at the Bretton Woods meetings, and in particular to White, despite their close collaborations. Keynes pictured the IMF as a type of global safety net for developing and developed countries alike, which would eliminate ongoing persistent debt problems. The International Bank for Reconstruction and Development (IBRD) that became known as the World Bank was designed at the meetings and began to function in 1945. Keynes may have emphasised the role of protector and aid designator of the World Bank and he hoped that the IMF could act as a world central bank with a reserve currency of its own that would create international reserves. However, the establishment of the IMF and the World Bank 'reflected [U.S. Assistant Treasury Secretary] Harry Dexter White's ideas rather than Keynes's, not because they were technically superior but because the Americans had the power' (Chandavarkar 2001).

By 1946 the IMF had real authority to *require* adjustments in member countries that appeared to be lagging behind more advanced nations in the global economy. The IMF had, and has, the power to act as a type of regulator and controller of world orders. The stipulation for use of IMF funds was that receiving countries would adopt *particular* forms of state, and production processes. Therefore the IMF had a powerful role to play in the formation of the New World order. During 1946 to 1958, major states set an example to other developing countries by adjusting their own national economies to adapt to the New World order of the time, Pax Americana. The Marshall Plan sealed the legitimacy of leadership within this historical bloc, via grants offered to countries recovering from the War. Aid provision seemed to be a quick solution with long-term benefits (Rupert 1995: 52–3).

Pax Americana: Relations of Production

In the post-war era, the primary mode of relations of production in the West involved tripartism, state corporatism, and central planning. Tripartism emerged as a negotiation tool to unify the three agents of large-scale industries: the state, employers, and employees. State corporatism incorporated tripartism into partnerships, meaning that labour took a participatory role in industrialisation, but enjoyed little real protection or job security. While the form of state remained similar after the Wars, the state's role was no longer to direct and control the economy as it had been during the War but was to manage it through central planning. This welfare nationalist state form had originated during the wars as a protective but controlling entity. For its cohesion, ideological consensus was necessary: wartime and post-war restoration facilitated nationalist mentality as well as centrally-controlled provisions distribution.

A mixture of Keynesianism and reformism predominated throughout the 1940s in political economics, though Cox names the mixed economy 'neoliberalism' (1987: 218). Cox's interpretation here should not be confused with the 'neoliberalism' of the more recent historical bloc. During the post-War era in England, a classic example of the mixed economy consensus is crystallised. The Conservative Party sought full employment and used monetary and fiscal techniques to regulate the level of aggregate demand, activities usually attributed to state behaviour within a Keynesian economy. However, simultaneously, the Labour Party sought public collective provision of goods. From 1945 to 1966, there was relative consensus between the parties. 'Mixed economy' in these years meant that major manufacturing industries were transferred to public ownership, an action applauded by Labour, since good service was the overall aim. On the other hand, free trade was endorsed, a position traditionally taken by the Conservative Party.

In England at this time, major manufacturing industries were national-ised if they met particular standards decided by consenting parties. The standards for nationalisation of industries were intended to gauge the following criteria: the extent of efficiency; whether or not industrial relations could be deemed satisfactory; whether the industry was holding a monopoly position; whether it retained too much investment of capital; or whether it was a supplier of basic materials. Simultaneously, workers became slightly more integrated into political life when trade unions were given a chance to speak at the Labour Party's annual conferences in the UK, to the extent that at some points speakers were too challenging for the Party. In 1966, Labour established the Board for Prices and Incomes. Any request for wage increases had first to be referred to this Board. This regulation was an indication that 'consensus' was beginning to wane. However between 1945–1966, the Nationalist Welfare State evolved into a new form and production and therefore took on a new character.

During the discussed period, social relations of production or accumu-lation were not drastically altered. But Pax Americana is distinct as an economic and political hegemony that assured hierarchical systems within corporatism. In developmental states, employers emerged victorious and enjoyed state support, while labour remained at the bottom rung (which is discussed in the following chapter). The 'hegemony' of Pax Americana is an era marked by increased American funding of development in penetrated states such as South Korea and the formation of the foundations for dependency. This historical bloc began to modify in the 1970s.

The 1970s can be characterised by what Rupert calls a 'laissez-faire fundamentalism' (2000: 44). Liberal globalization that led to neo-liberalism's global popularity for economic development included not just trade but also finance. During this period, the increase and ease of financial exchanges were affected by excess liquidity from US balance of payments deficits. Furthermore, the fixed rate regime and capital controls, implemented at Bretton Woods, saw their own demise. Rates of specu-lation and foreign exchange trade increased. American hegemony did not last, and Cox claims that this was evident from the late 1960s and onward, when America's 'consensual' fragility was revealed. A space revealed itself for a new organisation of the global economy: for new leadership, or dissent.

Neoliberalism

While much of the philosophy behind liberal and neoliberal economic theory is the same, the literature of Friedman and others differs slightly from the liberalism of Pax Britannica or Pax Americana. Neoliberalism is idealised within the recommendations of the Washington Consensus. The literature of Milton Friedman (1962), Stephen Haggard (2000), and others represents an ideology that requires increased incorporation and con-sensus of all groups within society into economic norms. These authors herald the supremacy of competitive capitalism and free markets, plus the need for labour market flexibility and constant national restructuring. Nations are driven toward membership in a growing community of knowledge-based economies, which are presented as an emancipatory process of development, providing 'freedom' in all aspects of social life (Leftwich 2000: 112). Neoliberalism is a political and economic doctrine that renews interest in the role of the state and governance in development. Particularly after the Asian economic crisis in 1997, observers accused nations of ignoring international norms of accumu-lation, and began to accuse nations of harbouring over-involved govern-ments, whose control and regulation of economies led to bloating and to the prevention of prosperity as a dynamic market economy. Neoliberalism was promoted as the way forward for recovery from the deficiencies of the past.

Neoliberalism originates in 1971, when President Richard Nixon overthrew the original gold standard and replaced it with a system of free-floating exchange rates. This controversial move symbolises a moment of transformation for a previous period of economic history. As the institutions created at Bretton Woods represent a managed international economy, so the collapse in 1971 represents a shift to less regulation and thus increased free market ideology, which I argue is the basis of Neoliberalism. Friedman of the Chicago School is perhaps one of the best known authors to condone a sophisticated neoliberal thesis. He advocates competitive capitalism as the paramount social economic model, believing that capitalism, when effectively instituted and socialised, provides freedom. Political freedom is conditional upon free markets, and a society that operates upon the principles of neoliberalism will theoretically find the benefits in all levels, and that education and income distribution will provide freedom from poverty. Of course, reality is often very different from the utopias that theorists visualise.

The 1970s set the stage for international neoliberal economic relations. Governments concentrated on international markets and outward planning. One of the first neoliberal development projects occurred in Chile beginning in 1973. The CIA, in this case, supported the coup against the 'Marxist' Allende regime, despite the fact that it had been popularly elected. Pinochet, the next leader, restructured the economy at the advice and prompting of consultants from the Chicago School of Economics including Friedman, who visited to advise him on how to apply a functional neoliberal state. Despite Friedman's confidence that capitalism under neoliberal policies is the ultimate choice, Pinochet's policies of trade liberalisation led to suppression of workers and various corrupt practices, causing mass social strife and eventually outbreaks of violence. Other countries took similar routes, such as in the case of Mexico, where, in the first year of North American Free Trade Agreement (NAFTA), wages decreased 40–50 per cent, and the cost of living rose by 80 per cent. The policies executed in Mexico for the sake of neoliberal restructuring resulted in the failure of thousands of small and medium sized businesses and the privatisations of more than 1,000 state-owned enterprises.

Whilst the 1970s paved the way for a neoliberal historical bloc, policy recommendations for developing Latin American countries were encapsulated in the 'Washington Consensus' in 1989. The 'Washington Consensus' is a term coined by John Williamson, Chief Economist of the World Bank in the South Asian Region and senior fellow at the Institute for International Economics. The Consensus is based on Williamson's ten policy recommendations for Latin American countries. These recommendations found a consensus with 'most of official Washington', and include:

1. Fiscal discipline.
2. A redirection of public expenditure priorities toward fields offering both high economic returns and the potential to improve income distribution, such as primary health care, primary education, and infrastructure.
3. Tax reform (to lower marginal rates and broaden the tax base).
4. Interest rate liberalisation.
5. A competitive exchange rate.
6. Trade liberalisation.
7. Liberalisation of FDI inflows.
8. Privatisation.
9. Deregulation (in the sense of abolishing barriers to entry and exit).
10. Secure property rights. (Williamson 1990)

These recommendations were part of a partnership between British Prime Minister Margaret Thatcher, and American President Ronald Reagan, whose own national policies heavily reflect the criteria within the Consensus. The conception of the Washington Consensus was particularly timely with the collapse of the Soviet Union. The disillusionment with Socialist ideology and Keynesianism may have sparked the urgency to utilise an alternative methodology for political and economic planning (Naim 1999).

While the Washington Consensus is only a set of 'recommendations', it provides foreshadowing of what would occur within the historical bloc of neoliberal capitalism in these early years and likewise greatly informs the restructuring requirements of Structural Adjustment Programmes (SAPs). Neoliberalism as an economic theory is based on the rule of market, on the liberation of free enterprise or private enterprise from government bonds, no matter how much social damage this causes. It is a system within which governments advocate greater openness to international trade and investment. Businesses and employers often reduce wages in the initial stages of neoliberal adjustment, by de-unionising workers, and pigeon holing workers as human capital rather than considering the importance of workers' rights. Governments eliminate price controls and allow total freedom of movement for capital, and goods and services likewise. In the public sector, governments typically cut public expenditure for social services, deregulate government regulation of anything that might diminish profits, even if it means negative impacts on the environment or health and safety. States furthermore sell any state-owned enterprises to private investors. And finally, in the ideology of Neo-liberalism the idea of communities is transformed, which is manifest in policy-making. The idea of public good is not condoned, and responsibility of the individual for his/her own affairs and survival appears to become universal. Martinez and Garcia, members of Comite Emiliano Zapata affiliated to National Commission for Democracy in Mexico, critique this process by documenting several cases of exploitation and inequalities instigated by the expansion of neoliberalism (Martinez and Garcia 1996).

Conclusion

In conclusion, this chapter has outlined a modern global history of capitalism to provide a background of global hegemonic struggles surrounding forms of state and production relations. Positivist IR theories based in realism have not deeply pursued these matters, but it is possible to evaluate several aspects of struggle utilising Cox's configurations of power (1981, 1987) and to explore the dynamic between forms of state, relations of production and emerging social forces.

Elite groups evangelised capitalist norms and set down liberal ideologies through the consolidation of groups of organic intellectuals across the globe, beginning in the era of hegemonic Pax Britannica. During Pax Americana, the World Bank and IMF directed the discourse on globalization and capitalism. This rhetoric involves the prescription of certain norms for economic development that are advocated in the terminology of the Washington Consensus and IMF restructuring require-ments, whose development programmes are often quite direct and explicit mechanisms of socialisation within nations. Those requirements have, over time, become increasingly integrated into an emerging transnational network of capitalist apologists who aim to educate societies accordingly. Because the final stage discussed here is not hegemonic, even according to Cox's criteria, social forces are positioning themselves in a war of position. Chapter 3 now looks at the way in which Korea has dealt with international hegemonic struggle over time by elite led development and the *trasformismo* of workers during the ongoing passive revolution. In order to understand how this has occurred, I identify conditions for this paralysis by looking at non-hegemonic forms of state as well as limited concessions provided to workers to keep them from successfully carrying out their own revolution.

3

KOREA'S HISTORY OF PASSIVE REVOLUTION

Introduction

Chapter 3 assesses the construction of a 'comprehensive concept of control' (Van der Pijl 1984; Overbeek 1990), or a project wherein the dominant class leads the restructuring of societies at many levels including production, which requires an assimilation of mentalities and the control of a potentially insurgent working class consciousness. This strategy is wrapped up in *trasformismo*, involving direct as well as indirect aims to supposedly overcome factional interests and class differences by providing a limited reward system to subordinated groups. Politically dominant groups aim to achieve hegemonic status by incorporating subordinate classes' 'needs' into its development trajectories, or what I argue is a form of *trasformismo* occurring under elite-led forms of state, wherein the capitalist class owns and manages the means of production. These two factors are what I have identified to be the conditions for passive revolution.

While there was a level of elite infighting during the stages of Korean history over the exact direction this country's development should take, conflicts of interests simply reinforced the claim that Korea's economic history is mired in hegemonic struggle. I am interested in the policies and strategies that effect workers' representation rather than what can be seen as outright oppression which has been an ongoing and consistently rearticulated theme throughout capitalist relations of production so to some extent, I must take note of elite infighting throughout development. Because Korea's political history is dominated by totalitarian governments whose intention has been to build a strong foundation for the proliferation of capitalism, it is impossible to qualify the extent to which elite battles have provided a space for possible representation for the wider population rather than carving a rut of oppression. This claim is substantiated by the recognition that even since democratisation, the management of workers' uprising is still steeped in top-down strategies that bear resemblance to earlier governments' approaches.

In the case of Korea, the government has offered a variety of concessions for workers to superficially incorporate them into development policies, but this has not occurred under consultation with workers and thus has not occurred under hegemonic consensus between social forces. *Trasformismo* is a limited inclusion tactic that aims to bring about consensus, or at the very least aims to convince people (in this case, workers) that elite-led operations actually benefit them more than take advantage of their vulnerability. Successful *trasformismo* will prevent workers from enacting a complete grass roots revolution against exploitative relations. So to qualify the characteristics of hegemonic struggle at the national level throughout Korean development, I look at the forms of state and ongoing strategies of *trasformismo* to note how passive revolution has been achieved. By following a similar pattern of periodisation of the previous chapter, the discussion demonstrates the impact that international hegemonic struggles had on this small nation, which has not been immune from international politics. It argues that nations' responses to what Cox claimed were at some points 'hegemonic' and at others, 'non-hegemonic' historical blocs are specific to each individual nation's case, but almost inevitably result in conflict and accelerated power struggles between owners of the means of production, and workers who act as producers but have only their labour power to sell. I argue that a close inspection of the history of Korean economic development demonstrates that the global hegemonic struggles outlined in Chapter 2 *have* significantly impacted this semi-peripheral nation but *have not* been conducive to hegemony within Korea itself. So the analysis begins to make sense of the impact that 'world orders' have had on the development of a small country that named itself the 'hermit kingdom' for years before finally opening its doors to international relations in 1876, when Korea signed its first international treaty with Japan. It also calls into the question the idea of 'global hegemony' itself, considering non-hegemonic relations in this semi-peripheral nation.

This chapter seeks out two conditions indicating passive revolution throughout four periods of Korean history, in conjunction with international hegemonic struggle. The analysis notes, within the first condition I have identified for passive revolution to occur, elite-led economic development and the restructuring of production. The second condition requires a look into the way that workers' needs have been re-articulated via *trasformismo*, as elite groups attempt to influence citizens' and workers' perceptions of accelerated development throughout Korean history.

Occupied/Colonial History During Rival Imperialisms:[1] Form of State and *Trasformismo*

Korea was the third East Asian nation to take a step toward inter-nationalisation; the Opium Wars of 1839–42 had opened China's doors, and Japan had met Commodore Perry's 'black ships' upon its shores in 1853. The United States did not make contact with Korea until 1882, and even then, a Chinese official managed the process of communication between these countries. Korea avoided interference from international forces in the early stages of its modern history but over time has not been immune from the national effects of elites' struggles for world hegemony.

This intriguing peninsula protrudes off the edge of eastern China and borders slightly at its northeastern tip with Russia, and has been historically manipulated by some of the world's most powerful players. The modern history of Korea starts with Japanese occupation which began in 1905 and then became formally annexed in 1910, and did not end until August 15, 1945. Japan had invaded several times before 1910 and has acted as a sometimes very brutal 'big brother' toward its neighbour. My analysis of Korea begins with a look into Japanese colonisation.

Top-down Production Restructuring During Japanese Colonial Industrialisation
This section discusses Japanese colonisation, or the early stages of industrialisation that occurred under elite-led conditions and often resulted in power struggles between those at the helm of restructuring and those affected, in particular, workers. Japan was a late-comer to compete in the world order of mixed imperialisms (1875–1945), although it had begun its preparations for world domination from 1871 to 1873 by sending out an 'Iwakura Mission' of Meiji oligarchs to study Western banking, technology, political systems, and infrastructures. Sending researchers to the United Kingdom and the United States, the mission was specifically executed to gain information on how other powerful nations

had gained leverage and power over other nations in a world whose traditional boundaries and identities increasingly appeared to fragment, and the 'international' was an emerging arena to be measured. Korea and Taiwan would be two of Japan's first experiments in imperial pursuits.

During the entire Tokugawa period, until 1868, Japan had been a relatively quiet neighbour, but 'had always had her eye on Korea' (Conroy 1960: 4). So when Japan invaded and colonised Korea in 1910, and proceeded to use her labour and resources to aid its own growth and to further its own imperialist initiatives, it may not have come as a surprise. As a component to imperial expansion however, Japan managed Korea's first industrial revolution under a developmental colonial regime. Japan forced Korean citizens into lives of propaganda-driven slavery, filched Korean land and distributed it to tenant sharecroppers, and built railways and ports so Japanese industrial workers could essentially 'eat Korea's rice in Japan'. In fact, from 1920–35, Japan increased food production in Korea specifically for export to Japan, following a classic colonial pattern. Japan also directed the building of roads and power supply systems, providing an infrastructure for their advancements. Choi (1989: 47) argues that the first period of industrialisation effectively destroyed Korea's traditional mode of manufacturing production, which had been based on a rural handicraft industry of weaving or producing hemp cloth. This was the beginning of the very forced opening of the Hermit Kingdom. Interestingly, the international community turned a blind eye toward Japanese occupation.

Japanese occupation marks the beginning of Korean modernisation and rationalisation. The colonising bureaucracy rationalised land relationships by fixing property rights and instigated industrial development. Cumings (1997: 149) comments that analysis of this process is often restricted to Japanese perspectives, whose narrative of this period of Korean history detracts from Korean citizens' experiences of colonial atrocities that have led to a lingering and widespread resentment toward Japan. Clifford states that some Koreans now would argue in favour of colonialism because it 'had the virtue of laying the foundation for subsequent economic development' (1997: 27). Vogel (1991: 90–1) sees Japan as a model for Korea's development. Japan held 'the primary source of capital and technology for South Korea's export-led market. Viewed from this perspective, Japan played the most critical role in promoting economic growth in South Korea' (Moon and Nishino 2002: 4). There is a certainly a proportion of the Korean population who would argue in this manner, but they are most likely to be those who have become members of the capitalist class and now, transnational capitalist class network as a result of Korea's development. This position tends to overlook the human trauma and political exclusion that has been a major factor of industrialisation.

For the supplementation of its imperial strategy at the onset of WWII, Japan invested in Korea's mining, chemical, railroad, and hydroelectric plant industries. The number of factory workers in Korea rapidly increased from 49,000 in 1921, to 80,000 in 1925, and jumped to 102,000 in 1930. In the pattern toward a dual economy, in all sectors, Japan gained benefits from Korea's modernisation. In 1937, Korea became the supply and production base aiding Japan's expansion into Manchuria. So although Korea could not defend itself in the global hegemonic struggles resulting in imperial intervention and war, its labour and resources played a complicit part in this ongoing struggle, via Japanese dominance.

In 1910, Korean people could not have imagined the changes to their very livelihood and social experience that were soon to emerge. Thirty years later, 420,000 mining, manufacturing, transportation and communication workers became the fire behind Korea's first exposure to industrialisation, solidarity and class consciousness emerged (Ogle 1990: 3). Japan was extremely oppressive toward Korean factory workers during occupation, forcing them and all citizens likewise to learn the Japanese language and adopt Japanese names. Under Japanese colonisation, Korean workers endured 'wage discrimination, long work hours and hazardous working conditions' (Kwon and O'Donnell 2001: 17). Most of the managers in the newly implemented factories were Japanese, but some Koreans were trained to manage in a similar way to the Japanese. Simmering anti-Japanese sentiment and resistance to the substandard working conditions led to the original formation of Korean class consciousness and the formation of labour unions.

Workers dealing with such oppression in the workplace joined a more general movement for independence from Japan, which roused a nascent labour movement. The March 1, 1919 Independence Movement was an event staged to protest Japanese occupation. 33 signatures of nationalist leaders were compiled in a public declaration against Japanese dominance. Chung (1995: 80) attributes anti-Japanese sentiment for bringing people together into a singular objective of resistance regardless of class position. These early defensive social movements indicate a mass recognition that it would take collective resistance to defend workers and other oppressed people against both external and internal oppression. In 1920, at the height of colonisation, 81 labour disputes broke out, involving 4,599 workers, and in 1930 there were 160 cases that involved 18,972 workers. Finally, the Japanese government drove the Korean labour movement underground in the last stage of its period of rule and in the 1930s and the voice of workers was effectively quashed.

Japanese Colonisation and Trasformismo

Mitchell's work on Europe's colonisation of Egypt discusses the disciplining of populations to instigate modernisation. Colonised citizens gain a 'new conception of space, new forms of personhood, and a new means of manufacturing the experience of the real' (1988: ix, xi) in relation to modernisation. This is reminiscent of my discussion of *trasformismo*, because the appeal to people's subjectivity allows a powerful role for ideas in the 'experience of the real' (ibid.). But Mitchell also argues that modernisation entails the direct disciplining of people and institutions, generated through educational processes in a colonial environment. Cumings (1997: 147) writes that Japan 'put its citizens through a regimen of public education that seemed perfectly designed to develop the industrious political subject, with the vices of self-surveillance and repression', and this tendency was translated into colonial practice. In the processes of hegemonic consolidation, states take an educative role in hegemonic consolidation (*PN*: 242). Unlike Mitchell's Foucault-inspired understanding of discipline however, a neo-Gramscian analysis cannot ignore the exploitative elements inherent to the discipline of workers and citizens under colonial rule or under any form of state for that matter.

During Japanese forced industrialisation in Korea, colonial leaders demanded 'efficiency' of workers rather than the historically developed kinship relations of production that had cultivated a subsistence economy, introduced the concept of training and work standardisation along targeted output requirements, and suppressed and controlled all aspects of Korean industrial education. Itoho Hirobumi, the first Residence-General, closed all pre-existing Korean technical, agricultural, commercial and 'correspondence officer training' schools, replacing them with one official training centre in Seoul in 1906 and several others in rural areas for the training of manual technicians 'required for Japanese exploitation of various Korean products' (60). Japanese-run schools did not offer qualified industrial education but only basic household-level industrial and manual education. In 1927, the first vocational place of education,

Hypsung Vocational School, offering commerce-focussed education was opened in response to Japanese increased demands on the industrial workforce. Hierarchical production relations during the colonial period were such that the Japanese forced workers to undergo training into particular skills, a relationship that is echoed in less explicit terms in later economic policy.

But between 1910 and 1919, there were four types of colonial practical schools: agricultural, commercial, industrial, and 'simple' vocational schools (KRIVET 1999: 108). Each practical school was designed to formulate the types of workers needed to organise an industrial economy suited for production of goods to be extracted by colonial leaders.

During the period of 'cultural rule' (1920–31), Japan rewrote the entire Korean education system, and during 'military rule' beginning in 1931, the colonial government as discussed above, demanded accelerated agricultural production. This would require ideological training intended to transform consciousness toward Japanese ways of thinking and working and thus a malleable workforce. The Japanese introduced new methods of training, which pushed beyond apprenticeships and kinship systems of craft acquisition skills but preceded formalised VET. While this form of education does not appear at first glance to hold *trasformismo* like qualities, it makes an appeal to an aspect of workers' subjectivities that transcends physical manpower. The Japanese were perhaps a mutation of British nineteenth century bourgeoisie who graciously forced training upon workers who were expected to passively and gratefully accept the good will of this activity.

As the war intensified, Japan soon realised its empire depended on output of production, and instituted an employer/employee relationship of what it called 'industrial patriotism' to encourage higher rates of production called *sampo*. From each subsection of each firm, one representative was chosen and given the responsibility to form a workers' organisation, or association. These associations were designed to provide workers with limited education on work efficiency, but each group was imbued with the intent to prevent worker disputes and unrest, as well as to increase productivity. *Sampo* is a form *trasformismo* in that it gave workers a form of authority in the workplace to manage associations, but in practice, prevented workers from formulating a voice, and re-instated their subordinate position as producers for the elite class. The message for workers was that their most important role was for increased output, and that their position required education toward this end, thus glossing over the completely hierarchical relations inherent to colonisation, and the slavery-like conditions that workers suffered.

So Japan placed ongoing pressure upon Korean workers to conform to their cultural, ideological, and practical standards for skills attainment in the workplace. This imperial nation named its development project or accumulation strategy in Korea one of 'modernisation', while Cumings calls it an early version of 'bureaucratic-authoritarian path to industrialis-ation' (Cumings 1997: 149–50). Thus Japan laid the foundations for Korean development. Whilst the colonial leaders did not gain much citizen *support* for leadership, *trasformismo* is noted in the way that the 'best' work positions and concessions such as found within the *sampo* were granted to workers who did not resist their directives.

Japan forced worker consolidation into its production strategies by requiring Korean workers to adopt 'Fordist' relations of production during the period of colonisation. During the period of rival imperialisms, American modes of production became influential internationally. In 1913 Ford opened the first moving assembly line, requiring a de-skilled production force. Mass production required cheap, mass labour, and this was in abundance in Korea. The US Fordist reorganisation of production inspired Japanese activity in Korea at the beginning of the twentieth century.

Gramsci discusses Fordism as 'an ultra-modern form of production and of working methods, such as is offered by the most advanced American variety, the industry of Henry Ford' (*PN*: 280–1). Fordism required both force and persuasion: 'a political regime in which trade unions would be subdued, workers might be offered a higher real standard of living, and the ideological legitimation of this new kind of capitalism would be embodied in cultural practices and social relations extending far beyond the workplace' (Rupert, *forthcoming*). In the postwar era, Rupert claims, the institutionalisation of Fordism allowed the USA to possess half the world's production (Rupert 1995). So it is no wonder Japan, one of the 'rival imperialisms', implemented this model within Korea during this period of passive revolution.

In 1943, as the war started to 'turn against Japan', the colonial power announced an 'Emergency Agenda for Education' and opened 25 more industrial schools by 1945, simultaneous to sending students to military factories rather than providing complete training. Koreans realised soon enough that the colonialist nation was more interested in exploiting their labour force than providing training that could allow their home country to compete against their captors, and resentment began to build (KRIVET

1999: 61–2). World War II did not end in Japan's favour, and soon enough, Korea was hurled into the next phase of national, social and economic restructuring.

Pax Americana I: US Occupation of Korea

In the first year of the 'hegemonic' historical period that Cox calls 'Pax Americana' (1981: 170–1), the USA assumed leadership over Korea, which would begin Korea's next phase of elite-led development within the conditions for passive revolution. When Japan finally surrendered in 1945 at the end of the Second World War, the USA entered centre stage in the South, where it still harbours thousands of troops in 2007, though it has begun to withdraw troops in the climate of the Iraq war.

In 1945, the US unilaterally decided to divide South Korea at the 38th parallel. There appears to be no rationale for this dividing line except that the capitol would fall within the same zone laterally with the US capitol, Washington DC (FRUS 1945: 1039; Cumings 1997: 187). Two young colonels decided where to designate the separating border, and neglected to consult with China, Russia, or Koreans themselves. But there was no staked adversity to this decision, and on the same day that General MacArthur ordered Japanese surrender via the General Order Number One, the 38th parallel divide was made official.

Cumings (1997: 185–9) stresses that the decade 1943–53 is very important for a complete comprehension of modern and contemporary political economics of Korea. During this period of Pax Americana, from 1943–47, the United States high diplomacy is termed by Cumings as going through an early 'internationalist phase'. Korea was forced to come to terms with a new identity resulting from the USA's international pursuits, i.e. to spread the message of democracy and fight Communism.

Korea found itself divided into two with Soviet troops occupying the north terrain beyond the 38th parallel of latitude, and the USA prevailing within the south. Politically, divisions reflect Cold War politics in that the north's leader was Russian-supported Kim Il Sung, and in the South, American 'democratic' influence was evident in increasing areas of society and politics with a little help from their new friends, the American military. With the collapse of trade with Japan, and the cut off from fertiliser that had been delivered from the northern area of the peninsula, production was in crisis, and widespread starvation was only prevented by American financial aid.

A complete American military government (AMG) took over the South from 1945–48. After these three years, the USA organised elections in the South with support of the United Nations Temporary Commission on Korea (UNTCOK), who claimed that it would allow for 'a valid expression of the free will of the electorate'. There was widespread resistance of separate elections between the South and North, as people believed that the North and South would reunify soon after the division. On 10 May 1948, UNTCOK oversaw the first general election in the south, despite the initial idea for election had been shared on both sides of the parallel, but a breakdown in discussions between the UNTCOK and the north led to a recommendation for a separate vote in the south, despite resistance from the South Korean population. Nonetheless, representatives drafted a constitution that gave an identity to the Republic of Korea. Three months later, the National Assembly elected Rhee, Syngman as the first President of the Republic of Korea (ROK). The North soon held elections and Kim, Il Sung in the North took Premier Leadership, a title taken over by his son Kim, Jong Il at the first Leader's death in 1994.

Between 1944 and 1946 manufacturing establishments fell in numbers by 44 per cent and manufacturing employment dropped by 60 per cent. By 1948, industrial output was 1/5 of the level in 1940. Rhee faced this political and economic turmoil when he took office as the first president of South Korea. Korean Democratic Party (KDP) representatives in the National Assembly were mostly composed of industrialists and land-owners, but this group opposed Rhee's autocratic leadership style. Rhee strengthened his executive powers through constitutional amendments in 1952, which gave him complete control of land reform. But land reform was not central to the leadership's development plans, and after land-owners had been dislodged and insurrection circumvented, the government shifted attention to urban areas. Urbanisation was a common global phenomenon at this time.

While the political elites were organising leadership of the new Republic, leaders of the labour movement hoped for a chance to move forward with its previously quelled objectives. While in the West, trade union associations did not profoundly utilise their functions as activist or interest groups until after 1918 (Gramsci 1921–26/1978), this process had been delayed even further in Korea by Japanese colonialism. In 1945, the year Japan surrendered, the left-leaning trade union movement had re-emerged in South Korea and the National Trade Union Council (NTUC) was established in November 1945. Members of the NTUC grew in numbers from 180,000 at its inception, to 553,408 within just two months. Between 1945 and 1948 the Council organised more than 3,000 strikes despite the fact that it had not gained fully legal status. In 1946, the AMG began to restrict the Council and allowed sole recognition for American-style union activity with pragmatic or business intentions. The Council reacted by declaring the 'September National Strikes' that began at the Seoul Kyungseong Railway Factory and quickly gained 264,000 workers' support. Government response to strikes resulted in 25 workers' deaths and 11,000 incarcerations, and a further 18,600 were forced from their jobs. The American military leadership learned of the Council's ties to the Chosun Communist Party, and in 1947, with heavily Cold War influenced overtones completely banned the NTUC.

The AMG replaced the NTUC with the General Federation of Korean Trade unions (GFKTU), which later became the Korean Federation of Trade unions (KFTU) in the 1960s. The Rhee government led this transition and organised the membership of 127,618 members by 1949, which marks

> ... the beginning of organised labour's incorporation by an authoritarian state in Korea. Incorporation meant that the Federation's functions were limited to supporting the political and economic interests of the state and Korean capitalism.
>
> (Kwon and O'Donnell 2001: 29).

Thus the growth of independent union movement was rapidly stunted in the early lifetime of the ROK. Unions that could have been representative of any interests rather than those of oversized conglomerates (*chaebols*) or of government whim were dismissed quite early in Korea's modern history.

Chaebols played a major role in Korea's development and cannot be overlooked in the discussion of the restructuring of production relations and *trasformismo* throughout Korean history. Ogle (1990: 29) attributes South Korea's incredible growth in its 'march to modernisation' to five factors: centralised government, centralised economic planning, foreign investment, export-led development, and the *chaebol*. The *chaebol*'s was designed after the Japanese *zaibatsu* and the combination of Chinese characters for *chaebol* are identical to *zaibatsu*, which means literally 'finance clique'. *Chaebols* are groups of companies that are owned and/or controlled by a family who manage from a central headquarters and are composed of subsidiaries operating in a collection of industries.

Characteristically, servants and politicians historically exchanged rent for political support or bribes, from *chaebol* leaders which led to bloating and was later seen as 'corruption'. Particularly after the Korean War, Syngman Rhee promoted import substitution and favoured specific industries through rents and credits, simultaneous to promoting over-valuation of the exchange rate and allowing high rates of protection and government procurement. The result of these corporate ties meant that *chaebol*s grew to mammoth proportions from their inception in the 1940s, but also contributed dramatically to Korea's accelerated development. Throughout the historical periods in this chapter, the *chaebol* has been the industrial basis for production.

Masfield and Schneider have documented the role of the *chaebol* and its relationship to policymaking, claiming that in fact 'trust between business and government elites can reduce transaction and monitoring costs' (1997: 13), a view that gives limited legitimacy to the series of authoritarian developmentalist governments that led this nation's development. Kwon and O'Donnell (2001) point out that an overly state-centric telling of Korean development overlooks the significance of the *chaebol* throughout the process.

But in its nascent years the enlargement of the *chaebol* would have been impossible without US aid. During the first years of Pax Americana following Japanese occupation, South Korea's relationship with the United States was not ideological alone. Korea actively 'attached' itself economically to America in the early period of its development, as American aid was in abundance in the post-Korean War years. During this period, the USA 'financed nearly 70 per cent of total imports between 1953 and 1962, and equalled 75 per cent of total fixed capital formation' (Haggard 1990: 55). The first Korean President, Rhee, Syngman was particularly skilled in getting funding from President Eisenhower, leading John Foster Dulles to call him an 'Oriental bargainer' (304). President Rhee spent aid money lavishly, often without telling even his closest officials how he did so. America saw South Korea as a good investment in the throes of the Cold War, and staunchly maintained partnerships with anti-Communist states. An obvious ideological split between the North and South Korean nations gave Rhee access to great amounts of American capital to fund his developmentalist import-substitution campaign.

After World War II, Korea plunged into the process of reconstruction and a second phase of industrialisation in a way that appeared to suit international demands in a climate of Cox's alleged American hegemony. The form of state in charge of Korean development during this time period can certainly be seen as a developmentalist state. *Corporatism* is a classic component of developmentalism, and again, the relationship between *chaebols* and the public sector provided a basis for much of South Korean economic development and has retained a high level of influence even in present day circumstances. Corporatism comes about when a ruler seeks to incorporate a wider range of voices into development plans, i.e. civil society and business, but the state is typically not as concerned with labour or the employed as it is with management. The developmental state model places the state in complete command of labour relations and often involves intimate business/political relationships of support.

Internationally, there appear to have been two powerful forms of state during the world order of Pax Americana, the mixed economic state, and the neomercantilist developmental state. This phenomenon did not bypass South Korea, which can be named within the latter category. The neo-mercantilist state is similar to pre-war Italian fascism in that capitalist development is enacted via passive revolution. The Korean state controlled labour relations and after 1947 with the ban of the NTUC, this was made official by the AMG who governed alongside Rhee until 1949. Trade unions were associated with Communist principles and in the Cold War climate were not looked upon favourably. President Rhee was a staunch anti-Communist and did not hide his prejudices. Despite ideological consensus evident in the elite echelons, I can argue that South Korea was not integrated into the supposedly hegemonic Pax Americana due to the throttling of workers' representation by way of independent unions in this era of state-led economic development.

Pax Americana II: Developmental Military Dictatorships

The next phase of Korean development during Pax Americana started when the United States withdrew troops from South Korea. In response to this action, the North, backed by the Soviet Union and China, attacked the South on June 25, 1950, initiating what is now known simply as the Korean War. It took three years and around three million deaths to return the South and North to a 'tense stand-off exactly where the fighting began' (Clifford 1998: 30). Particularly in the period following the Korean

War, Korean government and business elites aimed to attract investment and reconstruction aid from the international community of speculators and critics with a promise of rapid industrialisation. I argue that in the process, those in command of reconstruction and later economic development, completely overlooked the voice of workers and led Korea through another period of passive revolution using tactics of *trasformismo*.

At the time of the 1953 armistice with the North, President Rhee led Korea into a second round of modernisation. During his presidency (1948–60), Rhee strove to match his nation's global status with Japan and the West. Once again, with American funding and through considerable worker oppression, Rhee was able to autocratically apply an import-substitute strategy for this new round of industrialisation.

Post-war Restructuring: President Rhee's Form of State

But who was this powerful 'Oriental bargainer' with such strong ties to the West? The American CIA composed the first personality study of its kind about a non-American leader to reveal the psyche and character of President Rhee. The study states: 'the danger exists that Rhee's inflated ego may lead him into action disastrous or at least highly embarrassing to the new Korean government and to the interests of the USA' (CIA 1948). Rhee's government was in fact a template of Choson dynasty politics during which time the state and society were in almost constant conflict. The 'king' and 'legislature' of this first President's Republic behaved in a manner reminiscent of landed nobles who avoided accountability and a welfare role toward labour. Rhee would do whatever it took to create a 'full-blown, self-reliant industrial base with steel, chemicals, machine tools and the electric energy to run them' (Cumings 1997: 305), even if it took a complete oversight to the needs of workers. Nonetheless, Rhee was competitive, sharp, and high spirited, ideal attitudes for the cut-throat nature of capitalism.

After 1953, Korean economic policy was predominantly focussed on restructuring a war-torn, deteriorated infrastructure. President Rhee led the country through this initial period of restructure with considerable American and UN assistance. The UN Korea Reconstruction Agency encouraged Rhee to apply a rationalised program of import substitution and infrastructural development, and in order to achieve this, he would need to stabilise the exchange rate. This did not happen, and Rhee was ousted from office after it was discovered he had rigged the elections that kept him in office for 12 total years and had conducted various acts of fraud and corruption. Huge demonstrations erupted in the streets of Seoul when this was revealed. Students and workers formed alliances in antagonism to the government, demanding impeachment. After a widespread arraignment and his ousting, in 1960 a popular election brought Mr Chang, Myeon to presidency. This fleeting attempt for complete democratisation of the Korean government was unsuccessful however, as one year after the election a military coup led by General Park, Chung Hee dismissed Chang, and the General appointed himself President. Thus began the next era of authoritarian developmentalism of South Korea.

Second Developmental Dictator: President Park

General Park 'was a Japanese' (Moon and Nishino 2002: 6); indeed, at his death, the Ambassador Okazaki postulated that Park was 'the last soldier of Imperial Japan' (Okazaki 1984: 116). Park's name had been *Takagi Masao* during occupation and he had trained at the Japanese Imperial Military Academy. Perhaps as a result, his development plans intricately reflected Japanese industrial policy and Moon and Nishino (2002: 7) state that Park's:

> ... leadership style ... [was] greatly affected by his exposure to Japan, Japanese imperial education ... his preoccupation with command and obedience, emphasis on details, accuracy and precision, decisiveness, and overall militaristic mentality were such products of such pattern of political socialisation.

Thus the 'Japanese' man took power and began to organise his country's development, which would turn into a solid eighteen years of rapid, state-led development. President Park's military government has been called a developmental state, and the 'miracle on the Han' is often attributed to the state's control of the economy.

While President Rhee had been an autocratic ruler, Park started his period of rule with a revolutionary debut, and installed a Korean Central Intelligence Agency (KCIA) to seek to uproot what he called, with American inspiration, 'corruption'. Park rearranged all former President Rhee's leftover legal and political institutions and effectively centralised all power for economic decision-making to a powerful new Economic Planning Board (EPB). This regime soon became an icon of developmental authoritarianism led by a military government which thoroughly reflected his predecessor's era.

Park proceeded to censor the press and completely banned political parties, political organisations and unions, but despite these clearly repressive acts, he was not wholly unpopular and in 1963 announced he would hold a national referendum for continued military rule. His 'Democratic Republican Party' was narrowly successful. President Park thus began a series of industrialisation strategies at the advice of the World Bank and the US Agency for International Development (USAID), in the form of four Five-Year Economic Development Plans scheduled for 1962–6, 1967–71, 1972–6, and 1977–81.

During Park's first Development Plan, only unions that worked in cooperation with Park's strategies were allowed to operate. Park's government closely monitored and regulated the USA-created 'yellow' union, the FKTU, and in 1961 revised the *Labour Dispute Conciliation Law*, *Labour Committee Law* and the *Trade Union Act* to restrict political activities of multiple unions. The Labour Management Council was formed to promote unions' co-operation with the state.

In the 1960s and early 70s, Korea experienced both accelerated economic growth and a rapid process of political realignment. In 1972, President Park's government wrote the *yusin* (revitalization) constitution, and simultaneously overthrew his own Party, which he had founded in 1963. The *yusin* constitution was ratified under martial law, and effectively increased presidential power. The government was thus entitled to use martial law or garrison decree to respond to political unrest. From 1961 and 1979, martial law was affected eight times. For example on October 15, 1971 student protests sparked garrison decree and nearly 2,000 students were arrested. On October 17, 1972, nearly exactly one year later, Park proclaimed martial law. He also shut down the National Assembly, and arrested several opposition leaders (FAS 1999).

Koo (2001: 44–5) writes that the identity and class-consciousness of workers developed most prominently throughout the 1960s as a result of rapid industrial transformation and the impact this had on their day to day lives. The haste of transformation was 'remarkable' and at the expense of rural sectors forced farmers to become industrial wage workers and to move to city areas in droves. Manufacturing, however, was condensed to a few cities and the majority of workers were hired by large businesses such as the *chaebol* rather than in small and medium size businesses. The identity of the working emerged from a relatively homogeneous set of people who shared social background, demographic status, and skill level. Many workers were young women from rural families. Workers with a minimal amount of skill and with common levels of education and training were a classic feature of the Fordist mode of production. Until the 1980s, when 'industrial upgrading' of the economy began to differentiate labour, the working class shared a strikingly similar set of personal characteristics, work environments and conditions. Thus it is appropriate to discuss worker consciousness in relation to workers' role in production.

Park's most profitable industrialisation scheme was the Heavy-Chemical Industry (HCI) Promotion Plan. The early 1970s was marked by 'remarkable economic performance' (Moon 1999: 4), a result of government emphasis on export, aggressive industrialisation, and an improved balance of payments. Korea's 'catch-up' style of industrialisation was led by a developmental state, meaning that the state was intimately involved in adjusting both the market and the infrastructure of the country's economy (Amsden 1992). The HCI began in 1973 and during the 1970s the Park government supported the investment of private companies in development of factories and facilities for heavy industries. The government borrowed heavily from foreign sources in order to provide capital for its development initiatives.

During the 1970s the *chaebol* expanded rapidly at the direction and subsidisation of the government. Industrial 'priorities' were heavy machinery, non-ferrous materials, petrochemicals, steel, electronics, and shipbuilding. A corporatist government/business relations in South Korea prevailed, a relationship that excluded the voice of labour. The global historical bloc of Neoliberalism began, meaning that the hegemony of Pax Americana was in decline. The Park government however continued to direct a passive revolution.

In the 1970s, workers experienced unequal income distribution, few rewards for dirty and dangerous work, and a feeling of deprivation despite working for the fastest growing economy of the region. Union members began to fight with Union leaders and speak out against various new policies, discussed below. This occurred not only in the national and industrial peak organisations but also at the enterprise level. In Korea, income share in the lowest percentile decreased from 18.9 per cent at the beginning of the decade to 15.3 per cent in 1980. In the higher levels of income, on the other hand, income substantially increased. Whilst this figure rested at 43 per cent in the early part of the 1970s the top 20 per cent of incomes raised to 46.9 per cent by 1980.

The Special Act for National Security of 1971 allowed the KCIA and police liberty to oppress any labour uprising and to contain independent trade unions. But perhaps the most extreme reaction to these oppressions was the suicide of Chun, Taeil in the same year. The textile worker lit himself on fire in front of one of the well-known sweatshops in the centre of Seoul, in protest to the dire working conditions and the government's violation of the Labour Standards Act.

So during Pax Americana and into the era of Neoliberalism, a series of developmental regimes fashioned Korea's semi-peripheral status in the global economy. Korea's economy flourished very quickly and awed international speculators for several years. Despite constant labour protest, strikes, worker suicides and student uprisings, oppressed groups were not able to stop the daily atrocities that forced industrialisation accrued. So the first condition for passive revolution was maintained.

Trasformismo *during Developmental Dictatorships*

To keep workers from gaining power, which could have slowed the pace of development, elites resorted to *trasformismo* through building a managed solidarity between workers via an appeal to nationalist sentiment. From 1948–79, as has been discussed, two military bureaucratic presidents of Rhee, Syngman and Park, Chung Hee facilitated and directed modernis- ation under a regime of developmental paternalism, a form of state that is based on the idea that governments have a moral responsibility to the public. Both presidents appealed to workers' common sense regarding hard work and sacrifice for national prosperity and post-war recon- struction. Nationalism can reduce the risk of political dissent; it has the capacity to join opposing forces and proselytises a development ideology. This is a form of *trasformismo*, because it aids in 'revolution-restoration'; similar to what Gramsci noted in the formation of the Italian State as parties became closely aligned due to molecular changes of ideologies (Gramsci, *Risorgimento*: 157 in *PN*: 58).

But the appeal to common sense was not the only form of *trasformismo* evident during this time. President Rhee relied on UN assistance and US aid for reconstruction, and the USA took a paternal role as well over Korean education, making it look as though it would extend aid not in just financial terms but also in terms of public welfare. During Rhee's term of presidency, the United States took over the Education Bureau and formed an Educational Council. The 'beautiful imperialis[ts]' (Shambaugh 1993) reached out to Korea and helped the government appeal to the larger masses. Pro-modernisation commentators welcomed the 'beautiful' anti- Communist imperialists from the USA whose rhetoric claimed to have rescued Korea from the Japanese and saved South Korea from the Communism of the North, and US-led education reflected these convictions. 'Doing good for others' was the appeal to common sense that could support American and later IMF-directed construction of the Republic of Korea (KRIVET 1999: 114). Education institutions promoted the ideologically loaded slogans 'doing it for yourself', and 'working industriously'. A single-form system of education was introduced at this time, which was intended to provide an alternative to the Japanese totalitarian system. In the single-form system, vocationally trained students were not meant to be differentiated socially from students in the humanities, in the formal education system. An attempt to bring vocational training to the social status level of formal education is a form of *trasformismo* because it blurs social divisions and superficially empowers workers socially. In fact, vocationally trained individuals were not attributed the same level of social esteem as was associated with those educated in a formal institution. Later, during Park's era of leadership, within every vocational school and training centre the phrase 'skilled workers are the standard bearer of the modernisation of our country' was posted for trainees to read. Again, this is an appeal to workers' common sense regarding modernisation, ideas portrayed as though modernisation and convergence were to be the only options for their country's survival in times of global hegemonic struggle.

President Park envisioned four 5-year Economic Development Plans to accompany his accumulation strategy of export-led industrialisation. The first 5-year Plan encouraged guided capitalism, and actually stated that this 'economic system will be a form of "guided capitalism" … in which the government will either directly participate in or indirectly render guidance to the basic industries and other important fields' (49). The government thus committed itself to guiding the material restructuring of production, with high rates of cooperation from *chaebol*s, whose growth from small business status to large-scale conglomerates between the 1940s and 1970s enabled Park's industrialisation strategies.

During Park's first Plan (1962–66), more than 80 per cent of exports were of forestry and fishery products, agricultural products, and raw ores. 36 per cent of investment went toward infrastructure, and labour intensive industries of footwear and textiles were promoted and sustained by cheap labour, which was, and is still one of Korea's most fruitful resources. Ten of the largest *chaebol*s were diversified toward the Park government's policies and were led to manufacture light industries such as electronic appliances for domestic use and garments. The government extended its range of control by the promotion of training, according to a plan to train 8,000 workers, a number which quickly expanded to 9,000, then 10,000 individuals who would receive training over 18 months' time (KRIVET 1999: 119). In 1964, a vocational training bill was passed by the Ministry of Labour (MOL) that stressed the following points:

> ... the securing of labour power (skill, talent) in terms of quality and quantity is the one and only economic policy ... the authorisation and management of the results of vocational training by the state is appropriate in terms of skill management and will aid in the improvement of worker awareness ... the objective is to plan job improvement at the same time as economic development through the nurturing of skilled workers necessary for industry and other businesses by integrating the former job stability law and the skill acquisition system of a workers standard law.

These guidelines indicate the governments' direct leadership over the accumulation of industrial and manufacturing labour power. Amsden (1989: 63, 64) suggests that:

> The wheeling and dealing, horsetrading, and trafficking that characterised this process were reminiscent of the reciprocity that characterised relations between the state and the privileged classes under dynastic rule ... the state used its power to discipline not just workers but the owners and managers of capital as well.

During the second Plan, light industries remained key to export strategies, but heavy and chemical industries were introduced, leading to the restructuring of some *chaebol*s toward this strategy. New types of skills in the workplace were needed to accommodate changes, so the government restructured VET 'in order to supply the manpower necessary' for Park's Plans (KRIVET/NCVER 2001: 57). In 1967, at the beginning of Park's second economic plan (1967–71), the face of VET changed when the government formed a publicly funded Central Vocational Training Centre, with financial and supervisory aid from the UNDP and the ILO. Changes to VET were widespread, and most formal vocational education was soon provided directly within the state curriculum and was systematised and standardised in the 1960s. This change was the beginning of the government's project to internationalise worker VET programmes, and within the conditions of passive revolution was complimentary to, and not transformative of its overall political and economic development strategies.

A license-training process was implemented at this time and a basic law for vocational training in 1976 required large companies in 'certain industries' to provide in-plant training (KRIVET 1999: 131). In 1974, academic high schools with specialised vocational training programs were introduced for students who aimed to enter the labour force after graduation. Vocational high schools also provided students training that almost guaranteed work after completing the chosen course. These unique high schools were 'strategically established and supported by the central government as part of the plan to build a strong industrial state' (KRIVET/NCVER 2000: 9). Harbison (1961) encouraged NICs in the 1960s to develop a workforce capable of dealing with rapid modernisation and accelerated growth, despite the hazards that modernisation could pose to economies such as a labour surplus of unskilled workers or on the other hand, a surplus of unemployed intellectuals. To avoid these problems in human resources, Harbison recommended an emphasis on training of manpower, creation of incentives, and the provision of *rational* education. Incentives:

> ... encourage men and women to prepare for and engage in the kinds of productive activity which are needed for accelerated growth. To accomplish this, the compensation of an individual should be related to the *importance of his job in the modernising society*.
> [italics included by present author] (1961: 24)

Harbison advocated higher remuneration for jobs most needed to further the programme of modernisation. Experts like Harbison indicate that the formation of organic intellectuals around a development programme is not a new phenomenon of industrialisation, but is a prescription for success according to the measures of capitalist integration.

In terms of expectations placed on workers, Park's economic system required 'brutally long working hours, high rates of savings and investment, and a hierarchical, authoritarian system that rewarded those who succeeded and punished those who did not co-operate' (45). One of his dramatic speeches encouraged workers to take on the strenuous responsibility of fighting for a historic goal: 'We must work. One cannot survive with clean hands … smooth hands are our enemy' (47). This is an interesting mixture of elite-led development and the appeal to human sentiment or coercion with a limited attempt to garner consent, which if successful would have represented a hegemonic Korean nation. Park attempted to universalise the need to 'work hard' and to bring the nation together in a drive toward accelerated economic development. These activities are characteristic of *trasformismo* with regard to the appeal to national solidarity that would garner a complicit worker support for elite-led economic restructuring; activities that continued throughout the 5-year Plans. However, Korean workers did not simply follow orders. They participated in Park's development Plans begrudgingly and organised several uprisings and strikes because of muted union representation and inhumane work conditions, preventing hegemony from becoming realised.

Without worker consent, the government carefully guided the next two Plans in the years 1972–76 and then 1977–81, and workers were expected to comply with each transition. From 1972–81, the *chaebol* workforce increased from 25,000 to 154,000. It cannot be said that this was a period of hegemony, due to the absence of political harmony between workers and the government. Overall, during Park's 5-Year Economic Plans, the system of VET was marked by 'confusion' (Amsden 1989: 223). The government tried different strategies that would not challenge the accumulation strategy inherent to its 'plans' but without hegemonic consensus from all social forces, confusion was inevitable. Confusion was prevalent in two areas, having to do with the question of whether high schools or junior colleges should provide training, and secondly, whether the public or private sector should finance its provision. The confusion was partially resolved by an amendment to the Vocational Training Law, which required firms with more than 300 workers to provide in-plant training. However, there was no checking mechanism instituted and this law was deemed ineffective.

By 1976, 125,000 craftspersons passed the final exams in vocational training centres provided by one automobile business group, but Amsden claims that training was not comprehensive (224). Hyundai Construction, a subsidiary of the Hyundai *chaebol* group, was one of the first companies to reach out across the ocean in contracting, and workers were 'forced to upgrade the quality of their construction work, as required by U.S. federal regulations concerning subcontractors' (232). Then in 1977, the first year of Park's fourth and final Plan, there was an increase in foreign agreements for technology transfers, the majority of which were Japanese.

The government was beginning gradually to open its doors to foreign involvement and external advances into the market became increasingly evident. In 1975, Park's military government introduced a trading company system for export promotion, designed to 'enhance the international competitiveness' of the *chaebol*. The government granted general trading companies licensing to Samsung, Lucky Goldstar, Hanil, Ssangyong, Daewoo, Samhwa, Kumho and Hyundai, which have become some of the largest Korean *chaebols* today.

In 1978, Park was assassinated. Political unrest was brewing, and the Kwangju Massacre in 1980 marks the social chaos of the time. The fifth and final of Park's plans ended in 1981 as martial law was assumed by Chun, Doo Hwan. This interim government faced the first economic downturn since 1961: in the first half of 1980, the rate of growth was negative four per cent. Chun struggled to stabilise the economy following the internationally impacting oil shock and nationally high rates of inflation. He adjusted investment by reducing emphasis on manufacturing by 19.1 per cent and 41.9 per cent in the export industries. He claimed that he would build 'a society of democracy, welfare and justice' even as he established military rule (Rhee 1994: 157). His Triple Reform plan involved 'financial liberalisation, company unionism, and industrial rationalisation' (Kim, B. K. 2003: 56). Nonetheless, he did not abandon regulation of every aspect of the economy and society. Even the Monopoly Regulation and Fair Trade Act did not 'reform' the economy to the extent of promoting competition. Nor did it dismantle the *chaebol* which was becoming an increasingly powerful force in the Korean economy.

A new form of opposition movement, called *Uijang* (the Students' Movement), was simmering below the surface of social control. Students left university in thousands and took jobs in factories, with the intention of helping to organise uneducated workers. These radical students became the core of the labour movement and have been associated with democratisation in the late 1980s. Korean unionisation was highest in the craft industry and among production workers in manufacturing positions but finally in 1985, the first skilled workers strike occurred in the Daewoo automobile production plant. The strike was colossal and lasted for several months.

Labour Movement During Developmental Dictatorships

This section looks at political unrest during the period discussed above. Throughout the late 1960s and early 1970s, which was the beginning of the global hegemonic struggle of Neoliberalism, the government made a special effort to attract foreign investment because unstable industrial and labour/state relations could turn foreign investors away. To avoid this scenario, the government simply neglected to address the needs of labour, which it perceived as temporary, and as less important than the state's development drive. The government reasoned that labour had to be silenced and appeased. Strikes broke out in the late 1960s and early 1970s, after the very slim victory of Park's re-election that was later discovered to have been rigged. The poet Kim, Chi Ha (1980: 19) writes of the sacrifices that workers made for the development of their nation in 'The Road to Seoul':

> I am going. Do not cry; I am going.
> Over the white hills, the black, and the parched hills,
> down the long and dusty road to Seoul,
> I am going to sell my body.

In response to this eruption of protest, Park's 1972 Revitalising Constitution prohibited strikes completely in the state sector, local government, utilities, and public enterprises as well as privately owned business. In 1972 Park applied increased pressure onto unions, and in 1973, the Labour Disputes Adjustment Act was amended to prohibit collective bargaining without difficult-to-obtain certification.

Throughout the 1970s an underground anti-government labour movement was building. Workers were angered by very low wages received despite the rapid economic growth initiated by President Park. In the 1970s, the top 20 per cent of households earned more than 40 per cent of the national income. This is shocking when compared to the 16 per cent earned by the bottom 40 per cent. Furthermore, working conditions were often substandard and exploitative. The number of strikes from 1969–70 escalated from 70 to 101 (FKTU 1979: 567). Strikes were not usually organised within the controlled union structure, but were spontaneous and often very violent. Students and political activists from such organisations as the Urban Industrial Mission (UIM) formed partnerships and alliances with workers. The Mission prepared educational programmes for workers, 'to improve the social consciousness of workers and trade union members' (Kwon and O'Donnell 2001: 30). I visited the mission's headquarters in Seoul, Korea, in 2002 and met with one of the volunteers who gave me in depth information over the course of the day I spent there.

The UIM was originally named Industrial Evangelism, and was opened to convert factory workers in the Yeoungdungpo area to Christianity. However, the mission had little evangelical success, and after 10 years, the missionaries reconsidered their techniques when they realised that their social status as middle class individuals, as well as their friendships with the factory owners had discredited workers' perception and led to mistrust. The missionaries had explained to workers that servitude is a spiritual strength, but factory workers interpreted this to mean servitude to bosses, whose treatment of workers was not regulated or monitored. When mission workers realised this, they quickly changed their tactics, realising that people's day to day concerns needed to be addressed before any spiritual enlightenment could be achieved. Thus the UIM's political and educational focus transformed.

The mission began to organise education courses for female workers, realising that it was harder to draw in male workers who are traditionally the breadwinners in Korean families and put themselves at risk of job loss for any form of involvement. Factory bosses laid down rules stating that collective involvement of any nature was grounds for dismissal, but women were offered hobby clubs and cooking classes that were similar to Bible classes. These events brought people together and encouraged otherwise prohibited communication about work related topics, planting seeds for a revolution of shared ideas. The mission provided resources that the factory neglected, including information about workers' rights and unregulated education. Different from elite-provided education provided at that time, which did not encourage critical thinking or organic empowerment, the organisation encouraged workers to share ideas and work together rather than as separate individuals.

The UIM offered Labour Education classes to help workers organise more effectively. As a result, the establishment was soon threatened by the government with closure. In the 1970s, Reverend In, Myong Ju was jailed for three years. In the 1980s, one Australian missionary was taken to lunch by what he later realised were government officials trying to get information about the organisations' activity. However, the work continued, despite the fact that every General Secretary of the Mission had been jailed at some stage during their terms of office. But the commitment of leaders is a 'testimony', Mr England stressed, and an indication of a real need for support for South Korean workers.

Going back to the 1970s, the picture of ROK was bleak economically and politically. Inflation escalated, foreign debts were increasing rapidly, and economic growth was paralysed. Moon (1999: 6) argues that a group of dissidents at that time demanded for less government intervention and a complete overhaul or restructuring of the Korean economy in response to the downturn. Moon neglects to state whether dissidents emerged in the political circles or from silenced groups, and whether they opposed similar items to the labour movement dissidence. Nevertheless, President Park organised a team in 1979 to implement neoliberal-leaning stabilisation measures. In 1979 and 1980, there was a dramatic increase in labour disputes, and simultaneously, a relaxation of controls on press coverage of the activity, providing a rare chance to hear *Korea Herald* journalists' views on the two year period of struggle.

The 1980s: Democratisation and Neoliberalism

In the midst of political turmoil, President Park was assassinated on October 26, 1979, in a plot designed by Kim Jae-kyu, head of the KCIA at that time. An interim government was appointed from the Electoral College led by former Prime Minister Ch'oe, Kyu-ha. Interim President Ch'oe's government intended to pave the way for elections and constitutional reform, and restored civil rights to over 600 dissidents who had been oppressed under Park's regime. It seemed as though 1980 could be the year for final erasure of military leadership, and people across Korea met to discuss the drafting of a new constitution.

Despite President Ch'oe's original emancipating activity, workers continued to feel excluded. The most dramatic worker strike during this period was the mining strike at the Tong-won Coal Mine in April 1980. Strikers occupied the town for several days, paralysing all business and invading the police headquarters. Their aim was to gain increases in pay, and to see resignation of their Union leader who, strikers claimed, was in co-operation with management rather than on the side of workers. General Chun, Doo Hwan used this crisis opportunity to put himself in charge of the KCIA and secured his post as head of Defence Security Command. The American commander, General John Wickham, actually condoned the military involvement in politics and encouraged the government to act as 'watchdogs on political activity that could be de-stabilising' (*Asian Wall Street Journal* 1980).

While the Coal Mine strike resulted in a relative success for the fulfilment of worker demands, workers' militant strikes in other sectors, for example in those where women conducted most of the work, did not fare as well. Several strikes occurred in multinational corporations (MNCs) as well, such as the Control Data Corporation strike, where thousands of unskilled women assembled software products. They resisted layoffs of thousands of Korean workers: the company planned to seek cheaper labour abroad. Women who had lost their jobs demanded rehire, but were arrested and jailed. Some women did regain jobs, but on the condition that they 'sign a pledge of loyalty to the firm' (Deyo 1989: 80). The strikes in this period often 'followed on the heels of worker education and organisational efforts by middle-class, church linked labour organisations, such as the Urban Industrial Mission and the Catholic Youth Workers' (ibid.). Furthermore, during the political crisis of the 1980s, the FKTU, who remained co-operative with the government, did not condone or support strikes.

These strikes were soon accompanied by general demonstrations all over the country. In 1980, protesters took to the streets of Seoul and across the ROK with anti-government remonstration. Protesters demanded democratic elections, the removal of the *yushin* constitution, and the removal of Chun, Doo Hwan from the positions of authority he had seized. President Ch'oe promised he would consider their requests, but protest did not cease. General Chun proceeded to close all institutions of education, ban strikes and political activities, dissolve the legislature, and forbid slanderous statements made about the government. These oppressive moves sparked the Kwangju Incident, also known as the Kwangju Massacre, an event that echoed a huge anti-Japanese demonstration that had occurred in the same city years before.

Form of State: Continued Military Dictatorship

On May 18, 1980, hundreds of citizens of Kwangju took to the streets to protest martial law. Korean armed forces were deployed in Kwangju[2] and at least 500 citizens were killed in the first days of the conflict, with 900 missing. In response, on May 21, hundreds of thousands of citizens of Kwangju seized army vehicles and weapons, drove the army out of the city, and took control of the city for five days. American operational control of South Korea at that time continued to hold relevance under the US-South Korean Combined Forces Command. The Kwangju citizens' council asked for aid from the United States armed forces, but General Wickham was slow to act and was unsure about whose side to take. But when US troops were finally deployed to Kwangju on May 27, they demanded that citizens return all arms to the military and go home, and resistors were killed. US involvement in the Kwangju Massacre unsurprisingly has affected since the way Koreans have thought about American troops. Nevertheless, Chun's military recovered control, and closed political party headquarters and the National Assembly. Finally, General Chun, Doo Hwan seized power of the country, in what was to seem like a repeat episode of colonisation.

For the next seven years, President Chun did not relieve workers' oppression, beginning with the dissolution of the *Chong'gye* Garment Workers' Union that resulted in Chon, Tae Il's protest suicide in 1970. Frantic workers who had been members of the Union immediately went to the AFL-CIO Free Labor Institute and kidnapped the American director, and two protestors committed suicide. Chun sent the '*paekkol* (white skull) strikebreakers' to effectively break protesting workers' heads. In 1981, Chun executed a Purification Drive. What this meant was that he 'eliminated' politics and put '37,000 journalists, students, teachers, labour organisers, and civil servants into "purification camps" in remote mountain areas; some 200 labour leaders were among them' (Cumings 1997: 379). These purification camps were intended to rid the nation of any government opposition, and were extremely violent and oppressive. For the next six years, Chun was to rule Korea in the style of a military dictator.

April 13 Speech and Uprising Social Forces

In the spring of 1987, Korean police tortured a dissenting student to death, triggering widespread protests. Exacerbating the situation, on April 13, 1987, President Chun spoke formally to the nation, confirming that his government would not revise the constitution despite several meetings on the matter, and then proceeded to handpick his successor from the existing Electoral College system. The notorious April 13 speech caused a significant amount of both governmental and social upheaval and resulted in a split in the opposition New Korea Democratic Party. Kim, Young Sam and Kim, Dae Jung, who had both been members, left the Party and formed the Party for Peace and Democracy (*Pyeonghwa Minjudang*). Again, passive revolution indicates 'the constant reorganisation of state power and its relationship to society to preserve control by the few over the many, and maintain a traditional lack of real control by the mass of the population over the political and economic realms' (Showstack Sassoon 1982: 129). Reorganisation of political groups is another form of reassertion of control via *trasformismo*; there was no authentic break-off from the dominant party but the formation of another, but ideologically similar party.

Chun's April 13 speech sparked widespread dissent across South Korea. While previously, students and low-skilled workers had predominantly been involved in resistance activity, the year 1987 differed in that journalists, university professors, religious leaders, and skilled workers began to join in protest. Okonogi states that 'within Korean society, where religious feelings run deep and intellectuals are highly respected, these actions had a great impact' (Okonogi 1988: 26). Middle class citizens and skilled workers in protest joined unskilled workers and students, who had been most active in dissident behaviour, for the first time in the riots that followed. In the crisis of unrest, the government finally conceded in 1987 and agreed to reconsider a constitutional revision. Widespread unrest at this time shows the inability of the governments to gain hegemony; the government responded by making molecular changes to its rhetoric and trying to universalise consent for its strategies through *trasformismo*. However, this is not the end of the story.

The full onset of a more 'democratically' run Korea appeared somewhat incongruous with Korea's history of brutal colonial and state-engineered development. Kim and Moon attribute Korean economic development to the intervention of geopolitics; a market-moulding state; aggressive export promotion; formation of human capital and Confucian culture. Inherent to those factors several challenges for democracy exist. Kim and Moon claim that 'democratic opening in 1987 dismantled the template of developmental dictatorship' (56), but whilst democratisation changed the Korean political and economic climate to some degree, it did not directly follow that Korea could claim to be a successful case of integrated and hegemonic democratisation. Labour, management and the government held conflicting objectives, in the sense that workers wanted to see democratic practice in the workplace by way of bargaining power and work stability, but political leaders as well as management aimed to respond to market conditions for labour flexibility. Gramsci makes the following comment regarding hegemonic democracies: 'In the hegemonic system, there exists democracy "between" the leading group and the groups which are being "led", in so far as the development of the economy and thus the legislation which expresses such development favour the (molecular) passage from the "led" groups to the "leading" group' (*PN*: 56). This comment is consistent with Gramsci's understanding of consent as inherent to integral hegemony, which was not evident in South Korea even in the process of democratisation.

In 1987, after seven years of presidency, President Chun hand picked

Roh, Tae Woo for presidential candidate. Roh had been in close cooperation with Chun during the Kwangju incident and Chun felt that Roh would continue to effect military rule. Originally, the new Roh government relaxed its former intervention tactics, and business level negotiation between management and workers, or the attempt of such, became more common. Then in the years 1990–92 the government resumed an anti-union stance and membership began to decline. Employers supported the government's stance and implement neoliberal business strategies, including flexible wage systems based on performance evaluations, which was a kind of foreshadowing of the restructuring programmes led by the IMF and a host of MNC managers a few years later. The goal was to reduce labour costs while increasing productivity.

Neoliberalism and the Birth of Korean Democracy

The global historical bloc of Neoliberalism began in the late 1960s and early 1970s. Van der Pijl writes that the neoliberalism is identified by its capacity to raise 'micro-economic rationality to the validating criterion for all aspects of social life' (1998: 129). Here, I look at the way that South Korea, during democratisation and the first years of a 'democratic' form of state, dealt with the pressures of the neoliberal Washington Consensus[3] which demands intensive deregulation of trade and FDI inflows. One characteristic of Neoliberalism as an international framework of norms is that it, rhetorically anyway, does not tolerate non-'democratic' nations or a diverse brand of forms of state that were tolerated during Pax Americana. O'Brien notes that 'a system which allows union activity, but discourages it through legislation and uses market forces to reduce the power of organised labour is labelled *neoliberal*' (O'Brien 2000: 539). In the newly democratic Korea, a limited amount of union activity was permitted, but as is noted in the following sections, it was heavily resisted from the elite echelons. Neoliberalism began to pervade several aspects of life for South Koreans, and historically oppressed people began to cry out for a voice that had been stifled for so long under authoritarian developmentalist states. A remedy was finally prescribed, democratisation according to a Western standard. It remained to be seen whether this regime change and the mass production restructuring that would occur after the crisis ten years later would dismantle what seemed to be a stymied passive revolution.

The democracy movement was led by the *minjung*, a variety of social groups that included students, factory workers and white collar workers alike, self employed, small merchants in the city and farmers. *Minjung* is an organic resistance movement that Koreans believe emerges from a kind of spirit of history that demonstrates two crucial characteristics. First, advocates of *minjung* were Korean working class people and second, the objectives of *minjung* were to defend Korea from the unknown evils of global hegemony (Abelmann 1996: 24). While the concept of *minjung* originally represented an historical/organic Korean civil society, it has been argued that the movement is in danger of being co-opted and disempowered (Moore and Kim 2005).

But this historically subversive movement brought about social resistance to oppression throughout history, a movement that faces a crisis of identity, because resistance has become increasingly less viable despite its role in instigating a transition to democracy in 1987. Nonetheless, the *minjung* coalition of forces were successful in the sense that mass demonstrations in early 1987 were so disturbing that Washington was finally contacted, and President Reagan's advisors begged Roh and Chun to change their ways. Roh, Tae Woo then surprised the nation with a 'Declaration of Democratic Reforms', and on June 29, he promised the nation fair elections and more democratic policies.

Roh of the Democratic Justice Party took office in December of 1987. After a history of colonialism, authoritarian governments and war, Korean citizens held their breath to see what would come of the 'democratic' presidency. One of the first issues President Roh had to address was labour, whose voice should be heard under a democratic polity. As has been discussed, authoritarian regimes had silenced and punished workers, and there had been little dialogue between government and labour. Strikes in 1985, while still illegal, had become better organised and intelligently launched and the government continued to react negatively to uprising, calling leaders of the strikes 'impure'. But in 1987, as part of his first manifesto, Roh, Tae-Woo designed an 8-point plan that promised to give labour more say through relaxing its intervention in labour/management politics. In the summer of that year, labour organisation was finally legalised. From June 1987–June 1988, membership of Unions increased by 64 per cent. In June 1987 Korea can be said to have finally officially become a democratic state. The date of the Seoul-hosted Olympics was approaching likewise so the government self-consciously retreated from interference into labour issues.

First Years of 'Democratic' Form of State: The Great Labour Struggle
In the first few years of Korean 'democracy', several events took place
that gave citizens a renewed hope in their government. New political
parties that stood for democracy and resistance were formed and old
ones were revived. The Korean form of developmentalist state was
challenged in this period and several aspects of historical relations
between the state and society were dismantled. Censored books and
magazines began to pop up out of the woodwork in an anarchical
fashion and even conservative religious groups began to publish
ethical protests to the system of governance that had evolved into
Chun's Fifth Republic. Across the globe, other nations democratised
during this time period as well, including the Filipino 'yellow
revolution' of 1987 and two years later, the overthrow of Eastern
European communist regimes.

The Roh, Tae-Woo regime (1987–92) originally made claims that it
would reduce political oppression, but the 'nucleus of power remained
unchanged' (Song 1999: 10), and in terms of labour/state relations, little
changed in the preliminary stages of democracy. 1987–88 is what Mo
(1999: 101) calls the 'co-optation period'. During the first two years of a
democratic Korea, labour standards were reviewed and supposedly
strengthened. In this first period, however, Roh vetoed a reform bill put
forward by opposition parties and unions that would have permitted
public worker unionisation. Strike action erupted, and the number of
disputes rose from what had been an average of 171 per year, to 3,471 in
1987. The crackdown period, 1989–92, involved stringent crackdowns
on Union leaders and striking workers.

So the Great Labour Struggle of 1987–97 began with a challenge to the
traditionally hierarchical government/employer-led industrial relations
system and with a call for a 'democratic' aptitude. From 1987–89, trade
unions multiplied and labour disputes increased. Originally, the Roh
government relaxed its former intervention tactics and attempts for
business level negotiation between management and workers became
more common. The number of strikes declined in 1991, and at that point,
the MOL approached a discussion of labour law reforms, to include the
extension of a minimum duration of collective agreements, the allowance
of political activities by unions, a removal on the limit of union dues, and
the lift of spatial restrictions on strikes. However, the compromise for
these lifts on restrictions would be that labour would accept 'the
elimination of the ratification requirement for collective agreements and a

wage negotiation system based on a total compensation package' (1999: 102). No agreement was reached.

Nevertheless, election procedures were democratised and an election was held in 1993. The next administration led by Kim, Young Sam, 1993–97, was the first civilian government of the ROK. But conditions for democracy should ideally favour workers, and workers sought the removal of bans to multiple unionisms and on third party intervention in cases of labour/management struggles. Disappointingly, the Kim government usually sided with management, with the intention to formulate flexible labour market conditions. President Kim gave the labour force hope at first with his comparatively progressive attitudes toward reform, but he did not explicitly state how he intended to do so in his original manifesto, despite his democratic debut. Rhee, In Je, Minister of Labour at that time claimed in 1987 that 'the ban on union political activities is dead.' But there were no real changes to labour policies (Haggard and Kang 1999: 127). Roh, Tae Woo (1988–93) and Kim, Young Sam recognised the need to appease workers, particularly as flexibilisation became increasingly required by international investors for what they considered could be effective economic reform. Kim was quick to expect flexibility from workers, but neglected to simultaneously offer a full range of workers' rights. Labour relations were, thus, *not* appeased in the initial stages of democratisation. Finally in 1996 labour reform was announced, and wages and benefits for workers increased temporarily, despite claims that expenditure on labour would reduce international competitiveness.

Song (1999: 11) attributes gradual labour reform to Korea's 'reform' model of democratisation rather than 'rupture' democracy. The reform type is such that:

> ... old authoritarianism does not collapse completely and political power is shared between the old elites and opposition leaders ... fundamental changes are hardly expected ... it was natural [in South Korea] that labour codes remained almost untouched until 1996, and organised labour had no part in reform policies.

Thus the exclusion of labour continued, and workers were not granted a voice in any negotiation circles for several years. Despite democratisation it looked like passive revolution would continue in this semi-peripheral nation. Only elite groups had participatory rights to the process of reconstruction of labour relations. Even the Tripartite Commission, established in 1997, broke down after the first meeting due to KCTU members' disagreement with flexibilisation admissions within the original Social Charter. Policy making and application likewise continued to exclude labour opinion. While Roh had made efforts to address labour disputes, a history of oppression would not vanish and labour repression actually increased during the first years of democracy. President Kim's Minister of Labour Rhee, In Je made a concerted effort to reform labour laws despite the lack of more general governmental support. He sought to aid the re-employment process of workers who had been fired for taking part in union activities, investigated claims of companies' unfair labour practice and reviewed the MOL's directives. His plan included measures that would allow some striking workers pay in some situations, a change from the 'no-work, no-pay' standard that existed. Furthermore, more types of unions would be allowed, and the previous ban on third party intervention would allow unions inclusion in political activities. However, political pressures eventually dissolved Minister Rhee's plans, and he was replaced in 1993 as the MOL itself reversed its own earlier, more worker-conscious policy considerations.

Haggard and Kang (1999: 127) suggest a position that President Kim could have taken at this crucial early part of democracy. He could have taken a complete turn from past government attitudes and protected labour openly and addressed all its issues, simultaneous to opening up the nation economically. The model that focuses heavily on investments in human capital had been gaining support from the World Bank and was applied in many developing economies in Europe. However, the Korean government remembered one crucial fact that kept it from applying any drastic, socially conscious measures; that growth figures had shown a negative effect on productivity when labour costs rose. From 1987–95 wages grew 15 per cent per year, but productivity was low at 11 per cent. So while Kim, Young Sam made efforts toward complete democratisation and claimed non-interference as his primary position on labour issues, he prioritised economic reform at the surface level and did not address labour issues comprehensively.

Essentially, Kim chose the globally hegemonic route for political and economic decision making and overlooked the needs of his own population. Deyo calls Kim's form of state an authoritarian/state corporatism, which 'invites symbolic or co-opted participation in limited decision making, and in some sense, is at least nominally less exclusionary than simple exclusion' (1989: 108). Nonetheless, labour was incontrovertibly excluded from decision making during Kim's period of leadership.

Segyehwa: Trasformismo *within Democracy, Globalisation, and Neoliberalism*
In November 1994, President Kim declared that his vision of *segyehwa*, which means 'globalisation' in English, would 'lift the global role of the nation and make the life of future generations better' (Korean Embassy 1996); a 'globalisation first' method of development. President Kim told traditionalist senior officials and others who were staunchly against internationalisation or economic globalization that *segyehwa* was not the same thing. Kim claimed that his understanding of how globalization would proceed in South Korea was that it would positively affect several facets of society including politics, diplomacy, culture, the economy (but not 'economics'), education, athletics, and other non-economic factors (Bobrow and Na 1999: 183). President Kim told the international business community in a conference in 1996 that *segyehwa* represented Korea's push to eliminate corruption and the 'wrongs of history', and that his aim was to focus on 'transparency, openness, a clean government, and a clean society' (187). *Segyehwa* thus aimed to garner popular support for these ends in a classic attempt of *trasformismo*. Elites' aims were to convince the population through the promises of a 'clean society' and other concessions that simultaneous policy making was part of a nationally shared need to meet international standards, without a recognition of the affects of economic policy on people's day to day lives.

Kim, Young Sam's New Economic Policy zealously aimed to:

- Diversify business.
- Deregulate inward and outward investment flows, after 1995 OECD accession plan was to be materialised.
- Allow merchant banks to launch international business including foreign currency dealing and lease businesses (despite financial resource or level of experience in those areas).
- Secure support from big business (Kim and Lee 1999).

President Kim actively sought membership in the OECD from 1995, and hurriedly passed deregulation measures that advocated Korean overseas investment outlined in a Five Year New Economic Plan for 1993–7, as well as the Long-Term Economic Design for the Twenty-First Century.

Finance Minister Hong Hae and the President pushed for extensive capital market liberalisation, and announced foreign exchange deregulation in 1994. A dramatic opening of capital markets was hoped to have the effect of pressuring financial institutions to reach greater international competitiveness through mergers and acquisitions with foreign business in order to force corporations out of 'insolvent business ventures' (Kim, B. K. 2003: 70) that had become rampant. The government applied for OECD membership in 1995, and South Korea was accepted in December 1996.

Kim hoped that *segyehwa* could aid these steps toward OECD membership and that social forces could be harmonised with enough concessions to appease potential dissent in an era of rapid change. Kang claims that:

> *Segyehwa* dealt with the external challenges … in several ways. In response to market-opening measures targeting South Korea, *segyehwa* as a rhetoric served to give some political cover to Kim, Young Sam's government, which was unable to resist the United States' armtwisting. *Segyehwa* was used as a slogan enabling South Korea to acquiesce to market openings as part of its larger globalization drive. That is, *segyehwa* was a useful, if uncertain, psychological tool that helped the nationalistic South Koreans accept a measure of reciprocity in international trade.
>
> (Kang 2000: 85, 86)

President Kim was a popularly supported president at the onset of his leadership. His globalisation strategy was, at first, very attractive to citizens and its slogan became increasingly used in common speech and was thus a reconstruction of common sense, or *trasformismo*, amongst South Koreans. President Kim claimed that Korea would become globalized in a positive and beneficial way that would bring countries together, and planned to match democracy with his *segyehwa* politics. The implications were that Korea could become a partner to developed nations without becoming vulnerable to external markets and profit-seeking speculation. Nonetheless, his political project soon became associated with economic deregulation despite his ardent claims to separate the campaign from economic policy. Kim's administration recognised his exposure and pleaded powerless to his population, saying they would be left behind in the neoliberal global economy if Korea was not positioned to become competitive through deregulation. Kim's gambit was soon dismantled when it became evident that he could not keep his promise to avoid economics in his globalisation campaign, and citizens once again became frustrated with their stymied government, and did not elect his administration again after 1997. So Kim had found relative success at first with his *trasformismo* strategies but the manipulations of its original manifesto were soon laid bare. I can therefore claim that Korea was not integrated into Cox's supposed hegemonic world order, despite its relative economic successes throughout development.

In terms of labour policy, in 1996, only a year before the Asian economic crisis tested the resilience of the Korean economy, 11 'anti-labour' laws were passed which included provisions allowing employers to activate mass layoffs, and simplified procedures to hire temporary, part time, and replacement workers. The Employers Federation justified this by claiming that the new measures 'would be used only if firms were in extreme difficulties' (*Militant* 1997), a strange foreshadowing considering the actual 'difficulties' that would occur one year afterward. Alongside these assurances in 1996, the Federation offered to arrange 'development programmes that focus on vocational training' but 'neither union federation gave credence to the offer' (1997). So job flexibility was paired with a new form of 'security' in the form of vocational training. The labour force was, again, not figured into policy making, and Kim rapidly lost public support.

In fact, Kim's administration *blamed* labour for paralysing his newly engineered phase of deregulation and outward looking strategies. In the time of authoritarian leadership, the government utilised labour for its development strategies, as there was a surplus of relatively cheap labour. After formalised democratisation, workers began to demand higher wages and legitimacy of political activity. There were more labour disputes in between 4 July and 4 September 1987 than had occurred in the previous ten years.

Failure of Segyehwa *Clears the Way for Kim, Dae Jung*

To add to growing suspicions that Kim, Young Sam's strategies were not realistic or socially discerning and that worker/state dialogue was still paralysed, the first 'democratic' president was blamed for pulling the trigger for the Korean economic crisis in 1997. He had hoped to lead Korea into a new era of development, to free Korea from the shackles of military rule and to tear open its economy to the world, but he could not fulfil his aims under the expectations of investors and the international economy. The wider Korean community criticised the Kim, Young Sam government for its two faced policies. From a neoliberal position themselves, Kim and Moon (2000: 61) write that:

> [Kim, Young Sam's] globalization strategy was a dismal failure, resulting in an acute economic crisis even before his tenure had ended … during his term in office, foreign debts rose from USD 43.9 billion in 1994 to USD 160.7 billion in 1996, and USD 158 billion in 1997, while foreign reserve assets dwindled from USD 20.2 billion to in 1993 to USD 12.4 billion in 1997.

Kim and Moon attribute the inability of the Korean economic system to globalise to such factors as moral hazard, political/business synergies, the ongoing foreign exchange currency crisis, and limited, sporadic activity of foreign investors. They are critical of Kim's *Segyehwa* campaign by saying it was a 'premature and incoherent globalization strategy … the rhetoric of globalization overshadowed its substance' (ibid.). Their criticism is that the liberalisation of financial and capital markets was applied without related policy and institutional reforms. Korea had attempted to become a successful member of the historical bloc of Neoliberalism but had 'failed'. Therefore, the new President Kim, Dae Jung (who I will refer to as 'DJ Kim') came along to take that responsibility.

So DJ Kim, the new figure of hope, took centre stage. In response to the crisis, this former 'criminal' who had been jailed in the 1980s for active protest against Korea's legacy of authoritarian governments, requested a bailout sum of USD 57 billion from the IMF on 2 December of that same year. After a brief period during which Kim attempted to convince the nation that he would stave the most negative effects of structural adjustment that the reputed agency would require, the newly elected President made it clear that he would follow the IMF's direction. He wanted to lead his country into a new phase of development of reformism and internationalisation. The new President stated several times that his goal was to promote the country's attractiveness for Foreign Direct Investment (FDI).

The next chapter discusses in depth what happened when the new President took office and simultaneously faced the worst economic crisis of Korean history. DJ Kim's response to the crisis was to accelerate neoliberal economic development via the restructuring of several aspects of the economy, at the direction of the IMF. His intentions were to create a competitive global market player in a short period of time, particularly after its previously 'successful' growth of earlier decades.

The crisis hit Korea perhaps more acutely and devastatingly than other nations across the region, and drastic measures were taken to reform the economy to attract foreign capital and to try to avoid future crises. But crisis reform affected workers most directly and negatively due to corporate restructuring leading to an onslaught of redundancies. If workers could not keep jobs in the insecure post-crisis situation, they were expected to join VET programmes that would make them 'employable'. If workers were privileged to remain in positions of employment, they were expected to attend developmental VET that would aid in their retention of 'employability'. The government's hegemonic project was intended to involve workers by providing the means for workers to 'help themselves'. Yet, the required employability corresponded directly with the exact labour power needed to accommodate the elite-led accumulation strategy of neoliberalism, in response to the international historical bloc discussed in the previous chapter. The government formed partnerships with international experts who advised on approaches for labour market preparation for reform and economic recovery. The state's reformist strategies included revamped VET programmes in its aim to secure dominance against a potential revolutionary worker movement who disputed and still dispute the supposedly immutable phase of development toward neoliberal capitalism.

Soon the labour market was forcibly restructured in various ways after the IMF loan was implemented, with accompanying conditionalities. The following chapter addresses the case of *trasformismo* in the context of government-led reforms, bringing in the idea that international partnerships further guide state-led reformist development. The crisis led to a restructuring of employable skills and knowledge itself that became clear with post-crisis VET strategies.

Conclusion

Relations between the state and labour have undergone tremendous pressure throughout Korean history, and as the form of state has developed from colonial to 'democratic', various strains have been placed upon social forces. But a labour movement was evident to the extent described, and the sporadic but often violent eruptions of strikes and organisation in spite of ongoing oppression demonstrate that elite led development has not crushed the spirit of workers. The Korean government has behaved arduously to maintain some level of stability and passive control of the labour force, whether it is in the context of military dictatorship or attempted democracy.

Democracy is ideally meant to provide a forum for the voice of citizens, who are in this case, workers, but it appears that the government's intentions to develop and to later globalise took precedence over allowing labour to locate a political voice. Lang and Hines write that 'the subversion of democracy is nothing new' (1993: 107) in an environment of global free trade which underpins the ideology of neoliberalism. Often, workers are the first to suffer from the effects of an internationalising state, but in a democratic forum, it would be hoped that workers could find a space to channel a representative voice via independent unions. Workers have not been granted a political voice in Korea and have been co-opted into an elite led programme of economic development through the design and implementation of VET and through other forms of *trasformismo*.

So, workers' unrest has created an arena for potential social change, but it still does not appear that labour has had say in *how change is enacted* at any point throughout Korean modern and contemporary history. Over various periods which are trapped in passive revolutions, the government has acted to appeal to workers in unprecedented ways in order to facilitate a more saturated model of economics that will match global 'standards' for development.

There is a sequence of consistent, observable characteristics within the historic periods discussed here, pointing toward the adaptation of capitalism to historical circumstances as well as the prevention of hegemony at the local level. Conditions for passive revolution have been in place. First, Korean economic development has occurred under state leadership of its initiated accumulation strategies, without hegemonic integration. Second, elements of *trasformismo* or the progressive nature of VET and other elements that have been embellished to make hegemonic projects appear to substantially benefit workers within each historic period. In this chapter I observed the re-articulation of common sense, the appeal to nationalism, and elite-authored VET programmes, but as has been shown, resistance remained prevalent. Whilst molecular changes have applied in that VET curricula have transformed to accommodate the accumulation strategies of governments over time, the overarching appeal of capitalist integration into gradually emerging international norms has been the motivating force for elite-led, *trasformismo* driven and thus non-hegemonic, development. Only one of the conditions for passive revolution has been met; that of state led social change. *Trasformismo*-laden incentives have not resulted in complete circumvention of dissent but dissent has not led to complete overthrow of the exploitations evident within each time period. Thus complete revolution has not occurred from either side of the struggle. Korea's development trajectory has been evident within authoritarian forms of state, who have made attempts to 'involve' workers via *trasformismo*. Therefore, a passive revolution has been evident in this nation from Japanese colonialism to the early stages of neoliberalisation.

I have noted that within each time period international hegemonic struggles have had a significant impact upon the relations between workers and the state, and I argue that Cox's supposed 'hegemony' at the international level does not necessarily mean that 'hegemony' can occur within all nations. This calls into question the notion of international hegemony itself. Furthermore, because development programmes within Korea have been government organised with specific intentions, I can also claim that this research supports my claims that Korean workers' negotiation with accelerated development has not occurred in a vacuum, or via inevitable market forces, but involves specific, directed activities of the state and increasingly has involved external entities.

But is there a 'present significance' of passive revolution? The next chapter addresses this question by looking closely at the restructuring period that followed the Asian economic crisis 1997 by breaking down the restructuring process into three categories of forces: ideas, material capabilities and institutions (see Cox's first matrix in Figure 1). Crisis recovery in Korea has been a period of extensive reconsideration of Korea's position as an economic/political entity in the global environment, which I perceive a feature of the war of position and a time during which the previous historical bloc of authoritarian hegemony in Korea can be restructured. The 1997 crisis shook the nation of South Korea, and I argue that recovery and restructuring caused further adaptations of capitalism in three arenas. I seek out the conditions under which restructuring was applied, furthermore, to note how Korean VET has developed in the absence of hegemony.

As stated, the following chapter looks in depth at restructuring after the economic crisis of 1997 along three levels of association, ideas, material capabilities, and institutions. Shunning the determinism of positivist analysis, Cox's matrix allows a look into ongoing hegemonic struggles and of the dynamic between diachronic configurations of forces. This simplified model is intended to provide a basis for the analysis of Korea's economic and social restructuring that has resulted from the expansion of neoliberal capitalism, a phenomenon that has altered many facets of South Korea and has ultimately impacted peoples' day to day lives. In considering the restructuring of forces after the crisis, it is noted that increased international partnerships at several levels may show that the global political economic system of neoliberalism is finding new hegemonic 'allies' in East Asia. But perhaps most importantly, a nation/ state that is unable to achieve ideological hegemony locally and is only able to conduct economic development strategies by maintaining a passive revolution may also clear the way for widespread emancipatory dissent.

4

CRISIS RESPONSE AND IMF RESTRUCTURING: PASSIVE REVOLUTION IN THE KNOWLEDGE ECONOMY

Introduction

Previous chapters have discussed the historical background of a series of world orders which show the restructuring of South Korean production relations in a bigger picture. Within each world order, Cox (1987) has identified common forms of state characteristic to each period, as well as expansive norms of production he claims to have played a role in the consolidation or destruction of global hegemony. This chapter brings the story of South Korean development into a contemporary age, wherein the production parameters have shifted in the embrace of the Information Revolution.

Before the crisis, Western speculators had watched the rapid growth of the Asian Tigers with awe and were astonished at how rapidly South Korea recovered from the atrocities of the Korean War ending in 1953. In 1960, Korea's gross national product was aligned with Sudan and Ghana and still lagged behind India. Electricity was a novelty and cars still a precious commodity. However, in the following 30 years, Korea's growth averaged 9 per cent per year and by 1996, it could claim itself the world's eleventh largest economy. It had become the world's second largest ship-builder, the fourth largest electronics producer, the largest manufacturer of semiconductors, and the world's sixth largest steelmaker. South Korea was doing something right, and economists were quick to assume that policy-makers and business experts had discovered a promising new kind of capitalism; what some called 'Confucian Capitalism'.

But in 1997, when things went awry as a result of the Asian crisis, experts were quick to condemn nations for failing to note some of the most fundamental aspects of free market capitalism, and used the crisis to take on an increasingly pastoral role toward this sudden failed economy. Perhaps, experts reasoned, the Asian Pacific nations were not in tune with international norms of production and needed some guidance. So it became apparent that Korea had not been following all of the 'rules' of the Washington Consensus, and restructuring was necessary. This chapter looks at specific shifts to expectations from the labour market in the march toward globalising neoliberalism and all of its ideological baggage.

Economic crises can both unveil and re-establish historical relationships of exploitation between actors in the driving seat of expansive ideologies and production and groups who operate within what become compliant zones for dominant nations' accumulation. In the case of Korea, despite democratisation, economic and social reform after the 1997 crisis followed a similar trajectory to previous periods of development under the elite-led pattern of passive revolution. I aim to reveal how Korea experienced a domestic hegemonic struggle between social forces in the context of the presently expanding knowledge-based capitalist world economy that characterises what Cox claims to be a 'hegemonic' neoliberal historical bloc.

Crisis-related reform and restructuring is a process that must go beyond material reorganisation and in every case, must penetrate the core of the production force to become integrated. In this light, the chapter breaks down the transformation of production after the crisis through the analysis of three aspects for restructuring corresponding with Cox's first matrix: material capabilities, institutions, and the appeal to ideational intersubjectivity (Figure 1). This model highlights the dynamic interplay between social forces within the movement of history, and in this case during the attempts to restructure a society after economic crisis. While the function of Cox's theoretical tool is not to predict power relations between forces, I have identified an elite-led and transnationally motivated series of changes along each category. The role of what I have called the transnational capitalist class network (TCCN) has become augmented during the crisis restructuring period and onward, and this chapter looks at increased IMF, UNESCO, and ILO relations within Korea defined as increased incorporation into the expansive network of capitalist norms. The evidence of an increase in elite relations and influence without worker participation shows that the first category of passive revolution is again in effect during this period.

Sklair asks 'how does the capitalist class influence government and public opinion when it considers that its vital interests are affected?' (2001: 27). The question is answered here from a neo-Gramscian perspective, problematising the concept of *trasformismo* that involves an elite-led campaign in this most recent historical period of passive revolution. The *trasformismo* project in the Korean case existed wherein Kim Dae Jung's government involved workers in the political/economic agenda with various levels of penetrative strategies, the deepest of which exists in the minds of a population, thus revealing educational aspects of hegemony. Gramsci (*PN*: 350) maintained that:

> Every relationship of hegemony is necessarily an educational relationship and occurs not only within a nation, between the various forces of which the nation is composed, but in the international and world-wide field, between complexes of national and continental civilisations.

While infrastructural and material conditions can be restructured relatively easily according to IMF mandates, it is not as immediately straightforward to 'restructure' and re-educate people's skills, attitudes and behaviour, or to ensure cooperation of workers.

The Korean state's reformist strategy during the period of post-crisis restructuring intended to secure control over a potential revolutionary worker movement against IMF and transnationally-led development. Gramsci understood the dialectic, or the political movement of history resulting from the tension between thesis and antithesis, to be related to the variants between reformist and revolutionary politics. Showstack-Sassoon states that since 'reformism is a version of passive revolution [Gramsci] noted that one aspect of the strategy is the break up the struggle into finite moments' (1987: 213). Rather than allowing a dialectic moment to reach emancipatory fruition, the dominant class weakens the antithesis through fragmenting it into a 'series of moments, to reduce the dialectic to a process of reformist evolution' (Gramsci 1975b: 1328). It can be said that the Korean elite has constructed a reformist strategy that will promote the reform of work practices. Elite groups define this strategy as progressive and aim to appease workers from the instability caused by the economic crisis.

The TCCN moves in both implicit and explicit ways to proselytise production norms, ideologies, and practices. Whilst the 'globalization of capitalism' requires control of financial capital, it is incomplete without the ownership of 'political, organisational, cultural, and knowledge capital' (Sklair 2001a: 17). An effective tool for the expansion of hegemonic forms of knowledge is through education and the training of organic intellectuals who are sympathetic to the cause of periodised development. Education is a socialisation tool that produces a particular discourse intended to cultivate intersubjectivities.

More specifically, the Korean government, as well as KRIVET, business owners and managers, aimed to lead adoption of globally standardised norms of production particularly in newly invested and transnationally merged companies. 'The lesson for the working class is that the strategy of passive revolution will be attempted by the bourgeoisie' (Showstack-Sassoon 1987: 212–3). So the 'passive' dissemination of ideologically-led political/economic education could result in the cementing ingredient to leadership, via consent (Gramsci *PN*: 328). Van Apeldoorn (2002: 19, 20) writes that the world-view of a hegemonic group is only normalised through the adaptation of subordinate groups' needs into its own rhetoric. Because the bourgeoisie has not been capable of reaching hegemonic leadership status, it has enacted a passive revolution over time within South Korea.

Restructuring of Material Capabilities

The IMF Economic Program, applied on December 5, 1997 was broken down into three categories: 'Macro-economic Policies', 'Financial Sector Restructure', and 'Other Structural Measures' (IMF 1997). Within each category, the IMF made recommendations for the restructuring of Korea's economy. A major theme of the structural problems had to do with barriers to foreign investment. International investors had been blocked by the inability to acquire shares or to own majority stakes in Korean businesses, and domestically the financial market was not completely open to foreign banks or insurance companies. Japanese products had been historically restricted. Banks had followed the 'Japanese development model', meaning that the government backed lending to favoured industries with implied loan guarantees. *Chaebols* were too big, seen to follow non-transparent business practices, and occupied a disproportionate amount of the market. Kim agreed with IMF consultants who said that the crisis was a result of widespread problems in political and economic institutions including 'opaque corporate governance, bureaucratically driven financial institutions, and company unionism based on lifetime employment' (Kim, B. K. 2003: 53). Corporations demonstrated high debt-to-capital ratios, making them risky debtors for lenders either domestic or foreign. Thus these factors would all be reconsidered in the crisis recovery, restructuring period.

FDI Welcomed: Restructuring Businesses and Banks

The IMF required South Korea to invite a fresh wave of FDI, which was expected to mend corporate instabilities and debts that had partly 'caused' the crisis. What this meant in practice was a widespread termination of several banks and business bankruptcies, and a significant impact on thousands of workers' lives. The IMF started by shutting down nine insolvent merchant banks on December 2, 1997, requiring management to submit restructuring blueprints within 30 days. Trade liberalisation was also required in accordance with WTO commitments, including import licensing restrictions, trade-related subsidies, import diversification, and then streamlining and making the system transparent. Layoffs occurred due to restructuring of banks and corporations, and in many cases, happened overnight (KOILAF 2001b: 10).

Corporations, at the recommendation and requirement of the IMF, restructured around three basic tasks:

- *Managerial reforms*: accountability by divisions , computerisation of workflows, introduction of the open personnel system, innovations in work organisation and employee evaluation, improvement of the corporate culture.
- *Improvements in structural organisation*: trimmed, flat and matrix-based organisation, downsizing.
- *Transformation of the business structure*: M&A (mergers and acquisitions), business transfer, spin-off, business swap, outsourcing (KOILAF 2001b: 14).

These reforms were necessary, according to government-funded rhetoric, because 'Korea had failed to carry out voluntary restructuring during the periods of economic boom, and was finally forced to restructure itself within a short period of time immediately after the onset of the 1997 financial difficulties' (15).

After the crisis took hold in South Korea, corporations restructured around the surge of FDI and crisis managers instructed the Korean population to grow out of the 'culture' of foreign suspicion. Lee warns that 'Koreans as a group, whether they are industrialists, government officials, or citizens, should adjust to the idea of a global village. In the globalised era, no success can be expected from a xenophobic or nationalistic way of thinking' (Lee, H. K.1996: 82). This advice was taken through tremendous liberalisation and foreign business take-overs, seen to be a fundamental component of the IMF restructuring process.

President DJ Kim's government began:

> ... aggressively pursuing foreign knowledge-based firms and 200 global companies that have yet to invest in Korea. Fresh measures have been implemented to provide follow-up assistance to investors and services such as healthcare, education, and housing for foreigners residing in Korea are being upgraded.
>
> (MOFE 1999)

Investment and mergers and acquisitions were welcomed with the logic that foreigners' investment would be an excellent source of capital to repair Korea's economy and to push it forward into the age of the knowledge economy. A country that was nicknamed the hermit kingdom before division at the 38th parallel and was later very shy of foreign investment began opening the doors to investors with unprecedented welcome. Even hostile take-overs were permitted, and FDI from November 1997–November 1998 topped USD 6.9 billion, which was up 16.4 per cent from 1996 (Lee and Vatikiotis 1998). The Foreign Investment Promotion Act and the Securities Exchange Act cleared the path in 1998 for an investment influx and Korea quickly became one of the top investment sites in the global arena. The Korean government began to provide tax protection and offer advantages to investors that resulted in some cases with in complaints from domestic business about reverse discrimination (*Korea Corporate Finance* 2000). Director General Cho, Hwan-ik of the Ministry of Commerce, Trade and Industry stated that in 1999, 'the number of small and mid-sized investments valued at less than USD 100 million rose 44 per cent from January to November, to total 1,076 cases' (Korean Embassy 1999).

President Kim warned the nation that reform would not be painless, but that 'we shall practice the market economy fully and thoroughly, we shall open our market without hesitation' (DJ Kim 1997). He overturned historical antagonism of trade with Japan and other nations, and lifted barriers to Japanese products and restrictions on capital markets to foreign investors almost overnight. President Kim placed an emphasis on knowledge industry investment; his macro-level restructuring incentives were intended in the standard IMF fashion to organise industry around thriving sectors and eliminate non-prosperous sectors, and the MOL prioritised information technology (KOILAF 2001b: 13).

Restructuring of the Chaebol

Crisis reform was embraced at several levels, and as the *chaebol* was an exceedingly strong force in the Korean economy, it was the 'privileged issue' for discussion and renovation. The 'imperial' governance of corporations centred on single-owner families was blamed for much of the economy's problems (Kim, B. K. 2003: 53–4). Since the *chaebol* relations were strongly criticised and blamed for 'crony economic downturn of President Park, Chung Hee's era, Korea's ruling elite had viewed the *chaebol* with caution, arguing that these oversized conglomerates were the primary reason for Korea's growing economic problems. Speculators pointed fingers at 'crony capitalism', involving non-transparent loans procedures as linked with *chaebol*'s rapid and often, unmonitored expansion. Business/government ties led to rent-seeking, and soon what speculators name 'corruption and moral hazard' became a defining factor for the success of the *chaebol*. It was soon claimed that the *chaebol* contributed to, or even cause the economic crisis of 1997 (Mo and Moon 2003: 127). That year, eight of the thirty largest *chaebol*s in Korea collapsed, triggering a panic among policy makers and advisers who realised that the weaknesses of the developmental model of governance in a rapidly deregulating global economy.

The new President Kim was faced with this mounting problem and realised that in the nascent Korean democracy, he would have to identify a reform method suiting this form of state. He designed a 'five-plus-three principles' plan that *chaebol* leaders agreed to on 13 January 1998. The five agreements involved the most 'democratic' series of requirements seen in Korean economic history:

- Enhancement of transparency in accounting and management.
- Resolve of mutual debt guarantees among *chaebol* affiliates.
- Improvement of firm's financial structure.
- Streamlining of business activities.
- Strengthening managers' accountability (Mo and Moon 2003: 128).

The next year, 1999, Kim announced the final three parts of the Plan in his National Liberation Day speech on August 15:

- Regulation of *chaebol*'s control of non-bank financial institutions.
- Circular equity investment by *chaebol* affiliates.
- Prevention of irregular inheritance and gift-giving among family members of *chaebol* owners (2003: 129).

Kim provides an interesting critique of the history of attempted *chaebol* reforms and claims that workers' flexibility was one of the sticking points keeping complete transformation from becoming implemented. Particularly since 1987, leaders had begun to view domestic democratisation as a fundamental aspect of sustainable globalization. Nonetheless, attempts to reform worker/state relations and to successfully implement financial reform had been unsuccessful, and thus, this author is surprised that *chaebol* reform was similarly weak (Kim, B. K. 2003: 56). When faced with surplus capacity in manufacturing, the Ministry of Trade and Industry, rather than allowing business to collapse, created a system whereby banks persuaded *chaebol*s to focus attention on a 'few core businesses' rather than to effect wider reforms. '*Chaebol* policy' was instituted instead of '*chaebol* reform', and when previously amazing growth records slowed down, policy makers began to realise the disaster this may have caused. Mass media began to pay attention to *chaebol* reform, revealing that the *chaebol* had escaped taxes, enjoyed wage-controls and government assistance since their inception, and it quickly became clear that it would be difficult to convince these megaliths to surrender their favoured position (see Figure 4, Media Coverage of *Chaebol* Issues, 1990–2000). It was clear that policy reform would not be enough to restructure the *chaebol* however, and political relationships would have to change dramatically if reform was to become authentically manifest. Two related tasks of reform involve the reduction of rent-seeking and corruption, and to transform the expectations that 'private actors can shift risk onto the public sector' (Haggard et al. 2003: 8). This seemingly necessary evil was a crucial component within the era of restructuring and reform after the crisis of 1997.

Figure 4. Media Coverage of Chaebol Issues, 1990–2000 (Kim, B. K. 2003: 57)

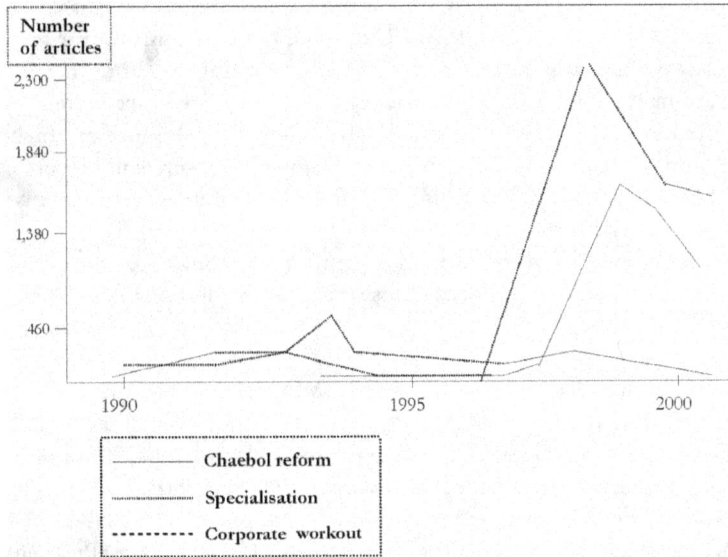

Restructuring of the Labour Market: Flexibility Required

In the context of corporate restructuring around FDI, workers were faced with the conditions of 'flexibility'. The SAP package's 'Other Structural Measures' states that for 'labour market reform ... further steps [will be taken] to improve labour market flexibility'. Previously existing labour laws did not provide for a 'flexibility in the labour market' (Park and Lee 1999) and would need revamping. President Kim declared in his inaugural address that 'intangible knowledge and information will be the driving power for economic development'. In this vein, flexibility was to become a primary factor for labour restructure.

A flexible labour force was one of the first objectives to invite inward FDI and to meet the expectations for conditionalities applied by the IMF package (Sohn and Yang 1998: 18). Korean economists stressed that 'We cannot avoid unemployment, business recession, price hikes and corporate bankruptcy. What we have to do is to make Korean companies competitive internationally through financial reform and corporate restructuring' (*Business Korea* 1998). Business Korea stressed that foreign investors would require flexibility of labour and that Korea had some work to do in this regard.

> Foreign investors are just around the corner. But, we are not yet ready to accommodate them. They would like to confirm if it is safe to invest in Korea and if it would be profitable. Foreigners are questioning if local companies run a transparent accounting system and if they can indeed streamline their businesses. In addition, they would like to know if Korean workers will be co-operative with foreign firms and will allow them to accommodate layoffs. Also, they would like to make sure if Korea is stable politically. Korea is a market attractive enough to foreign investors, but the problem is answering these questions raised by foreigners.

In 1998, analysts proposed that the IMF restructuring plan, which involved intensified opening to foreign investment, would result in 1 million layoffs of workers. The National Assembly in early 1998 began to make laws that were designed to 'make layoffs easier' (Strom 1998). The law eliminated the requirement for court approval for company layoffs and allowed multinational corporations a 'flexible' work force. President Kim declared in a televised speech during the heat of crisis reform that 'If foreign investors take over a local company, about 10 per cent – 20 per cent of workers may be laid off. But, their corporate activities would contribute to the national economy' (1998).

In 1999, Uh, Soo Bong of the Korean International Labour Foundation (KOILAF) gave a prescription for the facilitation of complete labour market flexibility. They are as follows:

- More flexible wage system is needed.
- Legal or institutional regulations not favouring 'various work forms' like contract labour, part-time or home-based work should be eased.
- Female work force should be encouraged, retirement age should be reduced, contract employment for public sector should be initiated.

- Education and training to produce and develop human resources.
- Labour market should make a stronger interconnected system and public employment services should be strengthened (Uh 1999: 50, 51).

This list gives an overview of the structural changes that were deemed to aid in Korea's recovery process from the economic crisis.

Unemployment, or the final impact of labour 'flexibility' in this context, increased dramatically as a result of the 1997 crisis. Yoon, Young Mo, International Secretary of the KCTU stated that 'M&As by foreigners [that] the law is encouraging will lead to mass dismissals' (Strom 1998). As expected, the unemployment rate that had rested as low as 2 per cent in 1995 dropped to 2.1 per cent in from the 'fall' in 1997 to 8.4 per cent in early 1998, which meant that about 1.7 million Koreans lost jobs nearly overnight (Rowley and Bae 2002: 534; Ledemel and Dahl 2001: 205). The country's jobless rate hit a 33-year high of 8.7 per cent in February 1998, and the number of jobless people was tallied at 1.78 million in the same month. A drop in new hires occurred as well, with a 5.3 per cent decrease in 1998. The economically inactive population increased by 5.5 per cent the same year. Workers began to interpret the word 'flexible' to mean 'fired' and reacted violently when in July 1998 serious layoffs began to take effect (43). By June 1999, 8.4 per cent of Koreans were unemployed, meaning 1,356,000 people were affected dramatically by the restructure of the material aspects of Korean society (KOILAF 1999).

The primary reason for layoffs, or 'employment adjustment' was to overcome the crisis of the firm (see Table 1). In the majority of cases, employees were compelled to quit under the 'honorary retirement programme' due to the severity of business downturns and lack of contracts (Park, D. J. et al. 2001: 129). The number of honourable retirees exceeded those dismissed. Before 1989, Koreans were accustomed to lifetime employment, which was part of the 'egalitarian and communitarian consciousness' of Korean society (126). In 1989, the Supreme Court designated the justification of dismissals if the following conditions were evident. The first condition was labelled 'urgent managerial needs', wherein all possible alternatives have been studied. The second states that if dismissals were unavoidable, employees would have to be selected for termination by 'reasonable and just standards'. Next, employers would be required to consult with Unions or employees on measures to avoid dismissal and setting standards for the selection process of dismissal. Conditions were formally legislated in 1996 but Union opposition prevented the bill from taking affect. An amended bill was drafted in 1997, but was immediately suspended for two years. Ministers decided, however, that limited agreed policy changes at the nascent Tripartite Commission were sufficient to write new laws in 1998 to fulfil the IMF's requirements for job market flexibility (127).

Table 1. Reasons for Adjustment. (Park et al. 2001: 129)

Reason	Firms	%
To make vacancy for promotion	7	2.9
To reduce excess of employees generated by automation	13	5.4
Corporate restructuring and downsizing	39	16.3
To reduce wage costs	31	12.9
To overcome crisis of the company	136	56.7
Merger and acquisition with other company	3	1.3
Others	11	4.6
Total	**240**	**100.0**

After the economic crisis, workers quit in droves when they realised the extent of the downturn and they hoped to be granted some retirement pay as well as severance that was sometimes available in what increasingly seemed to be unavoidable cases of dismissal. In fact, 35 per cent of firms used 'honourable retirement' to shed workers, which is considerably higher than the percentage of firms using straight dismissals. But attrition was the most widely used method of reducing employment. In 1998, 80 per cent of firms used this method, affecting on average 103 employees per company, whilst in 1999, 70 per cent of firms did the same, removing on average, 64 workers per company (140).

Job losses resulting from government and TCCN-led restructuring, in fact, divides workers into three broad categories of hierarchy. First, there are workers who are *integrated* into the system of management and research and development or who become organic intellectuals and often members of the TCC (Sklair 1997, 2001a, 2001b; Van der Pijl 1997, 1998). Second, workers in a more precarious position are subject to labour flexibility practices and minimal job protection. The third category consists of excluded groups. This final group includes workers in small low-technology enterprises and the unemployed (Cox 1999). The latter two groups are marginalised from the TCCN and from the Korean government's strategies, in the contemporary context of globalization.

Tense labour relations are a definite repellent for potential investors, but flexible workers can be dealt with accordingly. Typically, foreign companies are wary of an inflexible work force. In Korea the tradition of lifetime employment was not conducive to requirements for flexibility of the labour market and protest was on the horizon. The sudden permission of layoffs, after decades of guaranteed lifetime employment, was just one of the issues labour was suddenly expected to accommodate. President DJ Kim pleaded with workers to understand that the disappearance of jobs and resulting 'honorary/early retirement' (Kim et al. 2001: 129) would be *necessary* for the revitalisation of the economy. In many acquisition cases, 'early retirement' was the term used to describe the disappearance of a great number of employees at the merged plants. But labour flexibility would not immediately and naturally mesh with a Korean understanding of job security, although the government began to provide social safety nets for the unemployed. The phenomenon of such high levels of layoffs would not only disturb people's livelihood and families, but would also interrupt a pattern of what labour leaders interviewed called cultural norms[1] or a lifelong payment system that salaried people had enjoyed.

By August 1999, unemployment was above 1.4 million, for a total of 6.8 per cent of the labour force, compared to 2.6 per cent in 1997 (KOILAF 1999a). Wage cuts were offered in exchange for job stability, meaning that wage levels reached a 10.3 per cent decrease. Blue collar, white collar and managerial positions alike were threatened by the serious measures taken by companies at the direction of a global-minded government. Pressures escalated at this time. Safety nets and VET were concessions offered to workers who sought representation but received none. Instead, even as democracy was expected to take hold, they were given limited rights.

In 2000, the World Bank and the OECD reported on Korea's progress in incorporating itself into the global knowledge economy. Several aspects were examined, including redefining the role of the government, opening up the economy and promoting competition, FDI, efficiency of financial markets, corporate governance, addressing risks of the digital divide, social safety nets, enhancing flexibility in the labour market, venture capital, and strengthening intellectual property rights and enforcement. Each category includes three sections for comments on 1) situation up to crisis, 2) ongoing reforms, and 3) remaining issues. The 'enhancing flexibility in the labour market' section shows that Korea has worked to present a more flexible labour market to international speculation, as is shown in Figure 1.

In 2001, Chung Tae Sung, secretary-general of the Federation of Korean Industries (FKI) warned the nation that in a time of declining employment of young college graduates, only increased labour market flexibility could aid for a revival of industrial competitiveness and increase employment. Korea would have to revise corporate regulations on items such as 'days off' and 'special leave' and bring them into line with 'international standards, prior to the full-scale implementation of a five-day workweek system' (*Korea Herald* 2001). So even in 2001 Korea struggled to reform to international standards. What else would it take to convince the international business community of Korea's competitiveness and durability during the historical bloc of neoliberalism?

Institutional Restructuring I: Tripartite Commission and Limited Inclusion via *Trasformismo*

The material capabilities for production were thus thrown open to international pressures for change and the government promptly paid attention to IMF restructuring requirements. In a move to provide a more inclusive dialogue regarding steps toward restructuring, the Kim government established an unprecedented institutional forum for discussion called the Tripartite Commission, which held three important meetings at its inception but was ultimately unable to a consensus regarding discussed policy changes. The forum for dialogue was a chance for the elite to dictate both workers' and management's 'needs' in the era of restructuring via the *trasformismo* strategy of limited inclusion, which is what actually resulted in the failure of the Commissions.

The Commission's meetings illustrate the first post-crisis phase of domestic negotiation. From the onset, KCTU members believed that the Commission was created solely as a ploy to attract investment from the international spectrum rather than as a real political tool for unions and workers' rights in the crisis era. However, Lee and Lee (1999: 171) show that after parties came to limited agreements on several issues within the

Tripartite Commission, investors gained confidence in Korea's attempts to improve labour relations. KCTU representatives argued that government representatives were thus in a position of authority over the other participants in the discussions that ensued. The Tripartite Commission demonstrates the state's efforts to involve an increased number of voices into the restructuring project, which shows that the newly democratic regime was at least aware of workers' justified demand for inclusion. Nonetheless, this institutional platform for discussion was continuously unsuccessful. The government aimed to garner consensus, but ultimately, only coercion was evident.

Dialogue on Recovery: Social Pact of the Tripartite Commission

The First Tripartite Commission was established January 15, 1998. Representatives included at the government level representatives from three major political parties, the Labour Minister, and the Finance Minister. The Korea Employers Federation (KEF) and the Federation of Korean Industries (FKI) represented the employer/manager segment of the Commission. The Federation of Korean Trade Unions (FKTU) and the Korean Confederation of Trade Unions (KCTU) sent delegates to give union representation. The FKTU is a large umbrella union grouping with an average membership of 242, which is smaller than the KCTU, but in cooperation with the government much more than the militant KCTU.

All parties agreed that the economic crisis was partially the failure of each segment to prepare appropriately for economic difficulties (Tripartite Commission 1999: 169). The 'Tripartite Joint Statement on Fair Burden-Sharing in the Process of Overcoming the Economic Crisis' was attractive for the Commission's purpose. On February 6, 1998, 90 items were agreed at the meeting called 'Agreement to Overcome the Economic Crisis'. 21 issues were earmarked for further discussion. The Social Pact was initiated by the government and was composed of the following (Lee and Lee 1999: 172).

1. Management transparency and corporate restructuring.
2. Stabilisation of consumer prices.
3. Employment stabilisation and unemployment policy.
4. Extension and consolidation of the social security system
5. Wage stabilisation and the promotion of labour-management cooperation.
6. Enhancement of basic labour rights.

7. Enhancement of labour market flexibility.
8. Increase of export and improvement of the international balance of payments.
9. Other issues to overcome the current economic crisis.
10. Agenda for social cohesion.

Eleven Priority Tasks were discussed, with the hope to promote them at a meeting of the Subcommittee on Labour Relations (Tripartite Commission 1999: 7):

1. Securing the basic labour rights of teachers and government workers.
2. Recognition of the right of the unemployed to join non-enterprise-based trade unions.
3. Revision of the political fund act to ensure political activities of trade unions
4. Reduction of the statutory working hours (including reform schemes for holiday and leave systems).
5. Reform of the wage system.
6. Matters regarding punishment for the payment of wages to full-time union officials.
7. Matters regarding adjustment of the scope of essential public utilities projects.
8. Matters regarding activation of labour-management consultation on various levels, such as business type, region, etc.
9. Trade union organisation and bargaining structure (enterprise- and industry-specific improvement measures).
10. Improvement plans for the severance pay system.
11. Legislation of the basic act on industrial safety.

The 90 items agreed upon included consolidation of employment adjustment related laws and the reform of the wage system: reforms that would affect workers most immediately. The proposals, if followed by every member, were written to promote recovery from the economic crisis. The first *Social Pact* (above) included items that required government, unions, and management operational initiatives in a three-way trade-off system. However, 'trade-off' was an unfamiliar term, considering unilateral economic policy making of the past. Negotiation in the past had not been applied under conditions of consensus and was not easily executed.

Failure of Consensus and Union Reaction to Flexibility Law

While the Tripartite Commission was designed to encourage negotiation, the KCTU was heavily criticised by its members for accepting an early lay-off system (see #7 of social pact). The influx of foreign corporate take-overs has been directly related to the overwriting of the lifelong employment security law, and foreign companies were shy of an inflexible work force. Mr Yoon of the KCTU[2] claimed that just after the KCTU withdrew from the Commission, the government's permission to pass new laws to facilitate ease of employment adjustment was the initial violation to agreements. This would essentially clean officials' hands by way of passing a high level of responsibility to foreign companies for employee welfare (Strom 1998).

The KCTU withdrew participation from the Commission in response to pressure from its members after delegates agreed to the establishment of a 'flexible work force'. The Commission could not continue. 'Enhancement of labour market flexibility' was one of the first matters filed in the *Social Pact*, and before workers could be consulted was immediately categorised as being 'implemented'. The matter was an enactment of the Act Relating to Protection for Dispatched Workers. Labour flexibility, however, was the term used to grant layoffs 'should there be an urgent management need, or under the cases of mergers and acquisitions (M&A)'. The Act was a double-edged sword, as it granted permission of unions' increased political involvement from 1998, but simultaneously, labour laws were revised to permit employment adjustment and casualisation of labour.

The Korea Confederation of Trade Unions said it had no choice but to break away from the tripartite committee. Union leaders argue that under the government's unilateral reform program ... only the workers are forced to make sacrifices. KCTU has called the government to end mass layoffs. It also wants job security through shorter working hours and a greater social safety net for the two million unemployed. KCTU President Lee Kap-yong has offered to resume talks ... but only if the government comes up with measures to strengthen the committee's role and power. ... It said, unless the government stops its unilateral restructuring drive by next month's end ... it (KCTU) too will leave the tripartite body. So far, the government is taking a hard line stance.

(KOILAF 1997)

Not only the KCTU but also the Federation of Korean Trade Unions (FKTU), traditionally the government's trusty companion stated that if the government continued what they called unilateral restructuring moves, they would not participate in an organisation supposedly designed to give more voice to unions and by default, workers. The FKTU was in agreement when the KCTU reacted to downsizing and company take-overs, which shows an unprecedented move between two previously antagonistic groups. This reshuffling of social forces is part of the hegemonic struggle occurring during the negotiation for Korea's restructured future, a shuffle that unfortunately had little impact in the final outcome of decisions made at the Commission. Overall, the Commission itself is a form of *trasformismo* in the sense that the government organised the forum to demonstrate that it wanted to listen to previously excluded voices and to appear accommodating to workers who would suffer the greatest impact by the crisis. But workers' needs were quickly re-articulated into a discourse of 'flexibility', unions were pressured to come to a type of agreement, but ultimately, even the second and third commissions were unsuccessful because unions found little success in representing workers in this historically developmental state.

Second and Third Tripartite Commissions

After the failure of the first institutional arrangement to come to complete consensus on all pieces of discussion, in June 1998 the Tripartite Commission was revived with the hope of establishing more concrete goals and communication between members. Its new mission was to draft policy proposals to fulfil 'social agreements' of the original Commission and for tripartite policy-consultation and economic restructuring of banking, finance, and the public sector. The second Commission aimed to provide teachers' right to organise, to allow unemployed workers union membership, and to minimise 'potential confrontation' between parties. Barriers for agreement, however, included mutual mistrust over the issues of unpaid wages, collective agreements infringements, and employment stability (Lee and Lee 1999: 173).

The third Commission was inaugurated on September 1, 1999. Matters discussed at this Commission included wage payment of full time union leaders, wage system discrepancies, and union representation at the Commission. The Commission was and still is a forum for discussion and voting of members on issues proposed and included in the agenda, and so on, but it is not a legislative organ. It cannot pass laws. So discussion may be conducted at the table of negotiation, but resolutions are not laws.

While the main item differentiating the Tripartite Commission from previously attempted social dialogue models is the requirement for consensus, resulting in the paralysis of many discussed items and in turn, government has unilaterally taken steps to pass policies to suit its overall goals. There is a chronic lack of trust between members who have only associated in the past according to relationships based on hierarchies. The mistrust is also garnered from a history of 'policy means to impose controls over organised labour's demands and resistance, rather than promoting a democratic process of tripartite consultation and administering its balanced outcomes' (Lee B. H. 1999). The essence of negotiation is based of a complex body of rules that are both formal and informal, and the Commission as an institution was invented as a means to find consent between all three parties represented at the meetings. This nonetheless did not prevent government representatives from using historically repeated behaviour of imposing its authority and enacting policies. So the government typically has behaved as more of an authoritarian leader than a democratic entity at Commission forums.

Institutional Restructuring II: VET

As discussed, corporate restructuring in Korea resulted in a jump of the unemployment rate from 2.0 in 1996, to 8.1 per cent in the fourth quarter of 1998 which was the most vulnerable period of restructuring (UNDP 1999: 40). Material restructuring includes not just physical transformations of corporate realities, but has a significant impact on workers. As discussed in the previous section, corporate restructuring has resulted in mass layoffs of workers, and President Kim, the Ministry of Education and the MOL worked quickly to construct social safety nets for unprotected groups (OECD 2000: 20; KOILAF 1999:8).

Two agencies govern VET policymaking, the Ministry of Education, which looks after institutions of vocational education, and the Ministry of Labour, which manages vocational training institutions (KRIVET/ NCVER 2000: 8). Korea has historically provided training for youth as well as adults, and the institutions in existence in 2001 included vocational high schools, junior colleges, polytechnic colleges and vocational training institutes. But in the 1990s, young participants in VET decreased sharply, and in 1997 the government wrote an 'Act on promoting workers' vocational training in 1997' designed to promote attractiveness of VET for all entrants to the job market (KRIVET/NCVER 2001: 58).

New VET programmes were classified into 'initial training; upgrade training; and job transfer training' for re-employment of workers. Initial training was most often recommended for newly laid-off workers and involved general education co-ordinated with practical training, and secondly, basic training in knowledge and skills common to related occupations given by a training institution. Thirdly, initial training involved the cultivation and specialisation in knowledge and skills for 'employability' in the age of inflexibility. The new VET programmes are 'employment-maintenance' and 'employment-promotion'; introduced to provide compensation for laid-off workers (OECD 2000: 96–97) and an unprecedented chance for workers to take responsibility for employability itself.

For 'employment stabilisation' a few years after the economic crisis, KOILAF recommended specialised VET for unemployed workers most affected by corporate restructuring. In a summary of corporate restructuring and employment stabilisation policy released in November 2000 by the Ministry of Labour, specific training was promised at no cost to the worker, and training and food allowances would be distributed nationally. Training subsidies of up to 1 million won (1,067 USD) were suggested for individuals who desired to pay for training themselves. In 2001, the government claimed that it would prioritise construction and manufacturing training, and in the earliest period of 2001, it would focus on VET for re-employment (KOILAF 2000b: 4).

These programmes have been emphasised as an important factor in reform of the Korean economy (KOILAF 2000: 26), and are an attempt to mould what Gramsci named organic intellectuals into the ideology of neoliberal capitalism by way of the course material promising renewed employability. The next section discloses shifts taken in the education and research sector, in partnership with the government and international organisations, to accommodate restructuring. VET was expected save workers from the 'inevitable' fate of market economies; the *trasformismo* of workers' welfare once again came to the fore with the restructuring of VET in the crisis recovery period.

Shift to Knowledge Economy and Elite-led Goals for VET

The production characteristics of the Industrial Age involved mass production and mass consumption, and were more mechanical than relations now seen in the Information Age. The primary asset base during the Industrial Age lay in capital, labour, and resources, whereas the Information Age's assets lie in skills, knowledge, and innovation. Differences to nations' asset bases and expectations placed on the workforce demonstrate changes required in the context of the historical bloc of neoliberalism, and are manifest in a spreading number of developed and developing economies. Economies of flexibility and speed are reflected in the expectations of the populations that live within those economies and this is reflected in the expectations of labour. The World Bank 1998/99 World Development Report emphasises the role of knowledge for economic advancement and social well being, and heralds the development of a knowledge-based economic growth model as the ultimate goal for sustainable development. So how is this reflected by the need for new kinds of knowledge for employability in the era of labour market flexibility?

In the 1990s and early twenty-first century, specialised, knowledge-based economies became the ideal for nations seeking to compete at the global level. While industrialising economies were grounded in a mode of production of a more material and tangible nature, the neoliberal age has begun to celebrate 'knowledge' as the most important qualification for the specialisation of the economy. The new economies are 'required' to consolidate the main tenets of neoliberalism and to specialise according to their nationally specific qualities, whether it is human capital or another particular resource. Knowledge-based economies require a technologically driven highly skilled labour force, meaning that workers who are trained into the appropriate industries may be at an advantage to workers within traditional sectors.

So to remain *employable* in a knowledge economy, workers need to adapt to an entirely new set of codes involved in the production, mediation, and application of knowledge. The Linear Model shown in Figure 5 demonstrates a commonly accepted method of learning, one that is seen within the traditional pedagogical model used by academic institutions. According to the OECD (2000: 39), this model is outdated and cannot completely prepare workers for Information Age survival. The OECD stresses that this model of learning has been successful in the University, but these stages of progression in linear fashion are gradually becoming less useful for industry. Nonetheless, the model demonstrates three crucial aspects of knowledge that are negotiated in the industries of the Industrial Age.

Figure 5. A Linear Model

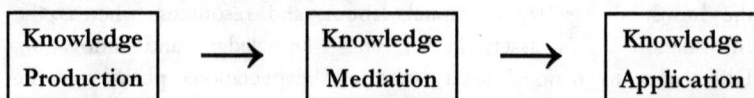

Knowledge Production	→	Knowledge Mediation	→	Knowledge Application

For success in a 'knowledge economy', new forms of learning however are important and knowledge is produced via a new set of exchanges, including:

- Commercial input to design.
- Feedback from users.
- University-industry interaction.
- Movement of knowledge embodied in people.
- Knowledge management in organisations (OECD 2000: 51).

Particularly around the turn of the millennium, experts began to stress the importance of knowledge for sustainable development. At the World Conference on Science in 1999, UNESCO experts declared that '... the future of humankind will become more dependent on the equitable production, distribution, and use of knowledge than ever before' (UNESCO 1999). The World Bank joined forces and encouraged the 'entire development community' to recognise the centrality of knowledge for development. The 'development community' was challenged to create the international public goods necessary to help developing nations survive in the knowledge economy (World Bank 1998/1999). Into the twenty-first century, on 20 December 2002, the General Assembly of the United Nations declared the UN Decade of Education for Sustainable Development beginning on 1 January 2005 (resolution 57/254).[3] UNESCO was given the responsibility to act as head agency for the management of a kind of discourse that underpins this decade, and was asked to draft an international implementation scheme. This scheme would include recommendations for VET across nations.

The ownership of intangible goods and services and the knowledge involved in their production drives competition in the 'new capitalism'. Workplace requirements have become less directly 'trainable' because the outcome is less obviously measured. The result is that workers are becoming increasingly removed and alienated from the final product. This has occurred in several industries, including information and communications and consultancy. Production of intangible goods within these industries requires new work styles and skills and new partnerships between sectors.

Training programmes began to prompt new forms of consolidation and convergence that would dissolve 'left-over' knowledge of cultural norms and practices, and ultimately fragment any terrain for resistance to state-led and internationally informed internationalisation strategies (Cox 1987: 253). New forms of knowledge became commodified assets in the international environment and were translated into Korea's VET programmes in order to train workers into what were seen as global norms of neoliberalism. Leadbeater believes that state guidance for this process has increased in importance due to 'its role in producing knowledge, through the education system' (1998: 379). The top-down relationship between the state and workers, even after the official declaration of democracy in 1987, allowed the state to implement institutions facilitating its neoliberal internationalisation economic drive(s) and to propagate elite and externally led accumulation strategies without consensus. Even since the transition to democracy, the legacy of authoritarian leadership has not subsided significantly (Kim, S. S. 2003: 39).

The Kim government began to manage unprecedented requirements for curriculum development and content via partnerships with international groups who maintain ownership of what is considered lucrative worker 'knowledge' in the contemporary context of neoliberal capitalism. In order to maintain control and to sideline potential social crises or uprisings in opposition to development strategies, or to initiate *trasformismo*, the Korean government intended to absorb any fragments of society that posed a threat through providing the means to obtain employable knowledge in the neoliberal economy. A congratulated role for VET programmes evoked the 'necessity' of workers' cross-national convergence of skills for Korea to remain a competitive global economic player. The 'Goals and Strategies of the National Human Resources Policy' as depicted by the Republic of Korea in a publication of 2001, 'Policy Visions and Goals for Korea's place as a knowledge economy are:

- Strengthening the capacity of individuals.
- Building social trust and cohesion.
- Creating new sources for economic growth (ROK 2001: 22).

The appropriate 'Policy Areas and Tasks' for these 'Visions' include the task to strengthen cooperation among businesses, universities, and research institutions for effective VET; and continuing education and training of workers by expanding commercially provided education and establishing technical schools and corporate colleges (22, 28). This government publication stresses that 'we must increase the opportunity of the low-income groups to receive vocational training through the vocational training for self-rehabilitation and employment promotion' (43). The government stated that it supports successful participation in training and employment via individualised supervision and by guaranteeing a decent standard of living by instituting the Law for Guaranteeing Basic Life for All Citizens (43).

'Making knowledge and human resources the driving force for further growth' became the priority for restructuring of VET. Goals at this time involved:

- Discovering and educating the gifted children at an early age.
- Developing knowledge and training workers for national strategic areas.
- Innovating the role and function of the university as a new engine for growth.
- Human resources development for upgrading the quality of the service industries.
- Developing professionals to produce knowledge capital (ROK 2001: 50–63).

The infrastructure necessary for these human resources development involved 'streamlining the system of distributing and managing knowledge' (ROK 2001: 82).

KRIVET: Institutional Support and Consolidation of Elite-led Development
An emerging dynamic between the national and international is seen in hegemonic struggles between social forces engaged in a battle for the establishment of a hegemonic production structure. What is seen in the Korean case is an ascendance of individuals who operate within the criteria of transnational norms by involving themselves with the TCCN. The network attempts to incorporate subordinate groups of workers into this paradigm by providing certain concessions but deliberately avoiding their political involvement. In the period of restructuring, the Korean government created a research centre specifically for the activity of restructuring work norms within its country to meet transnational

standards. KRIVET employs several researchers who are required to support, intellectually, the government's internationalisation initiatives within VET. The case study in further chapters discusses just one element of the elite-driven network that is expanding across the globe.

But perhaps the most important evidence of the government's attempts to reorganise according to supposedly immutable demands of expansive neoliberal capitalism is seen in the formation of organic intellectuals within one research institute. On 9 February 1996, the establishment of an unprecedented Korea Research Institute for Vocational Education and Training (KRIVET) was proposed as a part of the Educational Reform for the Construction of a New Vocational Education System. By 27 March of the next year, the KRIVET Act (Act. No.5315) went into affect. The Institute was then founded on 10 September 1997 as a government funded institution, just as the economic crisis erupted across Asia. Since 1997 KRIVET has controlled vocational education and human resources, and composed curricula that complimented the government's reform and recovery strategies. Researchers such as those working within KRIVET are increasingly part of an international network of institutions: Cox states that '... elite talent from peripheral countries is co-opted into international institutions in the manner of *trasformismo*' (1983: 173).

The MOL subsidised KRIVET with the aim to 'strengthen the vocational training system, in order to produce skilled manpower to meet changing industrial demands' (KOILAF 1999c: 108). In 1997, the MOL integrated a new form of vocational training programmes into formal education, and took over private vocational training institutions. At its inception, researchers within the Institute were asked to focus on the practical aspects of vocational training and *not* to explore the theoretical side of the issue. Later however, an increasing volume of international experts began to participate in the Institute's activities, as is discussed later in this section.

KRIVET has acted as a type of consulting firm for the government; as government ministries in South Korea typically enjoy a supplementary research institute of similar calibre. KRIVET's first responsibility was to give guidelines for qualification and background for the developing curriculum of vocational training in South Korea. Later, more responsibilities were placed on researchers having to do with comparative research projects, international performance standards analyses, and other data accumulation activities.

The Centre in Seoul has formed partnerships with the OECD, the ILO and APEC. The dialogue between these institutions and KRIVET is intended to integrate Korea into the extensive networks that now exist for VET conformity across nations.[4] There are partner organisations across the globe including the Centre d'Etudes et de Recherches sur les Qualifications (CEREQ) in France; National Centre for Vocational Education Research (NCVER) in Australia; Central Institute of Vocational and Technical Education (CIVTE) in China and General Organisation for Technical Education and Vocational Training (GOTEVOT) in Saudi Arabia (ILO 2001).

While neoliberal globalization takes particular characteristics in these diverse locations, there are cross-case expectations of nationally based workers, as put forward by members of the TCCN. UNEVOC is one example of an entity attempting to expand ideologies with a universal and essentialist tone, and sets the groundwork for the formulation of universalist convergence expectations. In 2002, the Seoul based UNEVOC Centre is involved not just with training programme design and co-ordination, but also conducts Korean vocational research that aids policy-making, training programme development, and the Centre considers individual workers' qualifications to permit national authorisation. Kang, S. H. emphasises the importance of worker preparation schemes for global competition within an international Knowledge Economy.

> The emergence of the knowledge-based society provides not only windows of opportunities, but also brings about uncertainty and greater challenges. Based on the bi-polarisation hypothesis about the knowledge-based society, the performance of knowledge may be much less than desirable in under-developed countries. As a result, these countries may experience an ever-widening knowledge gap compared to developed countries, due to an inadequate infrastructure for the expansion and application of knowledge, and due to a less competitive knowledge level.
>
> (Kang, S. H. 2000: 101)

KRIVET assumed the responsibility for worker training at the direction of the Ministry of Education and the MOL, and on 18 October 2000 it was inaugurated as the UNESCO Regional Centre of Excellence in Technical and Vocational Education and Training. KRIVET thus was transformed into one of the offices of the regional UNEVOC[5] centre for the Asia Pacific. This occurred as the General Assembly of UNESCO resolved to reinforce technical and vocational education and training via expansion of its the international program. The head office of UNEVOC was established in Bonn, Germany in September 2000 and has regional centres across the globe. In Seoul, UNEVOC has one main and three associate centres, located in the buildings of the Ministry of Education, in the Local Education Support Bureau and in the office of the Industrial Education Policy Officer at Korea Manpower Agency, and KRIVET.

So as a direct response to the economic crisis, the government took over all areas of vocational training at the same time as it established a partnership with UNESCO to formulate new curricula for general workers training. This was partly in response to the influx of MNCs who entered the economy rapidly in response to deregulation requirements; companies whose 'colonisation' of Korean industries required a particular kind of worker. Knowledge-based industries began to play an increasingly important role in the buoyancy of the Korean economy (Kang 2000: 101), and the workforce was incapable of fully adapting to this transformation. The government worked specifically with the ILO and UNEVOC to establish government-led, reform oriented VET programs. Whilst Koreans historically had been accustomed to on-site training after beginning a job that also offered lifetime employment, general vocational training within businesses was completely abolished in 1998. Workers were thus expected from 1997 and onward to fulfil government objectives for production and skill acquisition. The top-down nature of recommendations for skills acquisition indicates that workers' participation in development once again was elite-engineered, during the reform period.

The Presidential Commission for Educational Reform (PCER) designed the Second Education Reform Program which involved vocational education reform: the main change being an introduction of the 'Lifelong Vocational Education System' (KOILAF 1999c: 108). The Ministers of Labour instigated a campaign of the 'new labour culture' (KOILAF 2001: 11; Lee S. R. 1999: 1) (see below) in 1997, which was propagated into the next century. The campaign was designed to introduce new work training programs, involving classes, videos, and literature designed to prepare companies for foreign management and/or new policies. The main thrust was to implement a:

... total shift in perspective among workers and businesses, and the government will be necessary for Korea to compete in the new century, where national borders have lost their significance. Korea must observe a new paradigm of labour relations in which employers and workers are partners in every sense of the word.

(Lee, S. R.: 1999)

Simultaneously, On September 18, 2000, the Labour Reform Task Force was activated, a group chaired by the Vice Labour Minister. The Minister reminded the nation that 'labour sector reform is crucial to enhance competitiveness of an enterprise and a nation and improve living quality of workers in this era of unbridled competition' (MOL 1999). The following are some of the bullet points of the task force's objectives.

- Livelihood Protection Measure
  - Innovation in Operation of Job Security Centres and Manpower Banks
  - Establishment of a Three Year Plan for Vocational Ability
- Development
  - Diversification of labour diplomacy and international exchanges
  - Formulation of Measures to Expand Inter -Korean Exchanges and
  - Co-operation in Labour Sector (1999).

The fundamentals of the task force highlight the importance of labour capital and its capabilities in the reform period and articulate the strategies for its education. This process occurs predominantly through government relations with enterprises and most often aims to transform labour to meet premeditated behaviour targets. These new relations meant that the government was to become more deeply involved in VET programmes than ever before, through discourse with the research institute and involved negotiations about the content for skills training itself.

However, workers who are involved in VET programmes must also be convinced that their participation is beneficial to their lives, which is part of the incentive structure provided, and is necessary for *trasformismo* to be effective. To encourage voluntary participation, the government has offered businesses two forms of support for implementation of the subsidisation for implementation costs to employers, and paid leave for training to employees. This strategy is covered in section 4.5.5 and demonstrates new forms of incentive structure building for participation of employees and the unemployed in VET programmes. The next subsection discusses how the government has restructured VET itself with the vision of a skilled knowledge-based workforce.

Restructuring of Ideas and the Knowledge Structure: VET, Educative Strategy, and the Restructuring of Common Sense

The OECD (2000a) compiled a report entitled 'Knowledge Management in the Learning Society: Education and Skills'. The document aims to 'contribute to the understanding of knowledge and learning in the context of economic development and social cohesion' (2000a: 3). The OECD has worked with academics, policy-makers and private sector participants to compare 'knowledge processes' in information technology, engineering, the health sector and education. The publication is the product of four meetings held in Tokyo, San Francisco and Paris between 1997 and 1999. At each meeting, experts discussed 'issues and problems related to how knowledge and learning will become key drivers of social and economic change in the coming century' (3). Information was expected to provide consultation to developing nations who could become involved in the global knowledge economy as active members.

The intervention of what Gramsci terms 'a particular ideology, born in a highly developed country, is disseminated in less developed countries, impinging on the local interplay of combinations' (*PN*: 182) of culture and traditional ideology, that meet various new ideas infiltrating from international angles. Potential for conflict is high when national and international interests meet at the ideological/ideational level. Knowledge is not necessarily ideological, but because ideology represents a 'common sense' for societies, it is, ultimately, the most important cohesion of a society. Van Apeldoorn (2002: 48) states that at the 'superstructural level, we find the institutional context in which capital operates, referring in particular to the relative degree of embeddedness into specific national socio-political structures, including aspects of national (political) culture'. But, hegemonic struggles such as the struggle represented by ongoing passive revolution, operates most intimately at the superstructural level, within which ideas and ideology are manifest, because the composition of knowledge lies therein. If there is no pre-existing common sense within a population, which would be conducive to the strategies of a hegemonic class, then what methods will the dominant groups tend to use, in the struggle for hegemony?

How would the government convince workers to accept their 'flexibility' within the nascent knowledge economy of South Korea? As a safety net, the Unemployment Measure Training Programme[6] was drafted, and significant changes were applied to VET across the country. This Programme aimed to provide a substantial amount of vocational training and re-skilling, called also life-long learning, for the new unemployed, putting increased responsibility into the hands of workers for their own employability in a supposedly unchangeable trajectory of IMF controlled events following the crisis. The DOL terminated old vocational training programmes and invested an unprecedented level of funding into Polytechnics and training institutes, expanding the size of available instruction. Thus, the government began the process of restructuring for vocational training with urgency.

Unprecedented partnerships between education institutions also emerged, predominantly in the areas of computer, language (English), and vocational technical training. Increasing responsibility for this restructuring was delegated to the Department of Education (DOE). Traditionally in Korea, VET was headed by the Department of Labour (DOL), whilst vocational education, which is offered in schools, was headed by the DOE. After the economic crisis however, 'efforts have been made to integrate vocational education and training in order to deliver more effective vocational education and training to the users' (KRIVET 2000a: 8). 'Users' however, have no choice but to take part in training and are therefore constrained to 'passively' accept their only alternative for survival in the changing society and economy. New requirements were framed as beneficial for workers, but this claim is redundant because of the absence of negotiations regarding how employability would emerge in the era of recovery. The top-down construction of VET shows one of the characteristics for ongoing passive revolution. The way that VET has been proselytised as a safety-net for workers' survival in a supposedly immutable roller-coaster of market events is a case of *trasformismo*. Restructuring of South Korea's economy continued to demonstrate clear characteristics of passive revolution, with a re-articulated message that workers must consent to elite-led development strategies, and allow economic transformation, and in this case, restructuring, to occur.

The DOL announced plans to provide training programmes for 50,000 people in 1998 that would begin the process of 'inclusion'. That number increased to 162,000 when unemployment skyrocketed as a result of the IMF bailout package restructuring conditionalities in 1998. Public, in-plant and authorised training centres furthermore were asked to accommodate the influx of the unemployed. Ihm (1999) suggests that post-crisis training is a strategy of the Korean state to avoid taking a welfare-providing role: the state expected to see full employment of its economy after the period of healing. Training programmes were framed as a means to prepare the labour force for re-employment, armed with the new skills intended to carry Korea into the next phase of global-ready development.

Social relations of production include the formation of skills and the utility and applicability of those skills in the labour force. Cox (1987: 123) reasons that the increase of adoption of similar processes of production relations at the national level to liberal world order have transpired via British and later American inspired global hegemony, beginning in the early nineteenth century. This process requires 'tapping into' the national consciousness through ideological diffusion. The adoption of prioritised production relations in Korea has required more than a 'natural' evolution of norms, but has required top-down strategies of passive revolution. Without inclusion of the voice of workers, restructuring initiated by transnational entities and government groups has not led to case of hegemonic resolution. The government has co-opted VET through a prioritisation of transnational relationships and has overlooked independent unions and any other possible participation outside representatives of a particular elite class.

The restructuring of VET programmes was introduced in the period of IMF restructuring demonstrates that a restructuring of the Korean economy was activated with an inclusive strategy of knowledge-management. The role of globalizing professionals is the formation of knowledge and ideology within 'knowledge institutions [which are] research centres, universities, business colleges' (Sklair 2001: 139). The main work of globalizing professionals is to incorporate ideological cohesion toward World Best Practice (WBP), a global standard upon which national competitiveness depends. WBP is a label that refers to the gauging of nations' performance in the global economy, whose 'scores' are designated by globalizing professionals likewise. To support this initiative, globalizing politicians take on the responsibility of creating the legal space for the expansion of capital and for the ideology of national competitive-ness in a global world economy originating from IMF designation. The IMF '… has acted as the world's most powerful economic agency, enforcing neoliberal structural adjustment around the globe' (Gills 2000b: 393) and plays a part in setting the rules for 'universal' ideas guiding development and globalisation. This international 'machinery of surveillance' (Cox 1981) works closely with states to ensure sustained development through economic assistance, contingent upon norms integration.

A senior researcher at KRIVET[7] divided the nascent institutions of vocational training that emerged after the economic crisis into the following categories. The DOL heads these institutions.

1.   Public vocational training: Korea Manpower Association
2.   Vocational Training Institutes
3.   Polytechnics (associate degrees offered)

Dr Choi commented that in the United States, the DOL has very little power to regulate companies, although it takes on the responsibility for vocational training with intimate connections with private companies. Thus the DOL has no controlling power, unlike Korea, wherein the DOL has more control over what is actually taught, or the content of curricula of vocational training programmes. Before the IMF entered the scene and Korea began the route toward restructuring, the DOL had been involved more regularly in activities of mediation between employers and workers. After the crisis, the Department has been given increased responsibilities toward vocational training. In this section, I look at the educative strategies put into place that are intended to formulate an able workforce in the Korean knowledge economy, with impetus from international partnerships with the IMF and UNESCO.

Rationalisation of post-Fordism within the Knowledge Economy

For Korea to maintain its membership of the global capitalist system, the government would like Korean people to believe that changes and reform are inevitable, and that they must play their part in working toward this goal. Elites have, in this way, articulated workers' needs regarding the need to remain employable as the threat of unemployment has escalated considerably. Elite groups have not only articulated this need as common sense, but have provided a solution by way of internationally led and supported training programmes that teach workers skills required in the knowledge economy. Evidence of *trasformismo* is once again a part of Korean economic development and a method of preventing workers' participation in decision-making, but providing concessions during the crisis and subsequent restructuring of production.

So what exactly did the TCCN representatives, transpired by IMF/Korean state relations, expect of workers in the newly reconstructed nation? Gramsci noted in America, 'rationalisation has determined the need to elaborate a new type of man suited to the new type of work and productive process' (*PN*: 286). While Gramsci wrote about America specifically, he also noted the international expansion of 'work and productive process(es)' (286). Chapter 2 of this work outlines the expansion of production relations throughout history, and within the neoliberal phase of international hegemonic struggles, a particular form of production relations and employable knowledge has become expansive. In the neoliberal age, the most lucrative and 'employable' skills of workers changed rapidly. Particular relations of production became celebrated and disseminated by a network of capitalists who aim to involve as many nations' labour forces into its programme of leadership as possible.

Fordism celebrated the manufacturing worker's production of standardised output, which involved mass production, a hierarchical workplace, and state management of the economy in an industrialising world. This mode of production was not suitable for the information-based industries that began to dominate much of global markets, and the post-Fordist or Taylorist worker began to compete for employment in the global Knowledge Economy, also named the Information Economy (Gassler 2001: 112). Elements of post-Fordism are 'dominance of a flexible and permanently innovative pattern of accumulation … polarisation between skilled and unskilled workers …' (Jessop 1994: 261). The forces driving the transition to post-Fordism and the adaptation of workers to the global scenario involve the emergence of new technologies, and evidence of internationalisation of the state.

The key features of post-Fordism fall under the rubric of a 'flexible production process based on flexible machines or systems and an appropriately flexible workforce' (Jessop 1994: 259). In a post-Fordist knowledge economy, Amoore (1998: 49) notes that experts would like workers to believe that technology is the driving force of change for societies, and *not* vice versa. Again, the claim that capitalism is an immutable force was emphasised. Experts believe that a nation's somehow inevitably formed mode of production is the driving force for social change and production relations. The characteristics of post-Fordist relations of production involve a need for the flexibility of workers who can adapt quickly to rapid technological changes and job loss, which involves flexibility of training and skills acquisition, and flexible specialisation (Waters 2001: 80–6). Qualifications are increasingly required for any worker autonomy (Jessop 1997).[8] But perhaps the most important change in the emergence of the post-Fordist, neoliberal economy of global capitalism is the emphasis placed upon *knowledge* as an asset, rather than the emergence of industrial sectors and correspondent mode of production that perpetuated production relations within industrialising societies.

Kevin Cleaver, World Bank Director and author of the Bank report released in February 2002, reported that:

> Tapping into the Knowledge Economy goes beyond investing in communications and information technologies. It means having the capacity to use knowledge effectively by putting in place the right economic and institutional framework, giving people the skills they need to exploit these opportunities, and funding local innovation centres that guarantee the continuous flow of fresh ideas.
>
> (World Bank 2002)[9]

In this vein, there has been a surge in the demand for individuals with unprecedented skills, and a restructuring of Korean vocational training programmes has been enacted in a method of state-led adaptation into the hegemonic Knowledge Economy, within the post-Fordist era of relations of production.

The Asia Pacific UNEVOC Regional Centre in Seoul declares the following modus operandi in response to the emerging knowledge economy:

> We are dedicated to research on technical and vocational education and training (TVET) and human resources development (HRD), and supporting government policies to develop the vocational capacity of its citizens through TVET as part of lifelong learning.

The Centre began to emphasise 'knowledge management', inter-agency collaboration, capacity building and works to strengthen the UNEVOC Network. Its primary aims are, in consent with UNESCO's larger aims as discussed at the International Conference held in Seoul in 1999:

- To challenge existing education and training programmes to meet the changing demands of the world of work;
- Improving systems for education and training throughout life;
- Reforming the education and training process;

- Promoting access of special groups to technical and vocational education and training;
- The changing role of government and social partners in technical and vocational education and training; and
- Enhancing international cooperation in technical and vocational education and training.[10]

While this set up appears to benefit education institutions and uses positive terminology, what is actually occurring in Korea does not exactly match the humanitarian initiatives and the social safety net objectives of these changes. The provision of education of particular skills capabilities that support a particular type of shared meaning reduces the risk of social instability. If this 'provision', however is the only option for basic survival, then is it a concession, or part of a forced programme for modernisation, and thus a method of *trasformismo*?

Wellington (1987: 30) writes that the term 'skill' has expanded to include 'social and life skills, employability skills, communication skills, attitudes to work, and preparation for life skills'. The concept of 'skill' has blossomed into a range of ideas that include 'knowledge, thinking, understanding and motivation' (30). This phenomenon has occurred to facilitate expansive neoliberal ideology. 'Understanding' and 'knowing' could become skills on par with reading or mathematical skills, demonstrating a reformation of what would be seen as employable abilities. Workers' skills were traditionally connected to craft-based work. Mental and physical abilities were associated with direct production. The Special Programmes Division in the UK expanded on this concept to involve individual and general skills of communication and life skills, and particularly 'attitudes to work and a knowledge of working life'. Thus training took on a new meaning, and was distinguished from traditional apprenticeship methods. Brown and Lauder (1999: 50) write on an increase of income inequalities in the USA and UK between low and high-skilled jobs. Low-skilled jobs are increasingly exported to developing nations, and so the answer must be to 'give' unskilled workers the skills they require in order to compete for a pool of skilled positions.

In the period of recovery the government emphasised Korea's place in the world as a 'knowledge economy'. Kim reasoned that 'the ideas and the modus operandi of the industrial society of the past will not prepare us for adaptation and adjustment ... the time has come for us to positively transform our consciousness to fit the coming century' (Kim, D. J. 1997: 205). As Korean management and the government seek to mould society to accommodate knowledge-based development, it invites increased participation to fuse responsibility for this process.

> The knowledge society comes about through becoming a 'learning society'. Everybody (researchers, managers, workers) contribute to that process through sharing their distinctive insights and know-how in building institutions and social systems capable of holding/ memorising, mediating and continuously building new knowledge.
>
> (Nyhan 2002: 20)

The need for new forms of knowledge within the workforce arises with changes in production. During Fordism, workers were trained to work in particular ways that suited mass assembled production. Nyhan states that the crisis of European industry in the 1970s and 80s came about through a lack of appropriate knowledge for changes to Taylorist work expectations. Enhanced interest in 'knowledge' in education systems is a 'timely reminder of some of the fundamentals that have been lost' (30) through the assumption that adaptation will occur outside of clearly defined training. Adaptivity is a primary 'employable' skill in the knowledge economy.

The World Bank and OECD's 2001 review of Korean progress since the crisis shows that some amount of reform of education has been implemented, but more is needed to guarantee an appropriately skilled workforce for the growing knowledge economy in South Korea. Recommendations include the integration of skills instruction such as 'communication skills, capability to utilise ICTs, as well as increase possibilities for gaining field experience' (World Bank and OECD 2001: xv). These international organisations also advise partnerships between universities and industry, the enhancement of pedagogical training with emphasis on new knowledge and ICT, incentives for teachers such as performance based pay systems, knowledge sharing systems, and expansion of exchange programmes between Korean and foreign educational institutions. At this ideational level, these powerful institutions recommend several actions to improve Korea's chances of composing the work force needed and to 'provide better co-ordination between needs of the labour market and industry, and the supply of education' (xv).

Restructuring Employability: Demand for 'Knowledge Workers'

While the arena of skill formation in the United Kingdom is market-led, in Korea and in Japan, skill formation is traditionally state-led, and supply, rather than market-oriented. When the share percentage of ownership of the total market by 'foreigners', or non-Korean investors, rose from 2.24 in 1983 to at 9.11 in 1997, jumping to 18.6 per cent by late 1998 (the highest percentage since 1983),[11] the 'market' required a critical overview of the work force. This influx of foreign capital is located in the knowledge industry more predominantly than any other industry and this has created an increase in demand for skilled 'knowledge workers' (ROK 2001; Lee K. 2001) thus changing the nature of what it means in Korea to be 'employable'.

Knowledge and information as 'assets' are becoming increasingly valuable for nations to position themselves as competitive players in the global Knowledge Economy (OECD 2000:12–13). As the value of assets shifts from tangible to intangible, workers' supposed 'lag' in adjustment to expectations of what knowledge *is*, appears to require government led strategies to provide training that can hone capability quickly and efficiently (Leadbeater 1999: iv). The implications of a knowledge-based economy, which Charles Leadbeater names the 'new capitalism' (1998: 384) are that very specific types of worker knowledge and behaviour are expected for the increasingly important exploitation of human capital for development and will enhance national economies' competitiveness in this age of global neoliberal capitalism.

> The new capitalism, that of the Knowledge Economy, will be driven by the discovery and distribution of rival intangible goods— information and knowledge—created by largely intangible assets— human and social capital. These knowledge-intensive goods are best produced through collaboration and competition, partnerships and networks, which bring together public and private.

In this context, the Korean government has adjusted investment strategies, and has restructured VET programmes. The government in this way has requested that workers and civil society co-operate with its incentives for the changes in Korean development (ROK 2001: 12, 13).

Work within the information-driven global economy is characterised by very different skills than those that were in demand during the industrialisation eras of nations. Education systems and VET within developed nations have set a precedent for worker skills training and the Korean government decided that its own national curriculum should become internationalised to achieve enhanced global economic status (ROK 2001: 61–2). Korean workers have undergone several stages of state-led VET programmes historically. After the economic crisis however, the government is restructuring curriculum content, in communication with international groups who seek to gain hegemonic ownership of what is considered lucrative worker knowledge.

The urgency of economic recovery after the crisis in 1997 was thus the impetus to adopt a knowledge-driven economic model (ROK 2001: 7), and to become competitive in an increasingly global knowledge economy. Industry in South Korea has been changing, the 'Republic of Korea' states in one government booklet and therefore, the government is changing investment strategies to prioritise research and development. 'Until now', the booklet states, Korea has 'focused on research and development in medium-high tech industries, such as electronics, automobile, machinery and ship-building, in which it retains relatively high competitiveness' (7). 'Recently,' however, the government has changed its strategic investment into 'fields of new technology, such as IT'.

As has been shown, crisis reform involved restructuring of the labour market, and the very concept of employability and what constituted re-employability was thrown into disarray. If workers could not keep jobs in the insecure post-crisis situation, they were expected to join VET programmes that would make them 'employable'. If workers were privileged to remain in positions of employment, they were expected to attend developmental VET that would aid in their retention of 'employability'. The government's hegemonic project intended to involve workers by providing the means for workers to 'help themselves'. Yet, it corresponded directly with the labour power needed to accommodate its emerging accumulation strategy of neoliberalism.

In an interview with Dr Mee Souk Kim, Senior Researcher for KRIVET,[12] discussions focused on workers' situation with regard to training and how she, as a researcher in an 'elite' position conducting government-sponsored research, understood *employability* and its effect on workers in the context of economic restructuring. Dr Kim stated that management had developed different expectations and needs for training than workers in the post-crisis period. Workers were expected to seek qualifications and training for life-long learning, which would increase their mobility for job transfers and changes. Management in the restructuring scenario sought workers who could prove they had gained training in what Dr Kim called 'international skills'. Dr Kim reflected on a July 2002 newspaper article that stated that with the end of the contract system for labour, the average age to leave a job had become 38. Thus workers want new skills in order to keep up with changing expectations occurring in the increasingly flexible labour market and the high rate of worker turnover.

From 1998–9, unemployment was up to 8 or 9 per cent, but has declined to 3–5 per cent in 2002. People in the automobile and the computer industries were more likely to keep their jobs. However, the reasons for layoffs have now changed. During the economic crisis, many educated people lost their jobs due to external forces. Unemployment became the result of actual *unemployability* of individuals. I enquired about the origin of new requirements for work ability, thinking that a large amount of those are externally generated, so, to which 'external forces' could she be referring? Dr Kim stated that that new requirements come from companies themselves. However, 'company' itself is becoming an increasingly questionable term due to rapid changes in the structure of business due to inward FDI and take-overs of traditional Korean companies.

Thus corporate restructuring of Korean companies in the IMF led period resulted in unprecedented skills requirements that involved important repercussions on workers including employability itself. Cultural work practices and the knowledge and ideas that have surrounded their evolution have traditionally been slow to change. However, management in merged corporate environments very quickly placed unprecedented expectations on workers who struggled to reach the basic level of employability in a new phase of globalisation and development.

Unemployed workers after the economic crisis have been forced to accept their own 'unemployability' in the face of new skills requirements, and enter VET programmes that teach internationally accepted knowledge and ideas for self-improvement and skills development. Cox categorises 'ideas' twofold: firstly, habits and expectations are formed by 'inter-subjective meanings' and secondly, 'collective images of social order held by different groups of people' which are less inclusive than the first type (Cox 1981). Shared ideational interpretations of *employability* are neither immutable nor inevitable, and conflicting 'images of social order' can lead to a crisis of leadership. This demonstrates one of the contradictions of capitalism. Whilst orthodox economists claim that economic change opens up opportunities for the self-development of workers through life-long learning, it is soon clear that only a particular type of 'learning' and thus ideational structures are lucrative within what is presented by elite groups to subordinated workers.

The post-crisis Korean VET programmes are designed to prepare workers to take an active role in integration into certain fields of technology that are seen to require flexible workers who commit to a life-long plan of learning in order to remain employable. This knowledge is thus a commodified asset in post-industrial society, and can conceptually be provided by the public sector to the private, according to Leadbeater (1998: 379). State guidance for this process is actually increasing in importance due to 'its [the state's] role in producing knowledge, through the education system' (379). Jessop (2001: 63) notes that knowledge becomes commodified when it is artificially made scarce, as opposed to the commodification of labour-power that occurs when it enters the labour market and becomes employed in the labour process. The commodification of knowledge brings about an unprecedented role for the state, if it is to inspire a 'profound social reorganisation ... required to turn it [knowledge] into something valuable' (Schiller 1988: 32). As has been discussed in chapter 4, the inequality of state/labour relations throughout history has been facilitative to Korean economic development. This relationship has allowed the state, even after official declaration of South Korea's status as a democracy in 1987, to implement institutions facilitating the government's economic drive. While state activity in the Korean knowledge economy is *not*, as might be assumed, simply a replication of past authoritarian behaviour, it has acquired a position of knowledge management and is not *as* interested in institutionalising democracy as it is in economic recovery and preparation for the contemporary Knowledge Economy that characterises neoliberal capitalism.

The state has adopted a new perspective in both its methods and rhetoric in this initiative, to perhaps accelerate integration into the global economy after the economic crisis. In 1997, 13,888 firms were entitled to offer a 'Vocational Competency Development Programme' to employees (KOILAF 1999c: 109). This Programme involved training preparing workers for new work styles of individual performance and 'competence' (109). However, the increase in demand for knowledge workers exceeds drastically the demand for 'unskilled' (ROK 2001: 14). Furthermore, 'the wage gap between production workers and managerial/white collar employees has begun to widen since 1998, because production workers suffered more severe pay cuts' (Katz et al. 2001: 232). Top-down restructuring of what is considered employable knowledge and the best kinds of skills, thus had a significant impact on workers.

International Partnerships and Ideational Restructuring: Convergence for Flexibilisation
The rise of MNCs, who are 'the most important source of international economic exchange', have inspired a global transition to 'flexibility' (UNCTAD 1993). Rationalisation and foreign inward investment 'carry implications for the control of labour both directly through increased rationalisation and surveillance, and indirectly through its capacity to locate production in areas with "good" industrial relations records' (Littler and Salaman 1984: 83). In the contemporary era of neoliberal capitalism, we see an increase in both direct and indirect attacks on labour often through regulation of unionisation (ibid.). But, ironically, alongside both direct and indirect attacks on labour, we also see an extent of collective provision of things such as new welfare projects to do with housing, health services, increased investment in education, and central planning to achieve coordination of labour flexibilisation projects. Flexibilisation however results in severe insecurities for workers and my research has revealed that little recompense is offered except 'promises' of employability through lifelong learning and 'self-management'. The following flexibilisation policies are increasingly transnationalised in the Age of Information, as nations desire to become 'knowledge-based'.

a. Dramatic changes to job designs.
b. Functional flexibility: skills flexibility and transferable sills expected.
c. Numerical flexibility (which is a neutral sounding term for downsizing and outsourcing resulting inevitably in layoffs and redundancies).
d. Flexible and casualised working patterns and hours i.e. contracted, shift work, annualised, seasonal, part-time, agency and temporary work.
e. Wage flexibility.

Other characteristics of post-Fordist, 'rehumanisation' of labour are seen in the role of new technologies in reshaping work, and the extent to which this is creating new groupings of 'knowledge workers'. Relationships between managers and employees are also transforming by way of new forms of 'human resource management' and 'teamworking'. Service-sector jobs are on the rise, and are becoming rapidly feminised. Further gendered and racialised inequalities have emerged in relation to the scope and limits of 'equal opportunities policies', and discipline in the workplace, involving management surveillance, is further modernising in an increased number of nations across the world. Interestingly, there has been a relative absence of discussions of what this has done to the 'working class' both as a consciousness and in the day to day living of workers, despite the fact that corporations do little to mask their logic for implementing flexible policies as a means toward maximization of returns on capital investment despite the human cost.

In the post-Fordist age, leaders of neoliberal globalisation resort to what Harvey calls accumulation by dispossession (2004), which is a strategy to shift responsibility for people's welfare from traditional avenues to a new platform of investor whose ethical foundations or responsibility may not be expected in the same way or may have less legislative power as in the case of non-governmental or intergovernmental regimes (see also Burnham 1999). The impact of economic globalisation and the diffusion of information technologies has a large say in causing firms to 'go for lean production, downsizing, restructuring, consolidation and flexible management practices' (Lincoln 2001) as though there was no alternative, and the shift of responsibility to the private sector or the international 'community' is notable. The Korean state's reformist strategies included revamped VET programmes which was part of its aim to secure dominance against a potential revolutionary worker movement against neoliberal capitalism, which is the way that *trasformismo* operates.

In the contemporary age, the Korean government has formed international partnerships that have themselves been developing over many years and are seen to be stronger than international partnerships between revolutionary groups, or the network of unions that Robert O'Brien discusses (2000). This strength of membership has resulted in intergovernmental organisations' dominance over the dialogue on poverty-reduction, labour standards, governance and regulation as conducted by UN agencies and entities such as the World Bank and the WTO. The strength of the increasingly established and universally heeded dialogue can lend credibility to the Korean governments' relatively new decision to become involved in the expansion of networks alongside UNEVOC.

Even before the crisis, in the mid-1990s, in order to accommodate the state's objectives for internationalisation the Korean MOL began pursuing relations with international organisations to guide the nation toward development, and to model Korean VET programmes after those of developed nations, or to those of the 'convergence club' (Magariños 2001). The notion of convergence, or nations' abilities to replicate industrialised countries' development trajectories was both implicitly and explicitly an aspect of IMF restructuring schemes such as that applied to South Korea in 1998 and onward. Members of the 'convergence club' are advanced industrial countries, and the benchmarking of best practices for the creation of wealth emanate from those sites. There are various reasons given for the obstacles to convergence strategies, which result from several discrepancies discussed by Rowley and Bae (2002) including particular cultural value systems, or stem from the difference in varieties, or models of capitalism countries have demonstrated (Hall and Soisike 2001; Coates 2000).

Motivated by UNESCO's Project on Technical and Vocational Education (UNEVOC 2002a), the MOL institutionalised VET programmes to prepare workers for Knowledge Economy. The design and utility of such programmes demonstrate a gradually emerging state strategy to integrate workers, or labour; the group that has faced the least political participation throughout Korean economic development; *into* economic development not yet with a political participatory function, but as active, efficient, but flexible participants in the increasingly knowledge-based international economy.

UNEVOC's secretariat (2001) states that contemporary *shifts in job knowledge and skill* have opened a need for vocational educators to collaborate on projects across national and regional spaces such as the series of UNEVOC conventions. The Asia Pacific's greatest resource for development is manpower, according to experts at UNESCO, but is unrefined in its potential. The Asia Pacific coalition of UNEVOC emphasises 'innovativeness, creativity, adaptability, and self-learning' as the most attractive performance standards for workers in the Knowledge Economy, and holds meetings for educators to discuss implementation. The first principal strategy for training is 'entrepreneur-ship skills development'; one of the primary components of neoliberal economic growth as the entrepreneur is seen to be the controller of capital and the brains behind the system.

Thus, restructuring of knowledge and skills in Korea involved the government's establishment of relationships with multinational corporate power as well as international agencies whose intentions centre on the convergence of production relations, including employable skills. Having looked at the expansion of international partnerships, the next subsection goes more deeply into the content of skills training, to demonstrate the clashes in old styles of Korean work and the new expectations that are emerging in the post-crisis eras in conjunction with UNEVOC.

Restructuring of Content of VET Programmes: Performance and Individuality in the Workplace

The major changes introduced by VET programmes were in the areas of performance appraisal and payments systems, life-long learning, and individualisation of work simultaneous to the introduction of new kinds of networks with individually motivated contributions such as seen in the IT industry for software development. Several included elements resemble the characteristics of work in the post-Fordist age, such as new modes of control over the process of work. Some claim that in the post-Fordist production age, the stipulation for skills has become nearly completely replaced by the demand for workers' 'knowledge' (Aronowitz and DiFazio 1994: 83). The new systems have eliminated the core methods for climbing the corporate ladder, making the process more *individually* initiated rather than managed by hierarchical relations. New work styles have changed promotion and compensation techniques to fit individual performance, which were to be appraised by managers who were equally inexperienced in the new standards (Kim and Briscoe 1997).

Performance Appraisal and Payment Systems

Perhaps the two most difficult requests made by the government for labour discussed by the first Tripartite Commission in negotiation for restructuring of the labour market were labour flexibility and changes to the traditional payment system toward a *performance*-based system.

> Manpower with intelligence, skills, creativity and willingness, and the knowledgeable are critical for sharpening competitive edge in the era of infinite competition … it is becoming increasingly important to lay a solid ground for economic recovery through remodelling corporate infrastructure and creating an atmosphere where workers of ability are valued.
>
> (KOILAF 1999b: 11)

In November 1997, just as the economy began its dangerous slide toward crisis status, the MOL took a renewed interest in vocational programmes designed to achieve the above points. The Vocational Training Promotion Act No. 5474, December 24, 1997 began a trend by changing the titles of the VET facilities to vocational *ability development* training facilities, vocational training to vocational *ability development* training, vocational training instructors to vocational *ability development* training instructors, and in paragraph (2) of the same Article, public VET institutes were changed in name to public vocational *ability development* training facilities, and vocational training to vocational *ability development* training, respectively (MOL 1999). 'Ability', a relatively ambiguous term used repeatedly in the emerging training institutions, refers to a particular work ethic included as part of training procedures, a new priority toward a less tangible worker power than tangible skills alone. Workers are however expected to assume new responsibilities and skills for the international work standard regardless of their incongruence with the past work culture in Korean corporations and businesses. Green lists the following as problematic areas for an educative scheme of neoliberalisation:

- How to internationalise attitudes within education systems that have traditionally stressed national values and culture.
- How to co-ordinate skills supply and demand in increasingly volatile markets and with the pressures for political and economic neoliberalisation.
- How to generate the creative and innovative capacity required of future leading economies with education systems traditionally stressing passive learning and social conformism. (Green 1999: 254)

The promotions of new characteristics of labour performance include several elements that contrast with organically 'Korean' expectations of workers and evidence changes from Fordism to post-Fordism. Rowley and Bae (2002) observe how core ideologies of human resource flows, work systems, evaluation and reward systems, and employee influence can be systematically contrasted to new characteristics. The core ideologies for culturally Korean work practices include the prioritisation of an affiliate organisation over the individual him/herself; emphasis on collective equality; and community orientation over individual equity and market principal orientations. Kim and Briscoe (1997) note that traditional human resource management in South Korea is based on the emphasis of group harmony (*in hwa*). Incentives and bonuses were based *not* on individual performance but on that of the group. Team spirit was the formula for excellence in the traditional workplace. The new requirements of job mobility and flexibility and the development of professional and skilled workers soon took precedence over manufacturing work skills. However, the 'flexibility' rhetoric affects unskilled workers in more negative ways than skilled. While flexibility means lifelong learning and opportunities for some, it means job loss for many more.

A KOILAF publication recommends some 'basic directions' for the implementation of a performance-based wage system. Guidelines are designed to:

- Help workers and employers to find common ground on the introduction and operation of a performance-based system
- Ensure that the procedures for adopting a new wage system comply with the law and any counterproductive effect is averted
- Induce a simplified wage system (KOILAF 2002: 11).

Employers and workers were encouraged to introduce a profit-sharing system wherein profits exceeding targets could be shared equally. Management was expected to reveal expectations to workers openly and with transparency, so they could easily identify what types of performance would be expected. These suggestions aimed to democratise the performance-based system that required an entirely new set of performance requirements of individuals to take responsibility for their work and performance in the restructured economy.

Individualism and Life-Long Learning

Traditional Korean culture is said to be more community-oriented than individualistic. However, there was to be 'no choice' but for workers to adopt an individualistic attitude and to learn that style of work and other countries that have received aid from the IMF have experienced the same changes and *all* are facing the twenty-first century. Korea has had little time to account for cultural work styles, or for its Korean 'spirit', and will have no choice in the matter because of unlimited competition around the world, according to Minister of Labour, Mr Lee, Soo Young.[13] If labour fights with management, businesses will disappear.

Lee notes that the 'X' and the 'N' generations manifest more individual characteristics than previous generations, and a higher quality of education will be offered to the younger generation, so this will distinguish the workforce of the future. Employees will need to be 'creative, and they will also need to be able to adapt to rapid changes in society … employees should be given various opportunities to study continuously in order to adopt self-directed learning methods for absorbing new information' (Lee, K. 2001: 4). Individualism and life-long learning are crucial worker qualities that will be sought in the knowledge economy, and workers should prepare to demonstrate those skills.

Twenty experts and officials at the Korea Labour Institute (KLI) were brought together in 2003 to form a research team under the Qualification System Reforms Task Force (KLI 2003). The research team intended to come up with visions and innovations for the qualification system and to review changes to VET since restructuring of 1997 and onward. The study notes the shift towards learning for life and work, which is centred on the individual and states that 'decent work underpins individuals' independence, self-respect and well-being, and, therefore, is a key to their overall quality of life (2003). The study notes that every individual has a right to VET and compares Korea to several other nations including Argentina, Bolivia, Brazil, Chile, Germany, Guatemala, Italy, Mexico, and Spain, whose national constitutions accommodate for this. This 'right' is also acknowledged at the international level, for example in the Universal Declaration of Human Rights (1948) and the American Declaration of Human Rights and Obligations (1948). In the most recent phase of VET in South Korea, researchers at the KLI have decided that education is the right of citizens and is a crucial way to find access to employment, reduced likelihood of unemployment, and significant increases in life-cycle earnings.

The study claims that economic, social and technological factors cumulatively account for the growing emphasis on the individual in Korean vocational training and education. Contemporary production of goods and services has begun to rely on human capital, or on workers' individual and collective endowment of knowledge and skills. The 'individual' is the new citizen of society and has been granted the central place in statements of education learning, and training objectives. So the process of formal education and training was no longer isolated to the passing on information but envisions a society that prioritises a scenario of 'individuals learning to learn so that they can find out for themselves'. Factual knowledge itself is no longer enough, but individuals are encouraged to learn how to analyse, access and exploit information and in turn to devise and create new knowledge. Taking charge of one's own learning and ability to learn is the only way to survive or to 'live and work in the knowledge and information society'. VET makes individuals employable and productive and helps them escape poverty through mobility and choice. These statements, perhaps, do not sound controversial at first reading. But who decides what the VET provided, and to whom? Who decided that 'individuals' were to become the primary producers in Korea?

'Individuality' was not only part of a new concept of employability, but began to be associated with 'citizenship'. According to the EU Memorandum on Lifelong Learning (EU 2000), active citizenship refers to how 'people participate in all spheres of economic and social life, the chances and risks they face in trying to do so, and the extent to which they feel that they belong to, and have a fair say in, the society in which they live'. This incorporates ideas of participation as well as replacing ownership, similar to the ownership that is increasingly expected of nations' development (see Cammack 2001, 2002a, 2002b). *Trasformismo* as the appropriation of workers' needs has, in the knowledge economy, renewed emphasis on individuals and ownership of work and production, but ultimately, ownership and power is in the hands of elites, via industry investment and human resources management.

So individuals are now expected to take responsibility for their own employability and the government and elites have declared that VET is an important factor in this process. 'Life-long learning' is the way in which workers can adapt to rapidly changing economies over time, and the government (ROK 2001: 42) suggested a wide-spread series of facilities to support and incorporate life-long learning into the very core of Korean culture. National and regional lifelong education centres were to be developed. Libraries, self-governance centres, social welfare halls, human resources of women's halls, and citizens' centres were to be strengthened. A pilot project entitled 'learning clubs for tuning local culture into lifelong learning' was suggested. An information network was expected to emerge from this campaign and a database to organise information on professors, lecturers, and education programmes of educational institutions in relation to lifelong learning. One booklet, 'Occupational World of the Future' was proposed to offer workers access to available VET and other forms of education so that they, as citizens, could prepare themselves for new employability requirements in the knowledge economy.

Incentive Structure: *Trasformismo* at its Best

But in a nation with such a tumultuous history of unrest, how would workers react to drastic changes to the employment structure and labour market in South Korea? The government quickly honed in on aspects of employment that would prove to be the most volatile, and tried to create an incentive structure to circumvent uprisings in the atmosphere of rapid change and reform. Through framing the government-required training programmes as positive incentives for personal development and in the post-crisis era as a means to remain or to become employable in the midst of widespread lay-offs, the government applied a 'strategy on the part of the dominant power to gradually co-opt elements of the opposition forces-a strategy known in Italian politics as *trasformismo*' (Cox 1999: 25). '*Trasformismo* can serve as a strategy of assimilating and domesticating potentially dangerous ideas by adjusting them to the policies of the dominant coalition and can thereby obstruct the formation of class-based organised opposition' (1983: 166–7). The Korean government sidelined potentially dissident groups by providing a social safety net of VET programmes, to appease laid-off workers who are most likely to oppose elite-led accumulation strategies.

The study 'Educational and Training Program Situation in Korea' (2000c), shows 15.9 per cent of companies have taken part in internationalisation strategies via vocational training programmes. There are 191 new types of programmes being implemented and the number of companies who required participation increased year on year. As an example, Samsung adopted a 'reading management' training programme. Alongside this powerful *chaebol*, the leaders in reading management have been Mobile Telecom, Hyundai, Sunkyong and E-Land. At Samsung, employees were considered loyal, aggressive, and innovative. 'Samsung has had no strikes. Employees feel that their needs are met ... [Samsung] plans to increase its social responsibility' (Kim, E.-Y. 1996: 78). Reading management means that 'companies provide a list of required reading and say, "If you don't want to read them, leave"' (ibid.). These materials intended to give employees a sense of what would be expected of them in the crisis period. While *chaebol*s resisted overall firm restructure, they operated a 'radical remake ... forced by Asia's economic crisis to throw off old habits and quickly adopt new ways of business' with an immediate impact on employees (Baker 1998).

About half of employers surveyed by Park in his influential 2001 study said that the most difficult factor for firms in the process of employment adjustment and training was to convince workers of the inevitability of the process (see Table 2) (Park, D. J. et al. 2001: 144–5).

Table 2. Most Difficult Thing for Firms in Process of Employment Adjustment (Park et al. 2001: 145)

	Unionised	Non-Unionised	Total
Make [workers] understand the necessity of employment adjustment	73 (51.8%)	16 (39.0%)	89 (50.9%)
Consultation about the number to be adjusted	16 (11.3%)	5 (12.2%)	21 (12.0%)
Consultation about the criteria to select to be adjusted	28 (19.9%)	14 (34.1%)	42 (24.0%)
Consultation about the compensatory package	18 (12.8%)	4 (9.8%)	22 (12.6%)
Others	6 (4.3%)	2 (4.9%)	1 (0.6%)
Total	141 (100.0%)	41 (100.0%)	175 (100.0%)

The following items were ranked as the second, third, and fourth most difficult matters arising: 'consultation about the criteria to select who are to lose their jobs', 'consultation about the compensatory package for workers to be adjusted', and 'consultation about the number to be adjusted'. These were not favourable signs for the application, ease, or effectiveness of 'adjustment'. Management realised that sudden layoffs do not settle easily with workers, and sought ways to appease and help prevent backlash and resistance to what they had been told was a market-driven inevitability. Employment adjustment included several appropriated practices, including attrition, 'honourable' retirement, dismissal, and the category 'others', which refers to spin-offs or early retirement (128).

Management created regulations that introduced the idea of voluntary participation with incentives for participation in training schemes, which in some cases provided a rare option to secure employment in the midst of the crisis. New incentives for training participation were introduced under the Employment Insurance System (EIS), a system designed to appease job losses after the Lifetime Employment laws had been reversed (KOILAF 1999c: 112). The EIS:

> ... purports to popularise vocational training and enhance firms' competitiveness ... provides incentives such as subsidies and financial assistance to encourage individual firms to invest in the internal labour force, thereby improving labour productivity, employment stability and the firms' competitive edge in international markets.
>
> (58)

But the 'hottest issue' was how to encourage workers to participate voluntarily in Vocational Competency Development Programme (110). To encourage voluntary participation, the government offered businesses two forms of support for implementation of the subsidisation for implementation costs to employers, and paid leave for training (110). One KRIVET report (KRIVET 2000b) shows that workers who did not attend offered training programmes stated reasons such as lack of desire, or in some cases, a fundamental resistance to requirements for attendance. The study demonstrates that 47.4 per cent of attendees of training went as a response to direct employer instruction, whereas only 14.9 per cent attended training programmes voluntarily. Laid-off workers were opposed to forced training programmes because of unwillingness or because of a suspicion of the limited short-term benefits, demonstrating the lack of consensus for these initiatives.

I have claimed that Korea's economic development has been managed throughout history by a controlling government who have not been able to consolidate hegemonic consensus but have only led passive revolutions over time. Recovery and reform from the 1997 crisis has demonstrated similar characteristics. Not only has the government shown that it is once again, almost completely unswervingly taking unilateral charge of recovery at the guidance of the IMF, its programme of *trasformismo* by way of VET preparation has been unable to instigate workers' consent. Now I turn to a look into what appears to be a government effort of last resort to convince workers to change, this time, their entire 'culture' to appropriate elite-directed transformations.

There are three basic principles to the New Labour Culture Campaign as directed by the MOL in Seoul, Korea in 2001. The following section interweaves information obtained during a semi-structured interview with Mr Lee, Soo Young, Vice Director of the Korean Labour Management Co-operation Division and materials gathered from the Korea Herald newspaper and literature provided to me from the MOL. The reason for this research was to gain information about a 'new labour culture' publicised in the Korean media during labour market reform and to understand how the masterminds behind this campaign viewed changes to elite/worker/management relations. Furthermore, the interview was held to gain information about elite perceptions for how reform should proceed in the crisis-restructuring era. The New Labour Culture is a form of *trasformismo* because it is an elite -authored project attempting to display unions' and management's needs which involve cooperation with the government, but ultimately demonstrates that the government holds the final authority for the direction of changes.

Mr Lee discussed three principles and other points on the New Labour Culture, a campaign which aimed to transform Korean labour-management relations and which became a requirement for companies who wished to survive in the period of IMF restructuring. The three principles are:

1. *Trust and esteem*: the basic level to facilitate easy relations between labour, management, and government.
2. *Co-operation and engagement*: the action program.
3. *Autonomy and respect*: the goal between management and labour to eliminate the need and/or possibility for government intervention into business affairs, by solidifying a worker/management relationship.

Mr Lee defined *culture* in the interview by listing the basic activities of labour relations that include collective bargaining and strikes, as well as human resource management. Companies, he stated, should invest in Labour Culture training as a way to 'make labour unions co-operate.' A 12.2 per cent decrease in labour union membership in 1998 may indicate a higher level of co-operation, or that labour union members are learning that they should co-operate with policy makers by either leaving, or choosing not to join unions, despite the fact that union membership is their only chance to achieve legitimate representation. To achieve autonomy, like the third principle of the above list indicates, perhaps workers need labour unions as a tool to negotiate with the government if they feel that their autonomy is being challenged. Mr Lee stated that the autonomy supposition is a *goal*, not *reality*. He mentioned that labour leaders do not respect union laws, and often use violence to be heard, which is 'intolerable'.

As a solution, Mr Lee said that union members will have to change their 'minds'[14] and follow the laws. The most significant change, according to Mr Lee, will be union members' co-operation with laws and government policy. Unions are learning; they have started to follow the law gradually and realise that violence is generally ineffective. Besides, in the past, workers were not expected to take responsibility for the prosperity of their companies, but the IMF taught workers to be more loyal. Previous lifetime employment laws gave employees lasting job security but the looming threat of layoffs was an unprecedented incentive to demonstrate company loyalty. Mr Lee mentioned that Korea is in a period of transition and that there may be conflict now instead of co-operation, but that several positive changes will take place due to the IMF restructuring. He did not seem to understand the idea of 'culture ' with regard to traditions or intersubjectivities that develop over history and through repeated human interaction, but referred to percentages of labour union membership, company investment, and the models of modernisation (see Figure 6) for the New Labour Culture in reference to culture. Because Korea's labour history is so short compared to the United States and Japan, Korea would have to accelerate its development of 'modern' labour relations, assuming of course that the convergence model, laden with ideas of best practice in a shrinking world, is the only one available as authors Greider (1997), Schwartz (2000), Ohmae (1990) and Strange (1987) suggest.

The MOL introduced the idea of the New Labour-Management Culture in July 1999, and companies were given two months to hear about it, according to the 3 Phases printed in the *Korea Herald* (Wednesday, November 24, 1999). Companies were given 4 months to educate workers and 'change old thoughts and practices', and were expected to see reinforcement through awards given to model companies after the millennium. A sudden adoption of a new Labour Culture modelled after Japan and the United States (according to Mr Lee) is the MOL's prescription for business survival in the IMF age.

The final outcome of the Labour Culture project was intended to cultivate 'modern' labour relations. Mr Lee showed the model,

'Composition of future-oriented labour-management community' which was also published in the *Korea Herald* (Kim, M. H. 1999: 18), the most prominent English language newspaper in Seoul (Figure 6). The question now is whether people can quickly adapt to new institutional requirements, and whether Korean people's thought forms and culture can or will easily incorporate the new 'education' and 'training' of work habits and relatively ambiguous terminology that represents the 'New Labour Culture'. Mr Lee stressed that companies must invest in training if they wish to remain competitive and stable. There is 'no choice': Korea is facing a considerable loss of choices as a result of the economic crisis and IMF restructuring. But the crisis is the main reason for the need for a transformation of labour relations.

What quality marks the beginning of co-operation? *Trust*, according to the model prepared by the MOL (Figure 6). As a result of ongoing tensions for many years, there is little trust between workers, management, and policy makers in Korea. Since 1987, co-operation has been attempted, but without trust, there can be no success in labour relations. Trust will take time, but someone should make the first move, and according to Mr Lee, 'management' is the target. Management should learn to trust the government's IMF-inspired economic policy and successfully facilitate policy within their companies.

But isn't the 'IMF crisis' over? According to a statement by economic officials made a few days before the interview in 1999, the crisis was over, and Korea had begun the next phase of flourishing economic progress. So, did IMF restructuring change Korea's labour culture? Labour flexibility has certainly become a core theme in the restructuring of labour. Layoffs are usually justified as a temporary remedy for economic difficulties in Korea and ongoing restructuring of labour is a crucial element for the continuation of capitalism. Mr Lee noted that the possibility of being laid off, however, makes people work harder, and while they feel stress and fatigue now, their work will stabilise their positions. One change within the post-crisis era is that workers are realising the significance of their behaviour for company survival. In the past, workers and management alike were not as concerned about keeping their companies alive, partly because the government propped up lagging companies, and partly because there was less dependence on foreign investment. In the contemporary age, workers will have to take on increased responsibilities for their own employability as well as the wellbeing of their companies.

Figure 6. Composition of Future-Oriented Labour-Management Community (Kim, M-H 1999: 18)

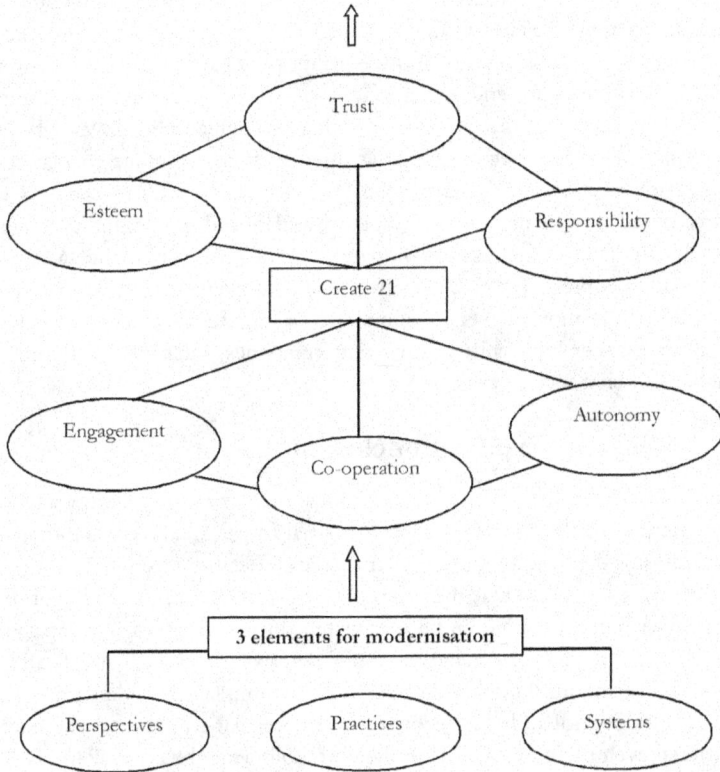

Unions must be government *partners* in the New Labour Culture. But will new laws implemented in the crisis-restructuring era reflect the needs and desires of workers? Mr Lee stated that *institutions* must change before laws can be made. The Tripartite Commission exists to facilitate policy changes; legal changes will be considered within the infrastructure of the Commission. It will take time for changes to truly affect relations. I reminded him of the *lack* of time that he had emphasised previously, of the urgency to change the Labour Culture to meet the standards of the United States and Japan. But with the same vision, he said, practices can be changed, since change depends on people's *minds*.

If workers do not follow the lead of management, and management follows the lead of the MOL's New Labour Culture mandates, then businesses will fail, especially those that are foreign-invested, and workers will lose their jobs. That was the message from Mr Lee. Perhaps the reality is less of an establishment of more equality of tripartite members than a reminder to workers and management of who is still in control; the Korean government. So in a world that is increasingly governed by corporate power and economic convergence, states continue to play an important role. Taylor discusses the 'myth of the powerless state' as a story based in examinations of Japan, Sweden and a handful of other developed nations that are incomparable to a majority of the 'world's states and peoples' (Taylor 2005). In actual fact, globalisation has inspired states to reposition power in sometimes new and inventive ways, i.e. through partnerships with government ministries, education and other factions of civil society, as has been noted here.

Conclusion

This chapter has identified the conditions for passive revolution within the interplay of three configurations of social forces, material, institutional and ideational in the period of restructuring after the crisis in 1997. See Table 3 for a final look at the extent of impact of collective dismissal on employees between 1998 and 1999, in the thick of the layoff campaign. Whilst the impact on regular employees experience of significantly increased attrition, 'honourable' retirement, dismissal and other types of layoffs, it does not address the impact on nonregular employees, who have suffered even more extensively in the years following the crisis (Park, D. J. et al. 2001: 128).

Despite the newly introduced idea of 'flexibility' of the labour force (an IMF restructuring requirement), it has been claimed that 'employable' workers enjoyed continuous work and have found it less difficult to gain re-employment. This means that less skilled workers were not permitted a significant voice in development strategy designs (neither historically nor contemporarily), and skilled workers were incorporated into elite-governed objectives via incentives and training opportunities. For less skilled workers on the other hand, training opportunities were a requirement. The incentive – or almost forced logic – was job retention and even then, job flexibility was an ever-present threat.

Table 3.
Impacts of the Enactment of Act Concerning Collective Dismissals on Regular Employees

1991 (March–December)

Number affected by act	Attrition		'Honourable' retirement		Dismissal		Others[1]	
	no. firms	%	no. firms	%	no. firms	%	no. firms	%
< 10	57	11.8	18	3.7	22	4.6	17	3.5
10–19	61	12.6	22	4.6	11	2.3	8	1.7
20–29	47	9.7	15	2.9	10	2.1	2	0.4
30–39	40	8.3	0	0	2	0.4	5	1.0
40–49	33	6.8	15	2.9	13	2.7	7	1.4
50 or more	142	27.1	101	20.9	17	3.5	25	5.2
None	103	21.3	312	64.6	408	84.5	419	86.7
Total	483	100	483	100	483	100	483	100
103	-	231	-	46	-	252	-	

1999 (January–end of July)

Number affected by act	Attrition		'Honourable' retirement		Dismissal		Others[1]	
	no. firms	%	no. firms	%	no. firms	%	no. firms	%
< 10	89	18.4	20	4.1	25	5.2	13	2.7
10–19	78	16.1	15	3.1	8	1.7	8	1.7
20–29	36	7.5	8	1.7	2	0.4	9	1.9
30–39	24	5.0	7	1.4	0	0.0	3	0.6
40–49	24	5.0	12	2.5	6	1.2	7	1.4
50 or more	84	17.4	22	4.6	3	0.6	15	3.1
None	148	30.6	399	82.6	439	90.9	428	88.6
Total	483	-	483	-	483	-	483	-
Average[2]	64	-	95	-	15	-	107	-

1. 'Others' refers to spin-off, early retirement, and so on. Spin-off is the process whereby capital stock of a division of a corporation is transferred to an altogether separate firm established be employees' buy-out, or management buy-out of the employees of the division (or subsidiary).
2. This means average number of employees per firm that carried out the programme.

(D. J. Park, J. Park and Yu 2001: 128)

Lee (2001: 6) recommends several items for the improvement for VET that can aid with workers' search for the 'unalienable right to live as an individual human being' and to become trained according to the appropriate skills within the knowledge economy, in order to become 'employable'. He stresses that the Lifelong Education Act in 2000 has provided the basis for this campaign and that several Lifelong Education Centres have benefited the public in this respect. Between 1997 and 2001, several policies have reflected the government's commitment to promote higher standards of VET, including the Promotion Act of Vocational Education and Training, the Basic Qualification Act, and the Act for the Establishment of the Korea Research Institute for Vocational Education and Training (KRIVET). However this has not been enough and five suggestions were given to strengthen this commitment, as follows:

- Provision of various opportunities for lifelong learning.
- Construction of a more flexible learning path.
- Strengthening of transition from learning to work.
- Active use of information and communication technology.
- More efficient system via distribution of role for private sector.

These suggestions in effect demonstrate the role of the government as manager for workers' experience with rapid economic changes after the crisis.

Trasformismo is evident in South Korea with governments' attempt to guide and finally re-establish relations between the state and workers, a relationship whose history is covered in the previous chapter. This relationship of tensions and non-representation returns to the point of the government and of antagonism and anger from the side of labour and from unions outside the FKTU. But, during crisis recovery, the invitation of foreign capital inspired a new face for labour/government relations represented in the formation of the Tripartite Commission and the New Labour Culture. The government has thus adjusted its tactics toward universalising a particular shared subjectivity and common sense in that it has promoted training programmes to accommodate globalisation and neoliberalisation in the context of democratisation. Workers are expected to reshape their concept of tripartite industrial relations, as well their expectations for permanent and long-term employment, and finally, their understanding of employability, knowledge, and skills in the expanding global system of economic and political hegemony which looks increasingly like a player within the capitalist knowledge economy. Thus, the restructuring of material capabilities, institutional capacity, and common sense itself has occurred in a state of passive revolution, and democratic freedoms have not been realised.

As discussed, the government encouraged voluntary participation in newly restructured VET programmes after the onset of the economic crisis in 1997. Incentives for the participation in VET have included several factors, and aim to make workers aware of their changing role in economic development of South Korea after the crisis. Government-required training programmes have been positioned as incentives for personal development, and in the post-crisis era are endorsed as a means to remain, or to become 'employable' after the enormous amount of lay-offs that occurred in the post-crisis restructuring period (UNDP 2000: 42). The restructuring of workers' needs and the replacement of responsibility for ownership of individual employability is the primary theme of *trasformismo* during this period.

Neoliberal capitalism, in the sense that it is the dominant ideology of the contemporary global world system has become increasingly pervasive at the direction of international forces and groups of the TCCN. I have explored how this ideology has been disseminated through society via the educative role the state has taken particularly in the era of IMF restructuring. There has been a tug-of-war dynamic perpetuated by the state, management and workers. Mentalities advocated and taught by groups of the TCCN are increasingly linked to the process of market liberalisation, rationalisation, and the adoption of capitalist values for economic development in the neoliberal knowledge economy. Governments formulate development with specific plans for material-level configuration such as restructuring of businesses and de-regulation of inward investment and permission of corporate take-overs. Workers' minds and acceptance of changes occurring during crisis recovery restructuring such as occurred in Korea in 1997 however may not be prepared for new work expectations inherent to the behaviours crucial for the cohesion and duration of material restructuring, indicating the possibilities for effective resistance and overthrow of passive revolution. 'Hegemony is like a pillow: it absorbs blows and sooner or later the would-be assailant will find it comfortable to rest upon' (Cox 1983: 173). Or, could it be that global hegemony does not, and cannot exist as evident through ongoing power relations between the state, with the bulwark of civil society, and workers? The next chapter concludes the analysis of ongoing passive revolution throughout Korean industrialisation and modernisation, looking at spaces for workers' resistance, and makes a final comment on the forms of state, production relations and hegemonic struggles within which Korean development has occurred.

5

CONCLUSION

A final look at the impact that international hegemonic struggle has had on South Korean economic development from the time that it was separated into two nations in 1945 confirms that capitalism is not an immutable force that is out of humanity's control, but it has been written and perpetuated by actors who are engaged in a global hegemonic project and an ongoing struggle. By way of an elite network of capitalists or the TCCN, 'universal' knowledge is increasingly becoming integrated into the elite echelons of societies, i.e. management and government. However, I have shown that this is not acceptable to workers themselves, whose historical resistance is only becoming stronger. Therefore I can argue that in spite of supposedly 'hegemonic' historical blocs that occurred during Pax Britannica and Pax Americana, Korea has not been capable of integrating the 'hegemonic' expansive norms of production by means of a consolidated, nationally-based hegemony, i.e. with consent from the wider population. This calls into question the validity of claims regarding international hegemony in any case, a point that Cox does not address.

Capitalism is not an immutable force but it is a global hegemonic project led by elite transnational capitalist networks and incorporated by nations under forms of state which have historically not necessarily been hegemonic themselves. I use the Gramscian interpretation of hegemony, which requires coercion plus consent, because there is something at stake: the voice of workers, which is typically left out of decision-making regarding economic development of semi-peripheral states that is needed to consolidate the global expansion of capitalism. I demonstrate that workers have not been fully silenced, however, by outlining the history of Korean forms of state and production relations, revealing ongoing resistance and struggles. In response to worker resistance, Korean governments have led a series of passive revolutions to 'help' workers adapt to capitalist norms. Economic development has been measured by the rapid growth of its GDP, and the government's development strategies have only more recently been questioned regarding inclusion of a range of voices.

Indeed, what form of state is necessary for nations to adapt to capitalist norms? Is it possible for semi-peripheral states to integrate to capitalist norms and achieve nationally consolidated hegemony? I argue that it has not been possible within Korea. I demonstrate this by revealing that the conditions for passive revolution have been achieved over time within South Korea. I show that international hegemonic struggle has *not permitted* this nation to attain consent between workers and the state, which is a condition for hegemony, within its own borders.

Throughout the chapters' discussions, I have asked whether neo-Gramscian theories are useful for the analysis of IPE in the contemporary neoliberal struggle for hegemony. I have argued that indeed, they are useful, because realism, neorealism, and liberalism are predominantly grounded in positivist epistemological roots and close more doors than they open for thinking about the movement of history, the relations between social forces and relations of production. I have asked how governments respond to and attempt to accommodate theorised hegemonic or non-hegemonic phases of world orders, and asked whether nations can appropriate global hegemony in a nationally hegemonic manner. I have found that this is *not* the case, and particularly in South Korea, international 'norms' for production have been required of workers by developmentalist, authoritarian governments. Unsatisfied populations have challenged governments over time and dissent has not subsided. Thus hegemony has not been achieved under the historically totalitarian governments, but passive revolution is the evident path of economic development.

Since democratisation, governments have consistently struggled to find consensus with the Korean population, and even after decades of provisions and tailor-made vocational education, dissenting workers have not been silenced except through violent police and militant response. In fact, government involvement and direction of VET is leading to exacerbated divisions between knowledge and skills of the working force. Workers are only employable in the contemporary age if they are capable of assuming the best knowledge needed for employability, who are increasingly divided from those workers who are left behind by these standards, and are expected to become trained to meet increasingly international norms. If workers protest these deepening divisions, and practice dissent in a form that threatens the implementation and advancement of VET programmes, it could lend evidence of the fragmentation of the international hegemony (Arrighi 1993). International notions of supposed 'best practices' (Appelbaum and Batt 1994) are seen as the way forward for a globally competitive labour force for the Korean knowledge economy, according to neoliberal demands and the most recent VET within Korea. It will be difficult to counter these increasingly imposed practices, but the struggle continues.

From the discussions of previous chapters, I aim to come to a conclusion regarding the trajectory of development that the Korean elites and TCCN have chosen for this nation. To this end, I outline the arguments hence. I review the questions I am compelled to think about in the bigger picture of the international political economy of expansive capitalism, and demonstrate how this both addresses these questions and opens doors for future research springing from the arguments I present. I will then discuss Korean citizens' dissent aimed at neoliberalism that has occurred in contemporary history: a phenomenon that raises significant questions regarding whether hegemony of development is secured within South Korea, even within the age of the knowledge economy.

South Korea in the Global Economy

The first chapter bestows a theoretical backbone to the argument of further chapters, highlighting Gramscian inspired ideas. A history of IR theory is thus traced, and I claim that the orthodox literature is embroiled in positivist epistemology and is thus inadequate for an analysis of global political economics. Positivist reasoning relies on the immutability and predictability of events and cases, but I pay credence to transnational historical materialism, noting that humankind plays a specific role in the formation of history. Others should further explore the place of historical materialism in IPE and integrate this school of thought, working to overcome the limitations that positivism poses.

Gramsci's theories emphasise superstructural elements of the con-solidation and prolongation of hegemony, which are useful for a look into one nation's struggle to adjust and adapt to international political economic norms in terms of 'necessary' cultural and traditional changes. Hegemony itself is an important concept because it provides an explanation for whether or not particular power relations during and after social change according to internationally prescribed development norms are sustainable, or whether subordinated groups will arise and seek leadership or at least hunt for representation in an exploitative environment. The development literature typically does not address the idea of hegemony from a Gramscian perspective, and the IPE literature often isolates examination to industrialised and developed nations with the assumption that convergence is the only option left (Taylor 2005). Without consensus, according to the Gramscian understanding, economic development will not become hegemonic and may or may not be sustainable in the long run. Without hegemony, populations will either overthrow the elites who control their destinies, or will remain at odds with their leaders. If development is authored by elite groups and is not fully accepted by the larger population, as I have shown to be the case in South Korea, it is still possible that a grass-roots revolution and overthrow of the elite classes could occur.

In the first chapter I also discussed the concepts of intellectuals, because the Gramscian depiction of these individuals is appropriate to grasp how hegemony is formed and disseminated at the local level. Because intellectuals have traditionally had privileged access to the 'curriculum' of ideological education, the message they portray in both the institution of education and in the workplace is paramount for the consolidation of superstructural co-option and consent, which Gramsci emphasises for the sustenance of hegemony. Further research could investigate cases wherein hegemony of liberal economic development has perhaps been hegemonic, such as within Western Europe, and contrast cultural norms that have allowed this consensus to occur.

The elite-led government strategy of passive revolution occurs in place of hegemony during a struggle for hegemony, or during a crisis of hegemony. I reason that passive revolution occurs in cases demonstrating two fundamental conditions. First, passive revolution requires elite leadership of a nation, and secondly, requires evidence of *trasformismo* that is a political strategy to co-opt and pre-empt successful uprisings from oppressed groups. After setting up the framework for the argument of the work, I present two chapters of rich historical analysis, to give a background for the empirical study of the economic crisis and the affect this has had on economic and social developments according to restructuring requirements in South Korea.

The second chapter sets a stage for a global history of 'hegemonies', as reasoned by Cox (1987), who modifies Gramsci's perception of hegemony to analyse the international expansion of production. His analysis is inspirational as it provides a discussion of several aspects of the growth of hegemonies, including institutional, material, and ideational, that have in some cases led to consolidated world orders. Chapter 2 organises this analysis into a historical analysis of forms of state and production relations during each phase of global history, in order to understand the appearance of hegemonic struggles from this angle.

The second chapter ends with an introduction to a proposed historical bloc of neoliberalism and the knowledge economy, or the most recent economic model that the government perceives to be the most competitive in the contemporary global economy. Production relations have changed, and workers are expected to catch up, and to maintain their own 'employability' within this historical period. Workers are increasingly given the responsibility to adapt and to 'own' their state of employability and to pursue the best kinds of knowledge and skills, in preparation for an increasingly unstable job market. Future research should look at how knowledge itself is used in the management literature to promote workers' responsibility for their own employability, such as is found in Moore (2006).

In the third chapter, I operationalise the concept of passive revolution that occurs in various forms during the absence of hegemony. The chapter revisits the concept of passive revolution and claims that elite-engineered accumulation strategies, plus the signs of *trasformismo*, are the codes of operative passive revolution rather than hegemony. Providing an analysis of worker/state relations in South Korea, the chapter begins to associate struggles for global hegemony with ongoing struggles at the local level in this small and historically secluded nation. I delve into the history of Korean worker/state relations over time, from Japanese colonisation, to the periods of developmental dictatorship that followed the exit of Japan, and finally look at the struggles leading to democratisation in the late 1980s. To develop my perception of passive revolution, I look at certain events throughout each time period that demonstrate conditions for passive revolution: elite-led development, and the push for *trasformismo*. From Japanese colonisation to the periods of developmental dictatorships and into the present, VET has existed as a tool of *trasformismo* and co-optation, in that it has been offered to workers as a way forward for their own personal development and as a substitution for labour empower-ment. 'Empowerment' has only been provided according to the demands of what are perceived to be internationally hegemonic norms, but workers have not historically been had any choice regarding involvement. As I note in Chapter 3 and below, workers have persistently rebelled against government-led development through strikes and direct action. Passive revolution is not a completed project, because it has not completely stifled exploited groups' voices. I argue that whilst passive revolution demonstrates a lack of hegemony in South Korea, it also demonstrates that hegemonic struggles between social forces have not resulted in a dispensation of consensual power favourable to all sections of society, but has remained at the level of government, civil society and the private sector.

The final sections of Chapter 3 look at South Korea's transition to democracy that occurred simultaneous to advancing globalisation and increased government-led opening of Korea's doors to deregulation and liberalisation of the market. Even this historical period did not occur at a time of national hegemony within Korea, and the chapter argues that political and economic transformation in South Korea has occurred within a passive revolution both historically and contemporarily. An avenue for further research begs the question of whether 'democracy' can be integrated within South Korea, or whether it is even *possible* to achieve economic growth and development within a democratic form of state in South Korea.

Despite Cox's perceived hegemonic world orders, Korea as a nation has not been able to hegemonically adapt or integrate into what Cox believes were internationally accepted production norms, which I demonstrate further in the fourth chapter. Within Chapter 4, I look at the complete restructuring of South Korea's economy after the economic crisis of 1997 at three levels of forces: material, institutional, and ideational (Cox 1981: 136; see Figure 1). I can conclude that previous elite-directed development did not accommodate each level of social interaction to the same extent and this can explain why it has not become hegemonically included into the international political economy. In short, there is no guarantee that Korea will become nationally hegemonic and universally accepting of changes in the contemporary neoliberal world order. This is particularly demonstrable because of ongoing uprisings and dissent, discussed in the next section.

Dissent: Past and Present

Chapter 3 paints a picture of the dissenting forces that have fought for years against capitalist, elite-engineered development of Korea. Perhaps the government thought that surface-level changes would quell this ongoing dissent, but frankly, it was wrong. Workers have not ceased to fight for a voice in contemporary times and this is evident through a number of more recent episodes.

Chalmers Johnson (1997) comments that the IMF's 'arrogant demands' could instigate widespread; even 'spectacular' reactions after the 1997 crisis. The most obvious voice of dissent emerges from the severely underprivileged and excluded groups. But because economic restructuring occurred at such a wide range of levels, resistance movements themselves must avoid focusing on only one level of occupation, as 'capital can always side-step such opposition' (Amoore et al. 2000: 25). Korean resistance has emerged from a widened worker consciousness of oppression, and from many arenas of the population including all workers of all socio-economic backgrounds, students, government workers.

Restructuring following the economic crisis triggered thousands of uprisings and demonstrations by labour groups, particularly labour union activists, including the Korean People's Action against Investment Treaties and the WTO (KoPA) on October 24, 1999. At that time, the People's Rally Committee had planned to submit a plea at the Asia Europe Meeting in Seoul protesting neoliberal globalization and structural adjustment programmes. Over 30,000 policemen had been positioned near the building where the meeting was to be held and there was violent repression when civil society leaders from religious, labour, human rights, and student groups tried to speak.

On 8 November 2000, Daewoo had announced its intention to lay off 3,500 workers, simultaneous to announcing it had gone bankrupt. Workers immediately retaliated in tens of thousands and blamed poor management and President Kim Dae Jung for the spread of neoliberal propaganda. Daewoo responded by stating that if workers did not back down, they would all suffer from job losses. The unions felt forced to accept the cuts. The next year, Daewoo workers staged one of the largest demonstrations and strikes against neoliberal globalisation in history. Whilst workers had staged various protests over the previous nine months, on 16 February of 2001 management announced that 1,750 workers would be laid off of that year. Union leaders told workers to continue to work at the Bu-pyung plant, which management had closed down, and to organise education sessions for workers' rights. Family members and other laid-off workers joined in this protest. 2,000 riot police were deployed to stop workers from working, and on 19

February, more riot police joined them to stop the direct action and injured many people in the ensuing struggle. In March, Daewoo announced that it would lay off 2,000 workers, creating more havoc, including the suicide of one dismissed worker. Workers blame 'neoliberal economic globalisation' for the disruption of their lives and continued the struggle (PICIS 2001).

In July 2001, the KCTU called a general strike against union oppression and to 'end the neoliberal structural adjustment regime of the Kim Dae Jung government' (Labournet 2001). The KCTU Central Committee invited all member unions and affiliated federations to stop work on 5 July, in response to ideological and physical attempts to disempower the KCTU. At the People's Rally again on 2 December 2001, 2,000 university students from around the nation gathered in Dongguk University in opposition to neoliberal education-related policies. The rally brought together people from various social sectors in solidarity, 'all angered by the neoliberal policies of the Kim administration, which has brought lay-offs and instability of jobs for workers, threat to the livelihood of small farmers and urban poor, and privatisation and liberalisation of basic social services.' (ibid.).

Despite speculation that the Korean economy was 'recovering' quickly from the worst effects of the economic crisis, dissent did not subside. In 2002, Korean government workers went on strike for the first time in history (PICIS 2002). They asked the government to legalise the Korean Government Employees Union (KGEU). At a pre-rally ceremony however, the police arrived, and violence broke out. Leaders were arrested and 600 members were apprehended at the incident. No resolution was reached. In 2004, KoPA staged a week of demonstrations before the American Chamber of Commerce, bringing together culture, environment, women and workers' groups who claim that neoliberal globalisation has 'seeped through and destroyed all aspects of our lives … [We] call for the stop to all negotiations for investment treaties and free trade agreements' (BASE21 2004). KoPA hosted debates and conferences to discuss globalisation's effects on health, education, the environment, and women, and a film festival of films that 'manifest the atrocities committed by transnational capital in various countries, and the struggles of the people' (2004). On 21 April, laid-off Korea Telecom workers were part of a group of about 100 protestors to hold a 'Global Day of Action' in Seoul.

So dissent has not subsided. Workers in South Korea are not satisfied with the restructuring and reform that was instigated after the economic crisis. This leaves me with several questions regarding the future of South Korea, particularly on issues of workers' job stability and training. What direction will the government take? The Korean population expected Roh, Moo Hyun, the president elected after Kim, Dae Jung in February 2003, to be able to restore their confidence because of his credentials as a human rights lawyer and a strong activist during the movement toward democratisation in the 1980s. After just over one year of leadership however President Roh was impeached for introducing a new political party in the run up to elections, and was exposed for having accepted millions of dollars from companies in the electoral race in 2002. Roh claimed that it is getting increasingly difficult to govern in the contemporary climate of international politics. Korean/US relations are becoming increasingly tense, the economy is eternally teetering on the edge, and the media and parliament are dominated with conservative viewpoints (BBC 2004). Even government leaders in the contemporary age of neoliberalism are bewildered with the future for South Korea.

The Chief Editor of the Labour Society Bulletin, Mr Yoon, discussed resistance to the growing trend of economic globalization in South Korea with me.[1] Within the union movement there are debates about globalization. Some individuals within both umbrella unions completely deny the legitimacy of the government's choice to globalize, while others are resigned to its inevitability. Responses must therefore be selective. However, the majorities of unionists are not interested in the underlying issue of globalization; the fight for better wages and work conditions are the bulk of union activity. I mused that much of the disputes surrounding these very factors can be attributed ultimately to the internationally driven restructuring process of the Korean economy. Mr Yoon agreed, but reminded me that most enterprise unionists are not exposed to these issues. He said that the most important objective for unions now is to find ways to slow down the process of economic globalization even without full access to knowledge of the issues. The union density is only 10 or 11 per cent, or 1.5 to 1.6 million workers are members of unions. This leaves 10 million uninvolved workers.

The Future

So what does the future hold for Korean workers? In an interview with a BASF union leader in 2002,[2] I learned that twice a year, union leaders attend management training (MT) for three days and two nights. Workers who are members of unions are permitted training 'whenever they need it' Mr Yoo told me; a provision that is rhetorically desirable for any self-interested worker. I asked, what sort of training is that? He assured me that the sessions involve training on union history, workers' values, worker mentality, environmental standards, and health and safety. Workers are also given on-the-job training once a month for two hours, to provide life-long learning. Furthermore, when new chemicals are introduced at the plants, Material Safety Data Sheets (MSDS) are presented in mandatory meetings for workers. White-collar workers are permitted to attend meetings and seminars in Germany for example the BASF 'Responsive Care' sessions, of the Korea Industrial Security Organisation (KOSHA). The government funds KOSHA to conduct seminars that are required of both white and blue-collar workers. So even after democratisation, the government is still heavily involved in the 'mentality' aspect of training, which is perhaps the most important facet of vocational education for neoliberalism to become integrated in South Korea. Gills notes that 'the relationship between capitalism and democracy is today, as in past generations, one of the most acute questions of our era' (2001: 235). This is an area that needs to be explored in more depth in future research that I plan to conduct.

Often, only privileged groups are meaningfully coerced in a process of *trasformismo* despite attempts to appeal to the lowest common denominator. Workers who filled, before the crisis, skilled or managerial positions have been largely able to retain employment. Those capable of adopting the new work requirements have been able to compete more successfully within the social scenario of economic crisis recovery and societal restructuring in South Korea (Koo 2001: 208; Park et al. 2001: 81). This process occurs as a very specific way of dealing with a larger scenario of global hegemony. In the South Korean case, elite levels of society: the government and the managerial capitalist class have automated internationalisation or globalization. New requirements made of workers have been applied under what are presented as immutable conditions, indicating that the 'choice' to participate, despite the voluntary nature of programmes, is not available. The empirical and textual data explains the changes of content and requirements of participation in VET in the following disempowered fashion: 'the demand for skilled workers has grown because of changes which have taken place in the manner and mode of employment' (KRIVET/NCVER 2000: i). Furthermore, 'restructuring has been sweeping the world economy, and no company in the market economy which is driven by the principles of competition and efficiency can be immune to the worldwide trend' (KOILAF 2001b: 15).

As has been discussed, restructuring during the crisis recovery period occurred in the context of the post-Fordist knowledge economy. This opens the space for unprecedented skills requirements on workers wishing to retain their positions of work, and presented a new concept of what 'employable' skills are in the contemporary setting. Education and training has been restructured in tandem with corporate restructuring, to provide the means for workers to keep up with the pace of change. My critique is that these changes have occurred not hegemonically, but show that the government is attempting to lead a passive revolution. The government has not involved workers' choice in the process of change, which is evident in various ways. For example, within the first Tripartite Commission, management and government forced the passage of documents that were not permissible by Union leaders.

Mr Yoon[3] talked about the differences between the two major umbrella union organisations, the Korean Confederation of Trade Unions (KCTU) and the Federation of Korean Trade Unions (FKTU). The KCTU, he described, represents the left wing of social democracy. Of course there are disputes within the organisation itself, but in 2000, the Union developed a report stating its desired policies and plans which, Mr Yoon stated, was too radical to submit to the National Congress. The FKTU, as discussed throughout Chapter 5 represents the right wing of social democracy. These splits were more recognisable before the economic crisis, however. After the crisis, the two were able to establish a better relationship because their members were faced with the same problems of worker layoffs and restructuring. The Joint Rally performed by both unions shows that they are not ideologically opposed to the same extent that they are opposed organisationally (in that the FKTU has been supportive of the government since its inception and the KCTU is militantly anti-government). The basic split between the two groups is the difference between FKTU's reformism and the KCTU's revolutionism, but in policy and practice, gaps are reducing. This appears to be another sign that *trasformismo* is occurring; that previously juxtaposed groups are becoming increasingly 'similar' in outlook and the rights of workers, which historically, the KCTU militantly fought for, appear to be increasingly dissolved in the ideological fusion that appears to be happening.

As seen by the historical trajectory of Korean economic development, capitalism has not fled this nation's terrain but has been re-articulated, in molecular changes since its introduction by Japanese colonisers. However, according to the conditions I demonstrate, the Korean government has been capable of arranging and managing passive revolutions during the extreme economic change of this semi-peripheral country. Korean workers have never been silent about their experiences of development and globalisation, despite the government's ongoing efforts to quiet them. Despite the illegality of Union activity, Unions stood firm. Despite concessions and the appeal to national sentiment, workers have resisted withholding of pay and poor working conditions evident throughout the course of dictatorships and accelerated development. It will be interesting to see whether the IPE literature will begin to take worker resistance seriously, and whether dissent will be successful in creating alternative projects over time.

During Japan's accumulation strategy of colonialism, workers were required to take on Japanese work norms. During the period of dictatorship from 1948–1993, Presidents expected workers to find comfort in nationalism and work for the benefit of their country, and to meet the standards as such. Even after democratisation, there was little relief in the workplace, as people have been forced to continue to keep abreast with 'market forces' that are preached as fundamental for national economic development. Finally, following the 1997 economic crisis, DJ Kim's government began to involve international groups toward worker skills improvements and convergence. Incremental changes have been predominantly engineered to meet government led strategies of accumulation, which are increasingly toward neoliberalism and the ascendance of a knowledge economy in Korea.

A significant critique that can emerge from this analysis is that economic restructuring in Korea privileged white-collar, highly skilled workers, particularly in the era of restructuring for neoliberalism. Privileged workers are those who were able to retain employment, often within companies who merged with MNCs. Despite the newly introduced idea of 'flexibility' of the labour force (an IMF restructuring requirement), 'employable' workers often enjoyed continuous work. This means that less skilled workers were not permitted a significant voice in development strategy designs, neither historically nor now; and skilled workers were incorporated into elite governed objectives via incentives and training opportunities. For less skilled workers on the other hand, training opportunities were a requirement. The incentive, or almost forced logic, was job retention and even then, job flexibility was an ever-present threat.

Various features are involved in a case of passive revolution that facilitate unresisted social and economic changes according to elite classes' motives. In order to avoid a crisis of hegemony at the national level (*PN*: 326), a passive revolutionary trajectory may inspire more direct authoritative action on the part of the government that takes the form of incentives for consent. *Trasformismo* is inclined to occur if fractions of civil society and in this case, workers themselves, begin to resist requests made of them. The government aims, via political restructuring of its relationship with and reparative attitude toward workers, to absorb fragments of society that might pose a threat to development or execution of its strategies through training. The ultimate goal of VET is to achieve widespread acceptance of decisions made at the exclusive and elite echelons of society. But this has not been effective and the government still faces significant worker resistance and dissent. The next step for research must be to address the questions regarding which of the contrasting hegemonic projects will succeed, the workers' or the government's? How can workers succeed in the ongoing struggles for material, institutional and ideational hegemony? Or will the government and the elite, transnational capitalist classes, maintain control?

Without hegemony in Korea, who knows what the future may hold? I have used a detailed picture of Korean governments' strategies to force workers into a supportive development force, via VET programmes. Korean workers have faced a great deal of pressure throughout history to accommodate to the state's accumulation strategies throughout various regime types. Over time, states have adapted vocational training curricula to match their development initiatives, and required workers to undergo this training under the conditions of passive revolution. While workers have born the burden of providing manpower for governments' initiatives, they are now responsible not just to the demands of the state but after the crisis also to international pressures for convergence of skills. The Korean governments' hegemonic projects; i.e. strategies to accommodate potential resistance groups via coercion; were articulated with progressive rhetoric, but did not result in ideological consolidation. Several dissident movements have accompanied each phase of regime change: anti-Japanese, anti-authoritarianism, and anti-neoliberalism and even democracy-suspicious groups (Shin 2000: 245) have emerged within each stage of Korean forms of state. Therefore I argue that while states' accumulation strategies have altered over time to appropriate and circumvent grass-roots revolution by way of limited concessions, elites' hegemonic strategies to engage consensus from all social forces have not been successful. So to conclude, Korea is not a hegemonic nation and has never been a hegemonic nation, calling into question whether global hegemony is a relevant or useful concept.

NOTES

Introduction

1. Antonio Gramsci, *Prison Notebooks* (1929–1935/1971) (*PN*), p. 310.
2. See for example Rowley and Bae 1998; McNamara 2002.
3. The leading Korean Gramscian is Choi, Jang Jip (1987, 1989). Gramsci's ideas were only introduced to Korea in the 1980s, as prior to this decade, censorship had prevented the reading of any Communist-related literature.
4. Here, Sinclair is quoting Gramsci from the *Prison Notebooks* (1929–1935/1971) p. 465.

Chapter 3

1. The chapter begins during an international hegemonic struggle that Cox names 'Rival Imperialisms'. Chapter 2 discussed a period previous to that of the global rivalry for imperialism, or the hegemonic period of 'Pax Britannica'. During this period, 'hegemonic' fundamentals of liberalism and capitalism were formed. I have not included a historical review of South Korean experience with this period of history because, since it closed itself off as a 'Hermit Kingdom', there is very little available information to observe relations during this time period. Barry K. Gills (2001: 240) writes that the origins of economic thought lie within Eastern political philosophy and that East Asia demonstrated signs of the formation of capitalist norms during pre-modern history as well, but for lack of space, I do not intend to pursue the possible avenues of research around these legitimate claims here.
2. Discussion in later years has been over whether troops were in fact drugged during the Massacre, as they did not appear to be completely in control of their own actions during this episode.
3. The Washington Consensus is a series of policymaking guidelines required of the nations of South America authored by John

Williamson, senior researcher of the Institute for Economy Policy in Washington DC in 1989. Williamson claims that these guidelines are in fact, 'the lowest common denominator of policy advice being addressed by the Washington-based institutions to Latin American countries as of 1989. The three big ideas here are macroeconomic discipline, a market economy, and openness to the world (at least in respect of trade and FDI)' (2000). The following is the list Williamson created on what he believes to be 'motherhood and apple pie' (2002) for developing nations:

1. Fiscal discipline.
2. A redirection of public expenditure priorities toward fields offering both high economic returns and the potential to improve income distribution, such as primary health care, primary education, and infrastructure.
3. Tax reform (to lower marginal rates and broaden the tax base).
4. Interest rate liberalisation.
5. A competitive exchange rate.
6. Trade liberalisation.
7. Liberalisation of FDI inflows.
8. Privatisation.
9. Deregulation (in the sense of abolishing barriers to entry and exit).
10. Secure property rights. (Williamson 1990)

Chapter 4

1. I interviewed BASF Yosu site Labour Union leader Mr Yoo, Young Hwa, 14 August, 2002.
2. I interviewed Mr Yoon, International Secretary of the KCTU, 8 August, 2002 at the KCTU Headquarters, Yeongdungpo, Seoul.
3. See http://www.unevoc.unesco.org/sustainable/index.htm.
4. The following VET programmes demonstrate very similar training curricula for knowledge-based training. In Singapore, for example, the Critical Enabling Skills Training (CREST) programme planned to enrol 100,000 trainees in 2001. (Refer to the Singapore Productivity and Standards Board, *Ranking of Singapore's Workforce by Business Environment Risk Intelligence*, Workforce Studies Series, 2001.) Germany's tripartite Alliance for Jobs agreed on the creation of

training places for 60,000 people in ICT up to 2003. In South Africa, a tripartite training authority in the ICT sector specifically was set up in 2000. See ILO *World Employment Report* 2001.

5. 'UNESCO's International Centre for Technical and Vocational Education and Training was established in September 2000. It is dedicated to developing and improving technical and vocational education and training in UNESCO's Member States. Its focus is on information exchange, networking and international cooperation.' UNEVOC (UNESCO International Project on Technical and Vocational Education) (2002a), Online, Available at: http://www.unevoc.de/

6. Translated from Korean.

7. I interviewed Dr Ji Hee Choi, senior researcher for KRIVET on 09 August, 2002, at KRIVET's headquarters in Seoul, Korea.

8. Also see Bonefeld and Hollaway (ed.) 1991; Amin (ed.) 1994.

9. The World Bank *Knowledge Economy Forum* was held in Paris in February 2002 and included presentations from representatives of Ireland, Finland and South Korea, all countries which have 'leap-frogged the development process through smart acquisition and use of knowledge'. World Bank (2002) *A Preliminary Strategy to Develop a Knowledge Economy in European Union Accession Countries*, prepared for the Knowledge Economy Forum (Paris, 20–22 February 2002) organised by the in coordination with the European Commission (EC) and the Organisation for Economic Co-operation and Development (OECD).

10. Information available on KRIVET website, Online, Available, http://www.krivet.re.kr/krivet-htm/eh/index.html

11. Statistics provided within an interview I conducted with Dr Young Hyun Lee, 09 August 2002, at the KRIVET headquarters, Seoul.

12. This interview was held on 09 August, 2002 at the KRIVET headquarters in Seoul.

13. This information was gathered from a semi-structured interview with Minister of Labour Mr Lee, Soo Young, Vice Director of the Korean Labour Management Co-operation Division in Seoul on December 4, 1999.

14. In 'Kunglish', or Korean inspired English, 'mind' means 'way of thinking'.

Conclusion

1. Interview I conducted in Seoul, Korea (20 August 2002) with Mr Yoon, Labour Society Bulletin Chief Editor at the Korea Labour Society Institute.
2. Interview conducted in Seoul, Korea (14 August 2002) with Mr Yoo, Young Hwa, Yosu site Labour Union leader, BASF. Thanks to Nicole Schiller for translating.
3. See endnote 1.

BIBLIOGRAPHY

Abbott, A. and O. Worth (eds.) (2000) *Critical perspectives on International Political Economy* (Basingstoke: Palgrave).

Abelmann, N. (1996) *Echoes of the Past, Epics of Dissent: A South Korean Social Movement* (California: University of California Press).

Abdollahian, M., J. Kugler and H. L. Root (2000) 'Economic Crisis and the Future of Oligarchy', in L. Diamond and D. C. Shin (eds.), *Institutional Reform and Democratic Consolidation in Korea* (Standford: Hoover Press), pp. 199–232.

Adamson, W. (1980) *Hegemony and Revolution: a Study of Antonio Gramsci's Political and Cultural Theory* (California: University of California Press).

——————— (1987) 'Gramsci and the politics of civil society', Praxis International 7, pp. 300–27.

Adorno, T. W. and M. Horkheimer (1944/1979) *The Dialectic of Enlightenment* (London: Verso).

Agnew, J. and S. Corbridge (1995) *Mastering Space: Hegemony, Territory and International Political Economy* (London/New York: Routledge).

Amin, A. (ed.) (1994) *Post-Fordism, Studies in Urban and Social Change* (Cambridge: Cambridge University Press).

Amin, S. (2000) *Capitalism in the Age of Globalisation: the Management of Contemporary Society* (New York: St Martin's Press).

Amoore, L. (1998) 'Globalisation, the Industrial Society, and Labour Flexibility: A Sense of Déjà vu?', *Global Society*, Vol. 12, No. 1, pp. 49–74.

Amsden, A. (1989) *Asia's Next Giant: South Korea and Late Industrialization* (New York: Oxford University Press).

——————— (1992) 'The South Korean Economy: Is Business-led Growth Working?' in D. Clark (ed.) *Korea Briefing 1992* (Boulder: Westview Press).

Annunziato, F. (1988) 'Gramsci's Theory of Trade Unionism', *Rethinking Marxism* 1 (Summer): pp. 142–64.

Appelbaum, E. and R. Batt (1994) *The New American Workplace: Transforming Work Systems in the United States* (Ithaca and London: Ilr Press, imprint of Cornell University Press).

Arato, A. (1981) 'Civil Society against the state: Poland 1981-2', *Telos* (47), pp. 23–47.

——————— (1981–1982) 'Empire vs. Civil Society: Poland 1981-82', *Telos* (50), pp. 19–48.

——————— (1990) *Revolution, Civil Society, and Democracy: Paradoxes in the Recent Transition in Eastern Europe* (Cornell: Centre for International Studies).

Aron, R. (1966) *Peace And War: A Theory Of International Relations* (London: Weidenfeld & Nicolson).

——————— (1967) 'What is a theory of International Relations?', *Journal of International Affairs*, 21 (2): 185–206.

——————— (1973) *Scientists in search of their conscience* (Berlin: Springer-Verlag).

Aronowitz, S. and W. DiFazio (1994) 'The New Knowledge Work', in J. Ahier and G. Esland (eds.) *Education, Training and the Future of Work 1: Social, Political and Economic Contexts of Policy Development* (London: Routledge), pp. 76–96.

Arrighi, G. (1993) 'The Three Hegemonies of Historical Capitalism', in S. Gills (ed.) *Gramsci, Historical Materialism and International Relations* (Cambridge: Cambridge University Press), pp. 148–85.

Ashley, R. (1981) 'Political Realism and Human Interests', *International Studies Quarterly*, 25, pp. 204–46.

——————— (1986) 'The Poverty of Neorealism', in R. Keohane (ed.) *Neorealism and its Critics* (New York: Columbia University Press), pp. 255–300: also published (1984), *International Organization* 38, 2, Spring pp. 225–86.

Ashworth, L. M. (2002) 'Did the realist-idealist Great Debate really happen? A revisionist history of international relations', *International Relations* Vol. 16, No. 1.

Asia Pacific Civil Society Forum (APCSF) (1997) *First Working Session Presentation of Theoretical Framework/Comment & Responses*, July 24, 1997, CDM, Rajendrapur, Online, available at: http://216.239.51.100/search?q=cache:qqZyQldfVNEC:apcsf.peacenet.or.kr/publications/2nd_assem/The%2520working%2520Session.doc+UNDP+definition+civil+sociey&hl=en&ie=UTF8

Augelli, E. and C. N. Murphy (1993) 'Gramsci and International Relations: A General Perspective and Example from Recent US Policy toward the Third World,' in S. Gill (ed.), *Gramsci, Historical Materialism and International Relations* (Cambridge University Press, Great Britain) pp. 127–47.

———————— (1988) *America's Quest for Supremacy and the Third World: A Gramscian Analysis* (London: Pinter).

Baker, M. (1998) 'Out With Confucius In Korea's Big Firms' *The Christian Science Monitor, International* March 11, 1998, Online, Available at: http://csmweb2.emcweb.com/durable/1998/03/11/intl/intl.6.html

Baldwin, D. (1993) *Neorealism and Neoliberalism: The Contemporary Debate* (New York: Columbia University Press).

Baran, P. (1967) *The Political Economy of Growth* (New York: Monthly Review Press).

———————— (1968) *Monopoly capital: an essay on the American economic and social order* (Harmondsworth: Penguin Books).

Barlett, D. L. and J. B. Steele (1996) *America: Who Stole the Dream?* (Andrews McMeel Publishing).

Barnes, T. J. (1995) 'Political Economy I: The Culture, Stupid' *Progress in Human Geography* Vol. 19 No. 3, pp. 423–31.

BASE21 (2004) 'Week of Action against Investment Treaties and Free Trade Agreements' *International Solidarity* No. 83, April 21 2004, Online, Available at: http://www.base21.org/show/show.php?p_ cd= 200001&p_dv=1&p_docnbr=16494 ('copylefted' by www.base21.org).

Bastiat, F. (1945) preface to *Harmonies economiques* cited in Loius Baudin (1962) *Frederic Bastiat* (Paris: Dolloz).

Bayart, J. F. (1995) 'The State in Africa', Longman, London, cited in Chris Hann's 'Philosophers' Models on the Carpathian Lowlands', in J. Hall (ed.) (1995), *Civil Society: Theory, History, Comparison* (Cambridge, Massachusetts: Polity Press), pp. 158–82.

Baxi, U. (2000) 'Human Rights: Suffering Between Movements and Markets', in Cohen, R. and S. Rai, *Global Social Movements* (London and New Jersey: Athlone Press), pp. 33–45.

Beaud, M. (1983) *A History of Capitalism 1500-1980* (New York: Monthly Review Press).

Bieler, A. (2000a) *Globalisation and Enlargement of the European Union: Austrian and Swedish Social Forces in the Struggle over Membership* (London: Routledge).

———————— (2000b) 'Labour and the struggle against neo-liberalism: a conceptualisation of trade unions' possible role in the resistance to globalisation', paper prepared for presentation at the conference

'Global Capital and Global Struggles: Strategies, Alliances, Alternatives', London, July 2000.

——————— (2001) 'Questioning Cognitivism and Constructivism in IR Theory: Reflections on the Material Structure of Ideas', *Politics*, Vol. 21 (2), pp. 93–100.

Bieler, A. and A. Morton (eds.) (2001) *Social Forces in the Making of New Europe: The Restructuring of European Social Relations in the Global Political Economy* (Basingstoke: Palgrave).

——————— (2003) 'Globalisation, the State and Class Struggle: A 'Critical Economy' Engagement with Open Marxism', *British Journal of Politics and International Relations*, Vol. 5, No. 4, pp. 467–99.

——————— (2004) 'A Critical Theory Route to Hegemony, World Order and Historical Change: Neo-Gramscian Perspectives in International Relations' *Capital and Class*, No. 82, pp. 85–113.

Biggart, N. W. (1990) 'Institutionalized Patrimonialism in Korean Business', *Comparative Social Research* 12 (USA: JAI Press).

Birchfield, V. (1999) 'Contesting the Hegemony of Market Ideology: Gramsci's 'good sense' and Polanyi's 'double movement'', *Review of Political Economy*, Vol. 6, No. 1, Spring 1999, pp. 27–54.

Birchill, S. (2001), 'Introduction', in Birchill, S., R. Devetak, A. Linklater, M. Paterson, C. Reus-Smit and J. True (eds.) *Theories of International Relations Second Edition* (Basingstoke: Palgrave Macmillan), pp. 1–28.

Birchill, S., R. Devetak, A. Linklater, M. Paterson, C. Reus-Smit and J. True (eds.) (2001) *Theories of International Relations Second Edition* (Basingstoke: Palgrave Macmillan).

Blustein, P. and Chandler, C. (1997) 'Behind the South Korean Rescue: Pressure, Speed and Stealth' *Washington Post Service International Herald Tribune* Monday 29 Dec 1997.

Bøås M. and D. McNeill (2003) *Multilateral Institutions: A Critical Introduction* (London: Pluto Press).

Bobbio, N. (1988) 'Gramsci and the Concept of Civil Society', in J. Keane (ed.), *Civil Society and the State: New European Perspectives* (UK: Verso).

Bobrow, D. and J. Na (1999) 'Korea's Affair with Globalization: Deconstructing *Segyehwa*', in C. I. Moon and J. R. Mo (eds.), *Democratization and Globalization in Korea: Assessments and Prospects* (Seoul: Yonsei University Press).

Bonefeld, W. and J. Holloway (eds.) (1991) *Post-Fordism and social form: a Marxist debate on the post-Fordist state* (London: Macmillan).

Bourdieu, P. (1996) *The State Nobility: Elite Schools in the Field of Power* (Cambridge: Polity Press).

Bottomore, T. (ed.) (1993) *A Dictionary of Marxist Thought* (Oxford: Blackwell). British Broadcasting Company (BBC) (2004) 'Profile: Roh Moo-hyun', Online, Available at: http://news.bbc.co.uk/1/hi/world/asia-pacific/2535143.stm

Brown, L. B. (1973) *Ideology* (London: Penguin).

Brown, P. and H. Lauder (1999) 'Education, globalization, and economic development', in J. Ahier and G. Esland (eds.), *Education, Training and the Future of Work I: Social Political and Economic Contexts of Policy Development* (London: Routledge), pp. 31–61.

Bryant, C. (1995) 'Civic Nation, Civil Society, Civil Religion', in J. Hall (ed.), *Civil Society: Theory, History, Comparison* (Cambridge, Massachusetts: Polity Press), pp. 136–57.

Burchill, S. (2001) 'Liberalism', in S. Burchill, R. Devetak, A. Linklater, M. Paterson, C. Reus-Smit and J. True (2001) *Theories of International Relations* (Basingstoke: Palgrave), pp. 29–69.

————— (2001) 'Realism and Neo-Realism', in S. Burchill, R. Devetak, A. Linklater, M. Paterson, C. Reus-Smit and J. True (2001) *Theories of International Relations* (Basingstoke: Palgrave), pp. 70–102.

Burchill, S., R. Devetak, A. Linklater, M. Paterson, C. Reus-Smit and J. True (eds.) (2001) *Theories of International Relations* (Basingstoke: Palgrave).

Burnham, P. (1999) 'The Recomposition of National States in the Global Economy: From Politicised to Depoliticised forms of Labour Regulation', in P. Edwards and T. Elgar (eds.) *The Global Economy, National States and the Regulation of Labour* (London: Mansell), pp. 42–63.

————— (1994) 'Open Marxism and Vulgar International Political Economy' *Review of International Political Economy* Vol. 1 (2), pp. 221–31.

————— (1991) 'Neo-Gramscian Hegemony and the International Order', *Capital and Class* Issue 45, pp. 73–93.

Business Korea (1998) 'Facing the nation' (Seoul: Business Korea Ltd).

Cammack, P. (2001) 'Making the Poor Work for Globalisation?', *New Political Economy*, Vol. 6, No. 3, November', pp. 397–408.

————— (2002a) 'The Mother of All Governments: The World Bank's matrix for Global Governance', in R. Wilkinson and S. Hughes (eds.) *Global Governance: Critical Perspectives* (London: Routledge), pp. 36–53.

————— (2002b) 'Attacking the Poor', *New Left Review*, Vol. 2, No. 13, Jan-Feb., pp. 125–34.

Cardoso, F. and R. Falleto (1979) *Dependency and Development* (Berkeley: University of California Press).

Castells, M. (1983) *The city and the grassroots: a cross-cultural theory of urban social movements* (London: Edward Arnold).

——————— (1989) *The Informational City: Information Technology, Economic Restructuring, and the Urban-Regional Process* (Oxford: Basil Blackwell).

——————— (1996) 'The Rise of the Network Society', *The Information Age: Economy, Society, and Culture* vol. 1 (Oxford: Blackwell).

——————— (1997) 'The Power of Identity', *The Information Age: Economy, Society, and Culture* vol. 2 (Oxford: Blackwell).

Castells, M., R. Flecha, P. Friere, H. A. Giroux, D. Macedo and P. Willis (eds.) (introduction by Peter McLaren) (1999) *Critical Education in the New Information Age* (Oxford: Rowman & Littlefield).

Central Intelligence Agency (CIA) (1948) *Prospects for the Survival of the Republic of Korea*, ORE 44-48, 28 October 1948, Appendix A, 'Personality of Syngman Rhee', CIA, 'National Intelligence Survey, Korea'.

Chandavarkar, A. (2001) 'A Fresh Look at Keynes: Robert Skidelsky's Trilogy, Finance and Development' (quarterly magazine of IMF, December 2001).

Chase-Dunn, C. (1991) *Global formation: structures of the world-economy* (Massachusetts: Basil Blackwell).

Cho, D. S. (1998) 'Korea's Economic Crisis: Causes, Significance and Agenda for Recovery' *Korea Focus*, January-February 1998.

Cho, S. H. (1984) *The Industrialisation of Korea and the Labour Movement* (Seoul: Pulbit).

Choi, J. J. (1987) 'The Strong State and Weak Labour Relations in South Korea: Their Historical Determinants and Bureaucratic Structure', in K. D. Kim (ed.) *Dependency Issues in Korean Development* (Seoul: Seoul National University Press) pp. 305–25.

——————— (1989) *Labour and the Authoritarian State: Labour Unions in South Korean Manufacturing Industries*, 1961-1980 (Seoul: Korea University Press).

Chomsky, N. (1988) *Language and problems of knowledge: the Managua lectures* (Cambridge, Massachusetts; London: MIT Press).

——————— (1994) *World orders, Old and New* (London: Pluto).

Chung, C. S. (1995) 'Confucian Tradition and National Ideology', in Wells, K. (ed.) (1995) *Korea's Minjung Movement*, Honolulu: University of Hawaii. p. 61–86.

Chung Nam Provincial School Board (1998*)* *The Basic Data for Career Education - High School* (1991), in M. K. Cho and M. W. Apple 'Schooling, Work and Subjectivity', *British Journal of Sociology and Education*, Vol. 19, No. 3.

Cicourel, A. (1964) *Method and Measurement in Sociology* (New York: Free Press).

Clifford, M. L. (1998) *Troubled Tiger: Businessmen, Bureaucrats, and Generals in South Korea* (New York: M. E. Sharpe).

Coase, R. H. (1937) 'The Nature of the Firm', *Economica* No. 4, November, pp. 386–405.

Coates, D. (2000) *Models of Capitalism: Growth and Stagnation in the Modern Era* (Oxford: Polity Press).

Cochrane A (1998) 'Illusions of power: interviewing local elites' *Environment and Planning A* volume 30, pp. 2121–32.

Cohen, J. L. and A. Arato (1994) *Civil Society and Political Theory* (Massachusetts: MIT Press).

Cohen, R. and S. Rai (2000) *Global Social Movements* (London and New Jersey: Athlone Press).

Comte, A. (1907) *A General View of Positivism* (London: Routledge and Sons).

Conroy, H. (1960) *The Japanese Seizure of Korea 1868-1910: A Study of Realism and Idealism in International Relations* (Pennsylvania: University of Pennsylvania).

Cook, T. and D. Campbell (1979) *Quasi-experimentation: Design and Analysis Issues for Field Settings* (London: Houghton Mifflin).

Cox, R. W. (1981) 'Social forces, states and world orders: beyond international relations theory,' *Millennium: Journal of International Studies*, Vol. 10, No. 2 (summer), pp. 126–55.

————— (1983) 'Gramsci, Hegemony and International Relations: An Essay in Method', *Millennium: Journal of International Studies*, Vol. 12, No. 2, Summer, pp. 162–75.

————— (1987) *Production, Power, and World Order: Social Forces in the Making of History* (New York: Columbia University Press).

————— (1989) 'Production, the State, and Change in World Order', in E. O. Czempiel and J. Rosenau (eds.), *Global Changes and Theoretical Challenges* (Lexington, Massachusetts: DC Heath).

————— (1989/1996) 'Middlepowermanship, Japan, and Future World Order', in R. W. Cox with Timothy Sinclair, *Approaches to World Order* (Cambridge: Cambridge University Press), pp. 241–75.

——————— (1992/1996) 'Towards a posthegemonic conceptualization of World Order: Reflections on the Relevancy of Ibn Khaldun', in R. W. Cox with T. Sinclair, *Approaches to World Order* (Cambridge: Cambridge University Press), pp. 144–73.

——————— (1993) 'Structural issues of global governance', in S. Gill (ed.) *Historical Materialism and International Relations* (Cambridge: Cambridge University Press), pp. 259–89.

——————— (1981/1996) 'Social forces, states, and world orders', *Approaches to World Order* (Cambridge: Cambridge University Press), pp. 85–123.

——————— (1985/1996) 'Realism, positivism, and historicism', in *Approaches to World Order* (Cambridge: Cambridge University Press), pp. 49–59.

——————— (1992/1996) 'Multilateralism and world order', in *Approaches to World Order* (Cambridge: Cambridge University Press), pp. 494–523.

——————— (1977/1996) 'Labour and Hegemony', *in Approaches to World Order* (Cambridge: Cambridge University Press), pp. 420–70.

——————— (1999) 'Civil society at the turn of the millennium: prospects for an alternative world order', *Review of International Studies*, Vol. 25, No. 1, pp. 3–28.

——————— (2000) 'Political Economy and World Order: Problems of Power and Knowledge at the Turn of the Millenium', in R. Stubbs and G. Underhill (eds.) *Political Economy and the Changing Global Order* (Oxford: Oxford University Press), pp. 25–37.

——————— (2001) 'The Way Ahead: Toward a New Ontology of World Order', in R. Wyn Jones (ed.) *Critical theory and world politics* (Boulder: Lynne Rienner Publishers), pp. 45–59.

——————— (with T. Sinclair) (1996) *Approaches to World Order* (Cambridge: Cambridge University Press).

——————— (with M. G. Schechter) (2002) *The Political Economy of a Plural World: Critical Reflections On Power, Morals, And Civilisation* (London: Routledge).

Croce, B. (tslt. C. M. Meredith, introduction A. D. Lindsay) (1914/1981) Historical Materialism and the Economics of Karl Marx (Transaction Publishers).

Cumings, B. (1984) 'The Northeast Political Economy', *International Organization* 38, pp. 1–40.

——————— (1997) *Korea's Place in the Sun: A Modern History* (New York, London: W. W. Norton and Company).

─────────── (1999) 'The Asian Crisis, Democracy, and the End of Late Development', in T. J. Pempel (ed.) *The Politics of the Asian Economic Crisis* (Ithaca: Cornell University Press), pp. 17–44.

Dale, R. (1985) 'Education and Training' in *Westminster Studies in Education* (Oxford: Carfax Publishing Co) vol. 7, pp. 57–66.

Davies, M. (1999) *International Political Economy and Mass Communication in Chile: National Intellectuals and Transnational Hegemony* (London: Palgrave).

Deyo, F. (ed.) (1987) *The Political Economy of the New Asian Industrialism* (Ithaca: Cornell University Press).

─────────── (1989) *Beneath the Miracle: Labour Subordination in the New Asian Industrialism* (Berkeley and Los Angeles: University of California Press).

Dexter, L. (1970) *Elite and Specialised Interviewing* (Evanson: Northwestern University Press).

Dicken, P. (1992) *Global Shift: The Internationalization of Economic Activity, 2nd edition* (London: Paul Chapman Ltd).

Domhoff, W. G. (1996) *State Autonomy or Class Dominance? Case Studies on Policy Making in America* (New York: Hawthorne).

Dos Santos, T. (1969) 'The Crisis of Development Theory and the Problem of Dependency in Latin America', in H. Berstein (ed.) *Underdevelopment and Development* (Harmondsworth: Penguin).

Drucker, P. (1993) *Managing in Turbulent Times* (Oxford: Butterworth & Heinemann).

Dutch Ministry of Economic Affairs (1995) *Strategy document: Knowledge in Action*, Online, Available at: http://www.minez/nl/home.asp?page=/nota/kennisen/hfd2.htm

Embong, A. R. (2001) 'Globalization and transnational Class Relations: Some problems of Conceptualisation', in J. Mittelman and N. Othman (eds.) *Capturing Globalization* (London: Routledge), pp. 92–106.

England, K (1994) 'Getting personal: reflexivity, positionality, and feminist research' *Professional Geographer* Vol. 46, pp. 80–9.

European Union Commission Staff Working Paper (2000) *Memorandum on Lifelong Learning* (Brussels, SEC 182), 30 October 2000, Online, Available at: http://ec.europa.eu/education/policies/lll/life/memoen.pdf

Farrands, C. (2002) 'Being critical about 'being critical' in IPE: negotiating emancipatory strategies', in J. Abbot and O. Worth (eds.) *Critical perspectives on International Political Economy* (Basingstoke: Palgrave Macmillan).

Fatton, R. (1991) 'Liberal Democracy in Africa', *Political Science Quarterly*, Vol. 105, No. 3, pp. 455–73.

Federation of American Scientists, Intelligence Resource Program, 'Korea: National Intelligence Service', Online, Available at: http://www.fas.org/irp/world/rok/nis.htm

Federation of Korean Trade Unions (FKTU) (1968) *Korean Trade Union Industry* (Seoul: Federation of Korean Industry).

————— (1979) Korean Trade Union History (Seoul: FKTU).

Femia, J. (1981) *Gramsci's Political Thought: Hegemony, Consciousness, and the Revolutionary Process* (Oxford: Oxford University Press).

Fieldhouse, D. K. (1982) *The colonial empires: a comparative survey from the eighteenth century* 2nd edition (London: Macmillan).

Fiori, G. (1996) *Antonio Gramsci: Life of a Revolutionary* (London: Verso).

Fisher, I. (1906) *The Nature of Capital and Income* (New York: Macmillan Company).

Fiske, J. (1987) *Television Culture* (London: Methuen).

Fontana, B. (2004) 'Hegemony and Power in Gramsci', paper prepared for delivery at the interim meeting of Research Committee 36, Political Power of the International Political Science Association, New York, 10–12 June 2004.

————— (2004) 'Hegemony', in *Dictionary of the History of Ideas* (New York: Scribner's).

————— (2000) 'Logos and Kratos: Gramsci and the Ancients on Hegemony' *Journal of the History of Ideas*, Vol. 61, No. 2 (April,), pp. 305–26.

Ford H. and S. Crowther (1922) *My Life and Work* (New York: Doubleday). Foreign Relations of the United States (FRUS) (1945) Volume 6.

Forgacs, D. (1988) *An Antonio Gramsci Reader* (New York: Schocken).

Frank, A. G. (ed.) (1988) *A Gramsci Reader, Selected Writings 1916-1935* (London: Lawrence and Wishart).

————— (1970) *Latin America: Underdevelopment or Revolution* (New York: Monthly Review Press).

————— (1971) *Capitalism and underdevelopment in Latin America: historical studies of Chile and Brazil* (Harmondsworth: Penguin).

————— (1978) *Dependent accumulation and underdevelopment* (London: Macmillan).

Frank, A. G. and B. K. Gills (eds.) (1993) *The World System: Five Hundred Years Or Five Thousand?* (London: Routledge).

Friedman, J. (1999), 'Class, hybridity and ethnification', in Olds, et al. (eds.) *Globalisation and the Asia-Pacific: Contested Territories* (London: Routledge), pp. 183–201.

Friedman, M. (1962) *Capitalism and Freedom* (Chicago: University of Chicago Press).

Fukuyama, F. (1993) *The End of History and the Last Man* (Avon Books).

————— (1999) *The great disruption: human nature and the reconstitution of social order* (New York: New York Free Press).

Furtado, C. (1963) *The Economic Growth of Brazil* (Berkeley: University of California Press).

Gassler, R. (2001) 'Globalisation and the Information Economy', *Global Society* Vol. 15, No. 1, pp. 111–18.

Gellner, E. [pseud. Philip Peters] (1984) 'The State of Poland', Times Literary Supplement, no. 4246.

Germain, R. (1997) *The international organisation of credit: states and global finance in the world-economy* (Cambridge: Cambridge University Press).

Germain, R. and M. Kenny (1998), 'Engaging Gramsci: international relations theory and the new Gramscians', *Review of International Studies*, Vol. 24, No. 1, pp. 3–21.

Gill, S. (1986a) 'Hegemony, Consensus and Trilateralism', *Review of International Studies* Vol. 12, pp. 205–21.

————— (1986b) 'American Hegemony: Its Limits and Prospects in the Reagan Era' *Millennium* Vol. 15, pp. 311–39.

————— (1990) *American Hegemony and the Trilateral Commission* (Cambridge: Cambridge University Press).

————— (ed.) (1993a) *Gramsci, Historical Materialism And International Relations* (Cambridge University Press).

————— (1993b) 'Epistemology, Ontology and the 'Italian School'', in S. Gill (ed.), *Gramsci, Historical Materialism and International Relations* (Cambridge: Cambridge University Press) pp. 21–48.

————— (1995) 'Globalisation, Market Civilisation and Disciplinary Neoliberalism' *Millennium: Journal of International Studies* Vol. 24, No. 3, pp. 399–423.

————— (2000) *The Dynamics of Democratization: Elites, Civil Society and the Transition Process* (New York: St. Martin's Press).

Gill, S. and D. Law (1989) 'Global Hegemony and the Structural Power of Capital', *International Studies Quarterly*, 33 (4), 475–99.

————— (1993) 'Global Hegemony and the Structural Power of Capital', in S. Gill's *Gramsci, Historical Materialism And International Relations* (Cambridge University Press: UK) pp. 93–185.

Gill, S. and J. H. Mittelman (eds.) (1997) *Innovation and Transformation in International Studies* (Cambridge: Cambridge University Press).

Gills, B. K. (1993) 'The Hegemonic Transition in East Asia', in S. Gill (ed.), *Gramsci, Historical Materialism and International Relations* (Cambridge: Cambridge University Press) pp. 186–212.

———— (1996) 'Economic Liberalisation and Reform in South Korea in the 1990s: A 'Coming of Age' or a Case of 'Graduation Blues'?', *Third World Quarterly* Vol. 17, No. 4, pp. 667–88.

———— (ed.) (2000) *Globalization and the Politics of Resistance* (London: Macmillan).

———— (2000b) 'The Crisis of postwar East Asian capitalism: American power, democracy and the vicissitudes of globalization,' *Review of International Studies*, Vol. 26, No. 3, July, pp. 381–404.

———— (2001) 'Re-Orienting the New (International) Political Economy', *New Political Economy*, Vol. 6, No. 2, pp. 233–45.

Gills, B. K. and D. S. Gills (2000) 'Globalization and Strategic Choice in South Korea: Economic Reform and Labour', in S. Kim (ed.), *Korea's Globalization* (Cambridge: Cambridge University Press), pp. 29–53.

Gilpin, R. (1972) 'The politics of Transnational Economic Relations', in R. Keohane and J. Nye (eds.), *Transnational Relations and World Politics* (Cambridge: Cambridge University Press) pp. 48–69.

———— (1986) 'The Richness of the Tradition of Political Neorealism', in R. Keohane (ed.) *Neorealism and its Critics* (New York: Columbia University Press), pp. 301–21.

———— (1987) *The Political Economy of International Relations* (Princeton, New Jersey: University Press).

Girling, J. (1984) 'Thailand in Gramscian Perspective', *Pacific Affairs*, Vol. 57, No. 3 (Autumn), pp. 385–403.

Giroux, H. (1983) *Theory and Resistance in Education: A Pedagogy for the Opposition* (London: Bergin & Garvey Publishers, Inc).

Godemont, F. (1999) *The Downsizing of Asia* (London: Routledge).

Gramsci, A. (1916-1935/1988) 'Intellectuals and Education', in David Forgacs, (ed.) *A Gramsci Reader, Selected Writings 1916–935* (London: Lawrence and Wishart).

———— (1921-1926/1978) (tslt. by Hoare, Q. and Smith, G. N.) *Selections from Political Writings* (London: Lawrence and Wishart).

———— (1949) *Il Risorgimento Opere di Antonio Gramsci*, Vol. 4 (Turin, Einuadi, 1947-72).

———— (1975) *The Modern Prince and other writings* (USA: Louis Marks).

———— (1975b) *Quaderni del carcere* (Torino: Einaudi editore).

—————— (1929-1935/1999) (tslt. Q. Hoare and G. N. Smith) *Selections from the Prison Notebooks (PN)* (New York: International Publishers).

Green, A. (1999) 'East Asian Skill Formation Systems and the Challenge of Globalisation', *Journal of Education and Work*, Vol. 12, No. 3, pp. 253–79.

Greider, W. (1997) *One World, Ready of Not: The Manic Logic of Global Capitalism* (London: Simon and Shuster).

Grieco, J. (1993) 'Anarchy and the Limits of Cooperation', in D. Baldwin (1993), *Neorealism and Neoliberalism: The Contemporary Debate* (New York: Columbia University Press), pp. 116–40.

Griffiths, M. (1999) *Fifty Key Thinkers in International Relations* (New York: Routledge).

Guerrieri, P. (1988) 'International Co-operation and the Role of Macroeconomic Regimes', in P. Guerrieri and P. Padoan (eds.) *The Political Economy of International Co-operation* (London: Croom Helm).

Guillen, M. F. (1999) 'Organised Labour's Images of Multinational Enterprise: Divergent Ideologies of Foreign Investment in Argentina, South Korea, and Spain' (unpublished, Pennsylvania, Wharton School, Department of Sociology, University of Pennsylvania).

Habermas, J. (1989) *The Structural Transformation of the Public Sphere: An Inquiry into a Category of Bourgeois Society* (Cambridge, MA: MIT Press).

—————— tslt. McCarthy, T. (1984) 'The Theory of Communicative Action', *Reason and the Rationalisation of Society* Vol. 1 (London: Heinemann).

Haggard, S. (2000) *The Political Economy of the Asian Financial Crisis* (Washington, D.C.: Institute for International Economics).

—————— (1990) *Pathways from the Periphery: The Politics of Growth in the Newly Industrialising Countries* (Cornell: Cornell University Press).

Haggard, S., R. Cooper, S. Collins, C. S. Kim and S. T. Roe (1994) *Macroeconomic Policy and Adjustments in Korea, 1970-1990* (Harvard University Press).

Haggard, S. and C. I. Moon (1993) 'The State, Politics, and Economic Development in Postwar South Korea', in H. Koo (ed.) *State and Society in Contemporary Korea* (Ithaca: Cornell University Press) pp. 51–93.

Haggard, S. and D. Kang (1999) 'The Kim Young Sam Presidency in Comparative Perspective', in C. I. Moon and J. R. Mo, *Democratization and Globalization in Korea: Assessments and Prospects* (Seoul: Yonsei University Press).

Hahm, C.-B. (1999) 'The Clash of Universal Ethics: Rethinking the Terms of the Asian Values Debate', paper presented at International Conference on Universal Ethics and Asian Values, Yonsei University, Seoul, Korea, 4–6 October 1999.

Hall, P. and D. Soskice (2001) *Varieties of Capitalism: The Institutional Foundations of Comparative Advantage* (Oxford: Oxford University Press).

Hall, S. (1991) 'Brave New World', *Socialist Review*, Vol. 21, No. 1, 1991.

———————— 'The Meaning of New Times', in S. Hall, D. Morley, K-H Chen (eds.) *Stuart Hall: Critical Dialogues in Cultural Studies* (London: Routledge) pp. 223–37.

Hall, S., D. Morley and K-H Chen (eds.) (1996) *Stuart Hall: Critical Dialogues in Cultural Studies* (London: Routledge).

Halpin, D. (2002) 'Human Rights in South Korea: Confucian Humanism versus Western Liberalism', paper presented at the spring Institute for Corean-American Studies, Inc. (ICAS) Symposium, May 8, 2002, U.S. Senate, Washington D.C.

Hamilton, G. G. and N. W. Biggart (1988) 'Market, Culture and Authority: A Comparative Analysis of Management and Organisation in the Far East', *American Journal of Sociology* 94, USA.

Hammersley, M. and P. Atkinson (1983) *Ethnography: Principles in Practice* (Tavistock: London).

Han, J. W. and L. H. M. Ling (1998) 'Authoritarianism in the Hyper-masculinized State: Hybridity, Patriarchy, and Capitalism in Korea', *International Studies Quarterly* 42, pp. 53–78.

Han, W. S. (1981) Minjung *Sohoehak, Sociology of the Masses* (Seoul: Chongno Sojok).

Harbison, F. (1961) 'The Strategy of Human Resources Development in Modernizing Economies', *Policy Conference on Economic Growth and Investment in Education* (Paris: Organisation for Economic Cooperation and Development), pp. 9–33, also reprinted in R. Wykstra (ed.) *Education and the Economics of Human Capital* (USA: Free Press), pp. 214–47.

Harvey, D. (2004) 'The 'New' Imperialism: Accumulation by Dispossession', *Socialist Register 2004: The New Imperial Challenge*, (London: Merlin Press).

Hegel, G. (1821/1952) tslt. with notes by T. M. Knox, *Philosophy of right* (Oxford: Clarendon Press).

Held, D. (1987) *Models of Democracy* (Cambridge: Polity Press).

Henderson, G. (1968) *Korea: Politics of the Vortex* (Harvard: Harvard University Press).

Herman, E. S., and Chomsky, N. (1988) *Manufacturing consent: the political economy of the mass media* (New York: Pantheon).

Herod (1995) 'The practice of international Labour Solidarity and the geography of the global Economy' *Economic Geography* Vol. 71, No. 4, pp. 341–63.

——————— (1998a) 'The geostrategics of labour in post-Cold War Eastern Europe: An examination of the activities of the International Metalworkers' Federation', in Herod A. (ed.) *Organising the Landscape: Geographical Perspectives on Labour Unionism* (University of Minnesota Press, Minneapolis) pp. 45–74.

——————— (1998b) 'Of Blocs, Flows and Networks, the End of the Cold War, Cyberspace and the Geo-economics of organised Labour at the fin de Millenaire', in Herod A. et al. (eds.) *An Unruly World? Globalisation, Governance and Geography* (Routledge: Londond) pp. 162–95.

——————— (1998c) 'Theorising Unions in Transition', in M. Pickles and A. Smith (eds.) *Theorising Transition: The Political Economy of Change in Central and Eastern Europe* (Routledge: London) pp. 197–217.

——————— (1999) 'Reflections on interviewing foreign elites: praxis, positionality, validity and the cult of the insider' *Geoforum* Vol. 30, pp. 313–327.

Hirst, P. and G. Thompson (1996) *Globalization in Question: The International Economy and the Possibilities of Governance* (Cambridge: Polity Press).

Hisahiko, O. (1984) (Kokka to Joho: nihon to Gaikou Senryaku wo Motomete), *The State and Intelligence: Searching for Japan's Foreign Policy* (Tokyo: Bungeishunju).

Hoffman, S. (1965) *The State of War* (New York: Praeger).

Holstein, J. and J. Gubrium (1997) 'Active Interviewing', in D. Silverman (ed.) *Qualitative Research: Theory, Method and Practice* (London: Sage), pp. 113–29.

Hong, W. (1988) *Relationship between Korea and Japan in Early Period: Paekche and Yamato Wa* (Seoul: Ilsimsa).

Horkheimer, M. (1937) 'Traditional and Critical Theory', tnslt. O'Connel, M. *Critical Theory: Selected Essays* (NY: Continuum, 1982). Online, Available at: http://www.undp.org/csopp/CSO/NewFiles/programmesglobalfmwrk2.htm#framewrk2.2

Hutchings, K. (2001) 'The Nature of Critique in Critical International Relations Theory', in Richard Wyn Jones, (ed.) *Critical theory and world politics* (Boulder; London: Lynne Rienner Publishers, Inc.).

Hyden, G. and J. Court (with P. Moore) (2001) 'Governance and Development: Trying to sort out the basics' (Tokyo: United Nations University Press).

Ihm, C. S. (1999) 'VET Reform and Lifelong Learning in Korea', *Journal of Education and Work*, Vol. 12, No. 3, 309–21.

Ikenberry, G. (2001) 'Getting Hegemony Right,' *The National Interest*, Spring No. 63.

International Herald Tribune (1998) 'It's not over yet for South Korea, as economy shrinks, many say problems are still getting worse', Friday May 22.

International Labour Organisation (ILO) (2001) *World Employment Report 2001*, Online, Available at: http://search.ilo.org/?Ilo+IloPublicHTML; then C:\TEMP\World Employment Report 20011.htm; or http://www.eclipse.co.uk/pens/bibby/wep/bib4.htm

International Monetary Fund (IMF) (1997) *Stand-By Arrangement: Summary of the Economic Program, Republic Of Korea* (December 5, 1997), Online, Available at: http://www.imf.org/external/np/oth/korea.htm

Jarvis, P. (1993) *Adult Education and the State: Towards a politics of adult education* (Routledge: London).

Jessop, B. (1990) *State Theory: Putting the Capitalist in its Place* (Cambridge: Polity Press).

———— (1994) 'Post-Fordism and the State', in A. Amin (ed.) *Post-Fordism: A Reader* (Oxford: Blackwell) pp. 251–79.

———— (1997) *L'Economia Integrale, Fordism, and Post-Fordism*, lecture prepared for Italian-Japanese Conference on Gramsci, Tokyo, 15–16 November 1997.

———— (2001) 'The State and the Contradictions of the Knowledge-Driven Economy', in J. R. Bryson, P. W. Daniels, N. D. Henry and J. Pollard (eds.) *Knowledge, Space, Economy* (London: Routledge) pp. 63–78.

Jessop, B. and N. L. Sum (2001) 'Pre-disciplinary and Post-disciplinary Perspectives', *New Political Economy*, Vol. 6, No. 1, pp. 89–101.

Johnson, C. (1997) 'To the North's jeers, Korea Fights to Survive the IMF' in *International Herald Tribune* Friday, 26 December 1997.

Jomo, K. S. (ed.) (1998) *Tigers in Trouble: Financial Governance, Liberalisation and Crises in East Asia* (London: Zed Books).

Jones, G. (1982) 'The Language of Chartism', in J. Epstien and D. Thompson, *The Chartist Experience: Studies in Working-Class Radicalism and Culture, 1830–60* (London: Macmillan).

Jones, L. P. and I. Sakong (1980) *Government, Business, and Entrepreneurship in Economic Development: The Korean Case* (Cambridge, MA: Harvard University Press).

Jose, A. V. (ed.) (2002) *Organized Labour in the Twenty-First Century* (Geneva: International Institute for Labour Studies).

Jwa, S. H. and J. I. Kim (1999) 'Korea's Economic Reform: Political Economy and Future Strategy', in C. I. Moon and J. R. Mo *Democratization and Globalization* (Seoul: Yonsei University Press), pp. 247–72.

Kang, C. (2000) '*Segyehwa* Reform of the South Korean Developmental State', in S. Kim, (ed.) *Korea's Globalization* (Cambridge: Cambridge University Press), pp. 78–101.

Kang, D. C. (2002) *Crony Capitalism: Corruption and Development in South Korea and the Philippines* (Cambridge: Cambridge University Press).

Kang, M. (1993) *One people newspaper*, 10-06-93, in K. Wells (ed.) (1995) *Korea's Minjung Movement* (Honolulu: University of Hawaii).

Kang, S-H. (2000) 'Human Resources Development in the Knowledge-Based Economy: Republic of Korea' in *Capitalizing on Knowledge Workers: report on the Asian Productivity Organization (APO) Symposium on Managing Knowledge Workers* held in Tehran, Islamic Republic of Iran from 2–5 October 2000 (APO).

Katz, H., W. Lee and J. Lee (eds.) (2001) 'The Changing Nature of Labour-Management Interactions and Tripartism: Is Co-ordinated Decentralisation the Answer?' (Seoul: Korea Labour Institute).

Katzenstein, P. (1978) *Between Power and Plenty: Foreign Economic Policies of Advanced Industrial States* (Wisconsin: University of Wisconsin Press).

Kavanagh, D. and P. Morris (1989) *Consensus Politics: from Attlee to Thatcher* (Oxford: Blackwell).

——————— (1990) *Thatcherism and British Politics: the End of Consensus?* (Oxford: Oxford University Press).

Keane, J. (ed.) (1988) *Civil Society and the State: New European Perspectives* (London, Verso).

Kelly, D. (2002) *Japan and the Reconstruction of East Asia* (Basingstoke: Palgrave Macmillan).

Kennedy, P. (1989) *The Rise and Fall of the Great Powers* (Fontana Press).

Keohane, R. (1981) 'The Theory of Hegemonic Stability and Changes in the International Economic Regimes, 1967-77', in O. Holsti, R. Siverson and A. George (eds.), *Change in the International System* (Boulder, Colorado: Westview Press).

———————— (1986) 'Realism, Neorealism, and the Study of World Politics' in R. Keohane (ed.) *Neorealism and its Critics* (New York: Columbia University Press), pp. 1–26.

Keohane, R. and J. Nye (1989) *Power and Interdependence* (New York: Harper Collins).

Keohone, R. and H. Milner (eds.) (1996) *Internationalization and Domestic Politics* (Cambridge: Cambridge University Press).

Keyman, E. F. (1997) *Globalization, State, Identity/Difference: Toward a Critical Social Theory of International Relations* (Atlantic Highlands, NJ: Humanities Press).

Kim, B. K. (2003) 'The Politics of *Chaebol* Reform, 1980-1997', in S. Haggard, W. Lim and E. Kim (eds.) *Economic Crisis and Corporate Restructuring in Korea* (Cambridge: Cambridge University Press), pp. 53–78.

Kim, C. H. (tslt. D. McCann) (1980) *The Middle Hour: Selected Poems of Kim Chi Ha* (New York: Human Rights Publishing Group).

Kim, D. J. (1985) *Mass Participatory Democracy: A Democratic Alternative for Korea* (Maryland: University Press of America).

———————— (tslt by the Blue House) (1997) 'Address to the Nation', December 19 1997, Article 6 #2, in C.-H. Sohn and J. Yang (eds.) *Korea's Economic Reform Measures under the IMF Program: Government Measures in the Critical First Six Months of the Korean Economic Crisis* (Seoul: Korea Institute for International Economic Policy) pp. 203–10.

———————— (1998) 'Facing the nation,' *Business Korea*, Seoul, June 1998.

———————— (1999) *DJnomics: A New Foundation for the Korean Economy* (Seoul: Korean Development Institute for the Ministry of Finance and Economy).

Kim, E. Y. (1996) 'Cultural Awareness', *Understanding Koreans* (Greenwood Publishing Group).

Kim, H. A. (1993) '*Minjung* socio-economic responses to state-led industrialisation', in K. Wells (ed.), *South Korea's Minjung Movement: the culture and politics of dissidence* (Hawaii: University of Hawaii Press), pp. 39–60.

Kim, M. H. (1999) 'Employers and workers are partners: new labour culture seeks co-prosperity through coexistence (Ministry of Labour)', *The Korea Herald* Wednesday, 24 November 1999, p. 18.

Kim, S. H. (1997) 'State and Civil Society in South Korea's Democratic Consolidation: Is the Battle Really Over?', *Asian Survey*, Vol. XXXVII, No. 12 (December), pp. 1135–44.

Kim, S. S. (2003) 'Korea's Democratisation in the Global-Local Nexus', in S. S. Kim (ed.) *Korea's Democratisation* (Cambridge: Cambridge University Press).

Kim, S. S. and D. Briscoe (1997) 'Globalization and a new human resource policy in Korea: Transformation to a performance-based HRM', *Employee Relations*, Vol. 19, No. 4, pp. 298–308.

Kim, Y. C. and C. I. Moon (2000) 'Globalization and Workers in South Korea', in S. Kim, (ed.), *Korea's Globalization* (Cambridge: Cambridge University Press), pp. 54–75.

Kim, Y. H. (1978) 'The Formation Process of the Modern Wage Labour', in Y. H. Kim, (ed.) *Structure of Korean Labour Problems* (Seoul: Kwangminsa).

Kindleberger, C. (1970) *Power and Money: The Economics of International Politics and the Politics of International Economics* (London: Macmillan).

———— (1973) *The World in Depression, 1929–39* (Berkeley: University of California Press).

King, G., R. O. Keohane and S. Verba (1994) *Designing Social Inquiry: Scientific Inference in Qualitative Research* (New Jersey and Sussex: Princeton University Press).

Kirk, D. (2001) *Korean Crisis: Unravelling of the Miracle in the IMF Era* (Basingstoke: Palgrave Macmillan).

Kondratieff, N. (1984) (tslt. G. Daniels) *The Long Wave Cycle* (New York: Richardson & Snyder).

Koo, H. (1987) 'The Strong State and Weak Labor Relations in South Korea', in Kyong-dong Kim (ed.) *Dependency Issues in Korean Development*, (Seoul National University Press), pp. 305–25.

———— (1993) 'The State, *Minjung* and the Working Class in South Korea', in H. Koo (ed.) *State and Society in Contemporary Korea* (Ithaca: Cornell University Press), pp. 130–62.

———— (2000) 'The Dilemmas of Empowered Labour in Korea: Korean Workers in the Face of Global Capitalism', *Asian Survey*, Vol. 40, No. 2, pp. 227–50.

———— (2001) *Korean Workers: The Culture and Politics of Class Formation* (Ithaca: Cornell University Press).

———— (2002) 'Engendering Civil Society: the Role of the Labor Movement', in C. Armstrong, *Korean Society: Civil Society, Democracy and the State* (London: Routledge), pp. 109–32.

Korea Corporate Finance (2000) 'Structural reforms on foreign investments' (London: Korea Corporate Finance).

Korea Employers Federation (1982) *Yearbook of Labour Economics* (Seoul: Korea Employers' Federation).

Korea Labour Institute (KLI) (1999) 'The Tripartite Commission: Surmounting confrontation and conflict is opening up a new labor-management culture', *Korea Labour Institute*, Seoul, South Korea.

———————— (2003) 'Learning for Work in the Knowledge Society' project for ILO *Revision of the Human Resources Development Recommendations: Infocus Programme on Skills, Knowledge and Employment*, Online, Available at: http://www.logos-net.net/ilo/150_base/en/report/rep_toc.htm

Korean Confederation of Trade Unions (KCTU) (July 15, 1998) 'KCTU Action Alert: Korean Workers Rise to Challenge the IMF Restructuring Program', Online, Available at: http://www.kctu.org/

Korean Confederation of Trade Unions (KCTU) (1998) 'KCTU Action Alert: Korean Workers Rise to Challenge Korea the IMF Restructuring Program' (Seoul: KCTU), Online, Available at: http://www.kctu.org/

Korean Embassy website (1999) (Ottowa, Canada), Online, Available at: http://www.emb-korea.ottawa.on.ca/right/news/news/Dec0299.htm

Korean International Labour Foundation (KOILAF) (1997) 'KCTU's walk out threatens labour-government-management relations', KOILAF local news, Vol.199902 No.99, Online, Available at: http://www.koilaf.org/cgi-local/news1.cgi?id=1364

———————— (1999a) 'Changes in the Employment Structure: Recent Developments, Current Labour Situation in Korea', (Seoul: KOILAF), Online, Available at: http://www.koilaf.org/publication/link16.htm#4

———————— (1999b) '1999 Guidelines for Collective Bargaining: Labor, Management and the Government' (Seoul: KOILAF).

———————— (1999c) *Labour Relations in Korea* (Seoul: KOILAF).

———————— (2000) *Unemployment Measures: From Desperation to Reconstruction* (Seoul: KOILAF).

———————— (2000b) 'Employment Stabilisation Policy Measures: Summary of Corporate Restructuring and Employment Stabilisation Policy Released in November 2000 by the Ministry of Labour' (Seoul: KOILAF).

———————— (2001a) 'Seminar for Foreign Investors: Stabilisation of Industrial Relations and Unemployment Measures' (Seoul: KOILAF).

———————— (2001b), 'For a Better Understanding of Restructuring' (translation of Korean-language manual originally published by Ministry of Labour) (Seoul: KOILAF).

————— 'KCTU's walk out threatens labor-government-management relations', Online, Available at: http://www.koilaf.org/cgi-local/news1.cgi?id=1364

————— (2002) '2002 Collective Guidelines for Collective Bargaining: Labour, Management and the Government' (Seoul: KOILAF). Korea Research Institute for Vocational Education and Training (KRIVET) website, Online, Available at: http://www.krivet.re.kr/cgi-bin/rabout.cgi and http://www.krivet.re.kr/krinet/runct/run5000fr.htm

————— (1999) 'Korea's Centennial History of Vocational Education and Training' (Seoul: KRIVET).

————— (2000a) 'Technical and Vocational Education and Training in Korea' (Seoul: KRIVET).

————— (2000b) 'Participation Factor of Training Programmes' (Seoul: KRIVET).

————— (2000c) 'Educational and Training Program Situation In Korea' (Seoul: KRIVET) (in Korean).

KRIVET/NCVER (2000) 'Linkages between Vocational Education and Training Providers and Industry' (Seoul: KRIVET; Australian National Centre for Vocational Education Research Ltd [NCVER]).

————— (2001) 'Adult Retraining and Reskilling in Korea and Australia' (Seoul: KRIVET; Australian National Centre for Vocational Education Research Ltd [NCVER]).

Krasner, S. (1983a) 'Structural Causes and Regime Consequences: Regimes as Intervening Variables', *International Regimes*, S. Krasner (ed.) (Ithaca: Cornell University Press), pp. 1–21.

————— (1983b) 'Regimes and the Limits of Realism: Regimes as Autonomous Variables', *International Regimes*, S. Krasner (ed.) (Ithaca: Cornell University Press), pp. 355–68.

Kuhn, T. (1996) *The Structure of Scientific Revolutions* (Chicago: University of Chicago Press).

Kwon, S. H. and M. O'Donnell (2001) *The Chaebol and Labour in Korea: The Development of Management Strategy in Hyundai* (London: Routledge).

Labournet (2001) *Korea Confederation of Trade Unions Calls General Strike, Reports by KCTU and Korean Federation of Chemical Textile Workers Unions (KFCW)*, Online, Available: 02/07/01 http://www.labournet.net/world/0107/korea1.html

Landy, M. (1991) 'Socialist Education Today: Pessimism or Optimism of the Intellect?' *Rethinking Marxism* 4 (Fall): pp. 9–23.

Lane, T. D. (ed.) (1999) *IMF-Supported Programs in Indonesia, Korea and Thailand: A Preliminary Assessment* (IMF).

Lang, T. and C. Hines (1993) *The New Protectionism: Protecting The Future Against Free Trade* (London: Earthscan Publications Ltd).

Langguth, G. (1996) 'Dawn of the 'Pacific Century?'', *German Foreign Affairs Review*, Vol. 47, No. 4.

LaPalombara, J. and S. Blank (1976) *Multinational Corporations and National Elites: A Study in Tensions* (New York: The Conference Board).

Larrain, J. (1996) 'Stuart Hall and the Marxist Concept of Ideology', in S. Hall, D. Morley and K-H Chen (eds.) *Stuart Hall: Critical Dialogues in Cultural Studies* (London: Routledge), pp. 47–70.

Laver, M. (1997) *Private Desires and Political Action* (London: Sage).

Leadbeater, C. (1998) 'Who will own the knowledge economy?' *Political Quarterly*, 69 (4) (October–December 1998) pp. 375–85.

——————— (1999) 'It's not just the economy, stupid', *New Statesman*, 27 September, pp. iv–vi.

Ledemel, I. and E. Dahl (2001) 'Public Works Programs in Korea: A Comparison to Active Labour Market Policies and Workfare in Europe and the USA', in F. Park, Y-B Park, G. Betcherman and A. Dar (eds.) *Labour Market Reforms in Korea: Policy Options for the Future* (Seoul: World Bank and Korea Labour Institute), pp. 196–214.

Lee, B. H. (1999) 'Social Dialogue and Unions' Involvement in Korea' (Seoul: Korea Labor Institute).

Lee, C. S. and M. Vatikiotis (1998) 'Open Sesame', *Far Eastern Economic Review*, Hong Kong, 24 December, Vol. 161, No. 52.

Lee, H. K. (1996) 'Democratisation of the Korean economy and Implementation of Nord-Politik', *The Korean Economy: Perspectives for the Twenty-First Century State* (New York: University of New York).

Lee, K. (2001) 'New direction of Korea's vocational education and training policy', paper presented at International Conference on TVET, Adelaide, Australia, 2001.

Lee, S. H. (1993) 'Activation Of Civil Society In South Korea', *Pacific Affairs*, Vol. 66, No. 3, pp. 351–67.

Lee, S. R. (Labour Minister) (1999) quoted in Kim, M.-H., 'Employers And Workers Are Partners: New Labour Culture Seeks Co-Prosperity Through Coexistence', *Korea Herald*, Wednesday, 24 November, p. 18.

Lee, W. D. and B. H. Lee (1999) *Labour Relations in Korea, Korea International Labour Foundation*, Seoul (KOILAF).

Leftwich, A. (2000) *States of Development: On the Primacy of Politics in Development* (Cambridge: Polity Press).

Lew, S. C. (1998) 'The Structure of Domination and Capital Accumulation in Modern Korea,' paper presented at the 4th PACKS meeting, University of British Columbia, Vancouver, Canada, 10–16 May.

————— (1999) 'An Institutionalist Reinterpretation of 'Confucian Capitalism' in East Asia', *Korea Social Science Journal* Vol. 26, No. 2, pp. 1–16.

Lewis, W. A. (1984) *The Rate of Growth of the World Economy* (Taipei: The Institute of Economics, Academia Sinica).

Lim, W., S. Haggard and E. Kim (2003) 'The Political Economy of Restructuring', in Haggard, W. Lim and E. Kim (eds.) *Economic Crisis and Corporate Restructuring in Korea* (Cambridge: Cambridge University Press) pp. 1–34.

Lincoln, M. G. (2001) *Global Trends and Work Patterns*, unpublished paper given at the First International Global Studies Association Conference, 2–3 July 2001.

Lindauer, D., J. G. Kim, J. W. Lee and E. Vogel (1997) *The Strains of Economic Growth: Labour Unrest and Social Dissatisfaction in Korea*, (Cambridge, MA: Harvard University Press).

Linklater, A. (1990) *Beyond Marxism and Realism: Critical Theory and International Relations* (London: Macmillan).

————— (1998) *The Transformation Of Political Community: Ethical Foundations Of The Post-Westphalian Era* (Cambridge: Polity Press).

Lipschutz, R. (1992) 'Reconstructing World Politics: The Emergence of a Global Civil Society', *Millennium* 21, pp. 391–420.

Littler, C. and G. Salaman (1984) *Class at Work: The Design, Allocation and Control of Jobs* (London: Batsford).

Locke, J. (introduction by Russell Kirk) (1690/1955), *Of Civil Government Second Treatise* (Chicago: Henry Regnery).

Luxemburg, R. (1919) 'The General Strike, the party and the Unions', *Avanti!*, Milan. From A. Gramsci, 'State and Civil Society', *Selections from Prison Notebooks*, pp. 233.

Lynch, C. (1998) 'Social movements and the problem of globalization', *Alternatives*, 23, pp. 148–73.

McEachern (1990) *Expanding State: Class and Economy in Europe Since 1945* (Basingstoke: Palgrave Macmillan).

McNamara, Dennis (2002) *Market and Society in Korea: Interest, Institution and the Textile Industry* (London: Routledge Advances in Korean Studies).

McRobbie, A. (1982) 'The Politics of Feminist Research: Between Talk, Text and Action' *Feminist Review* 12: pp. 46–57.

Macpherson, C. B. (1964) *The Political Theory of Possessive Individualism* (Oxford: Oxford University Press).

———— (1973) *Democratic Theory* (Oxford: Oxford University Press).

Magariños, C. A. (Director-General of the United Nations Industrial Development Organization) (2001) 'Managing UN Reform: UNIDO's Need-Driven Approach', Presentation at the Royal Institute for International Affairs, Chatham House, London, speech presented 21 September.

Mandel, E. (1975) *Late Capitalism* (London: NLB).

Manning, C. A. W. (1962) *The Nature of International Society* (London: Macmillan).

Mardin, S. (1989) *Religion and Social Change in Turkey: The Case of Bediuzzaman Said Nursi Suny Series in Near Eastern Studies* (Albany: State University of New York Press).

Marshall, A. (1890) *Principles of Economics* (London: Macmillan).

Marsh, D. and G. Stoker (2001) *Theory and Methods in Political Science* (New York: Palgrave).

Magariños, C. A. (2001) Director-General of the United Nations Industrial Development Organisation Managing UN Reform: UNIDO's Need-Driven Approach, Presentation at the Royal Institute for International Affairs, Chatham House, London, speech presented 21 September 2001).

Mandel, E. (1975) *Late Capitalism* (London: NLB).

Manning, C. A. W. (1962) *The Nature of International Society* (London: Macmillan).

Mardin, S. (1989) *Religion and Social Change in Turkey: The Case of Bediuzzaman Said Nursi Suny Series in Near Eastern Studies* (Albany: State University of New York Press).

Marshall, A. (1890) *Principles of Economics* (London: Macmillan).

Marsh, D. and G. Stoker (2001) *Theory and Methods in Political Science* (New York: Palgrave).

Martinez, E. and A. Garcia (1996) 'What is Neo-liberalism? A Brief Definition for Activists', paper presented at Intercontinental Encounter for Humanity and against Neoliberalism (27 July–3 August 1996) in La Realidad, Chiapas.

Marx, K. (1887/1999) *Capital* (A New Abridgement) (Oxford and New York: Oxford University Press).

—————— (1869) 'The Eighteenth Brumaire of Louis Bonaparte', reprinted in K. Marx (1973), 2nd edition, D. Fernbach (ed.) *Surveys from Exile* (London: Harmondsworth, Penguin).

Maseide, P. (1990) 'The Social Construction of Research Information' *Acta Sociologica* Vol. 33 No. 1, pp. 3–13.

Mason, E. S. (1990) *The Economic and Social Modernization of the Republic of Korea* (Cambridge, Massachusetts: Harvard University Press).

Melucci, A. (1989) *Nomads of the present: social movements and individual needs in contemporary society* (Philadelphia: Temple University Press).

Merriam, S. (1998) *Qualitative Research and Case study Application in Education* (San Francisco: Jossey-Bass).

Mestrovic, S. G., G. Stjepan and C. Mestrovi (1998) *Anthony Giddens, the Last Modernist* (London: Routledge).

Michalet, C. A. (1982) 'From International Trade to World Economy: A New Paradigm,' in H. Makler et al., *The New International Economy* (London: Sage), pp. 37–58.

Mies, M. (1983) 'Towards a Methodology for Feminist Research', in G. Bowles and R. D. Klein (eds.) *Theories of Women's Studies* (London: Routledge).

The Militant (1997) 'S. Korea General Strike Answers Antilabor Laws', Vol. 61, No. 2, 13 January.

Ministry of Finance and Economics (MOFE) (1999) *Breaking New Ground: Korea's Economic Transformation* (Seoul: MOFE).

Ministry of Labour South Korea (MOL) (1999) 'Labour Sector Reforms Gaining Speed: Ministry of Labour decides to operate The 2nd Term Labour Reform Task Force', International Co-operation Division, Online, Available at: http://www.molab.go.kr/English/English.html

Mitchell, T. (1988) *Colonising Egypt* (Cambridge: Cambridge University Press).

Mittelman, J. (1996) *Globalisation: Critical Reflections* (Boulder, CO: Lynn Reinner).

—————— (1998) 'Coxian Historicism as an Alternative Perspective in International Studies,' *Alternatives* 23, pp. 63–92.

Mo, J. (1999) 'Democratization, Labour Policy, and Economic Performance', in J. Mo and C. I. Moon (eds.) *Democracy and the Korean Economy* (California: Hoover Institution Press), pp. 97–134.

Mo, J. and C. I. Moon (2003) 'Business-Government Relations under Kim Dae-Jung', in S. Haggard, W. Lim and E. Kim (eds.) *Economic Crisis and Corporate Restructuring in Korea* (Cambridge: Cambridge University Press), pp. 127–49.

Modelski, G. (1978) 'The Long Cycle of Global Politics and the State', *Comparative Studies in Society and History* 20, pp. 214–38.

Moo, K. B. (Chairman, National Labor Relations Commission) 'Labor Dispute Resolution in Korea, with Special Reference to the Problems of Foreign Investors.' Seminar for Foreign Investors: 'The Governments Policy on Core Labor Issues (including stabilization of labor-management relations)', Online, Available at: http://www.koilaf.org/publication/link15.htm

Moon, C. I. (1999) 'Democratization And Globalization As Ideological And Political Foundations Of Economic Policy', in J. R. Mo and C. I. Moon (eds.) *Democracy And The Korean Economy* (California: Hoover Institution Press) pp. 1–34.

Moon, C. I and J. Nishino (2002) 'From Between Learning and Policy Innovation: Japanese Economic Institutions and South Korea's Economic Policy since the 1960s', paper presented at ISA New Orleans 2002.

Moore, P. (2006) 'Selfwoven Safetynets: the Crisis of Employability for Knowledge Capitalism', *Global Society*, Vol. 20, No. 4.

———————— (2005) 'Revolutions from Above: Worker Training as *Trasformismo* in South Korea', *Capital and Class*, No. 86, pp. 39–72.

Moore, P. and J. Kim (2005) '*Minjung* Filmmakers and the South Korean State: Power Struggles and Hegemony during Democratisation', Institute for Asia Pacific Studies (IAPS), University of Nottingham, Online, Available at: http://www.nottingham.ac.uk/iaps/new_onlinepapers_main.htm

Morikawa, H. (1992) Zaibatsu: The Rise and Fall of Family Enterprise Groups in Japan (Tokyo: University of Tokyo Press).

Morgenthau, H. (1948) *Politics Among Nations: The Struggle for Power and Peace* (New York: Knopf).

Morton, A. D. (1999) '*On Gramsci*', *Politics*, Vol. 19 (1), pp. 1–8.

———————— (2000) 'Mexico, Neoliberal Restructuring and the EZLN: A Neo-Gramscian Analysis', in B. Gills (2000) *Globalization and the Politics of Resistance* (Basingstoke: Macmillan), pp. 255–79.

———————— (2001) 'The Sociology of Theorising and Neo-Gramscian Perspectives: The Problems of 'School' formation in IPE', in A. Bieler and A. D. Morton (eds.) *Social Forces in the Making of New Europe: The Restructuring of European Social Relations in the Global Political Economy* (Basingstoke: Palgrave), pp. 25–43.

——————— (2003) 'Structural Change and Neoliberalism in Mexico: 'Passive Revolution' in the Global Political Economy' *Third World Quarterly* Vol. 24, No. 4, pp. 631–53.

Munck, R. (2000) 'Labour in the Global', in R. Cohen and S. M. Rai (eds.), *Global Social Movements* (London and New Jersey: The Athlone Press), pp. 83–100.

Murphy, C. (1994) *International Organisation and Industrial Change: Global Governance since 1850* (Cambridge: Polity Press).

Naim, M. (1999) 'Fads and Fashion in Economic Reforms: Washington Consensus or Washington Confusion?' *Foreign Policy Magazine* (26 October 1999), Online, Available at: http://www.imf.org/external/pubs/ft/seminar/1999/reforms/Naim.htm#I

Neufeld, M. (1995) *The Restructuring of International Relations Theory* (Cambridge: Cambridge University Press).

Oakley, A. (1981) 'Interviewing Women: A Contradiction in Terms?', in H. Roberts (ed.) *Doing Feminist Research*. (London: Routledge).

——————— (1998) 'Gender, Methodology and People's Ways of Knowing: Some Problems with Feminism and the Paradigm Debate in Social Science', *Sociology* 32(4), pp. 707–32.

——————— (1999) 'People's Ways of Knowing: Gender and Methodology', in S. Hood, B. Mayall and S. Oliver (eds.) *Critical Issues in Social Research: Power and Prejudice* (Buckingham: Open University).

O'Brien, R. (2000) 'Labour and IPE: Rediscovering Human Agency', in R. Palan (ed.) *Global Political Economy: Contemporary Theories* (London: Routledge) pp. 89–99.

——————— (2000) 'Workers and World Order: the Tentative Transformation of the International Union Movement', *Review of International Studies* Vol. 26, No. 4, pp. 533–55.

O'Connor, J. (1983) 'Historical Materialism Reconsidered: Forces of Social Production or Social Forces of Production?', paper delivered at the Gramsci Institute's Conference commemorating 100th year of Marx's death, Rome, Italy, November 16, 1983 (unpublished), Online, Available at: http://www.msu.edu/~rudya?Soc816?OC-Cooperation.htm

Ogle, G. E. (1990) South *Korea: Dissent Within the Economic Miracle* (Atlantic Highlands, NJ: Zed Books).

——————— (2000) 'Pushing Ahead with Reform in Korea: Labour Market and Social Safety-net Procedures' (Paris: OECD).

Ohmae, K. (1990) *The Borderless World: Power and Strategy in the Interlinked Economy* (London: Collins).

Okazaki, H. (1984) *The State and Intelligence: Searching for Japan's Foreign Policy* (Tokyo: Bungei Shunju).

Okonogi, M. (1988) 'South Korea's Experiment in Democracy', *Japan Review of International Affairs*, Spring/Summer, pp. 24–41.

O'Leary, D. and V. Dunleavy (1987) *Theories of the State: the Politics of Liberal Democracy* (London: Macmillan).

Organisation for Economic Co-operation and Development (OECD) (2000) *Knowledge Management in the Learning Society: Education and Skills* (Paris: OECD).

Overbeek, H. (1990) *Global Capitalism and National Decline* (London: Unwin Hyman).

——————— (1993) (ed.) *Restructuring Hegemony in the Global Political Economy* (London: Routledge).

Overbeek, H. and K. van der Pijl (1993) 'Restructuring Capital and Restructuring Hegemony: Neo-liberalism and the unmaking of the post-war order', in H. Overbeek (ed.) *Restructuring Hegemony in the Global Political Economy* (London: Routledge), pp. 1–25.

Pak, J. H. (1985) 'Examination of the characteristics of masses in terms of social class', *Study of social classes in Korea* (Seoul: Hanul).

Pannekoek, A. (1938) *Lenin als filossof* (Amsterdam: De Vlam).

Park, C. K. (ed.) (1980) *Essays on the Korean Economy: Macroeconomic and Industrial Development in Korea* (Hawaii: University of Hawaii Press).

Park, D. J., J. Park and G.-C. Yu (2001) 'Assessment of Labour Market Response to the Labour Law Changes Introduced in 1998', in F. Park, Y.-B. Park, G. Betcherman and A. Dar (eds.) *Labour Market Reforms in Korea: Policy Options for the Future* (Seoul: World Bank and Korea Labour Institute), pp. 125–50.

Park, F. K. and J. H. Lee (1999) 'The Social Impact of the Financial Crisis: Labor Market Outcomes and Policy Responses in Korea' (Seoul: Korea Labour Institute).

Parmar, I. (2002) '"To relate knowledge and action': The Impact of the Rockefeller Foundation on Foreign Policy Thinking during America's Rise to Globalism, 1939-1945', paper presented at International Studies Association (ISA) Convention, New Orleans, Louisiana, 2002.

Paton, C. (2000) *World, Class, Britain: Political Economy, Political Theory and British Politics* (Basingstoke: Palgrave Macmillan).

Peet, R. (1991) *Global Capitalism, Theories of Societal Development* (London: Routledge).

Plamenatz, J. (1970) *Ideology* (London: Pall Mall Press Ltd).

Policy and Information Centre for International Solidarity (PICIS) (2001) 'Daewoo collapses to Global Capital', Newsletter No. 81 (Seoul: PICIS), Online, Available at: http://www.nadir.org/nadir/initiativ/agp/free/imf/asia/korea/

————— (2002) 'Latest from Korea 5th November: Govt workers on strike!', statement from Korean Government Employees Union (KGEU), Online, Available at: http://www.nadir.org/nadir/initiativ/agp/free/imf/asia/korea/1105gvt_workers_strike.htm

Pollack, A. (1997) 'Seoul gets $55 billion in IMF aid: a humbled nation accepts Fund's largest-ever rescue plan', *International Herald Tribune New York Times Service* Sunday, 4 December 1997, pp. 7–8.

Power J. (1995) 'G-7 Should Give Keynes New Look' (San Francisco Chronicle, 19 June), Online, Available at: http://www.lightparty.com/Economic/G7.html

Purnell, R. (1973) *The Society of States: An Introduction to International Politics* (London: Weidenfeld and Nicolson).

Pursiainen, C. (2000) 'Trends and Structures in Russian state-society relations', *Politics of Civil Society: A Global Perspective on Democratisation, Network Institute for Global Democratisation,* NIGD Working Paper 2, pp. 19–27.

Putnam, R. D. (ed.) (2002) *Democracies in Flux: The Evolution of Social Capital in Contemporary Society* (USA: Oxford University Press Inc.).

Republic of Korea (ROK) (2001) 'Human Resources Development Strategies for Korea: Human Resources Knowledge New Take-off' (Seoul: Republic of Korea).

Rhee, J.-C. (1994) *The State and Industry in South Korea: the limits of the authoritarian state* (London: Routledge).

Ribbens, J. (1989) 'Interviewing: An Unnatural Situation?' *Women's Studies International Forum* Vol. 12, pp. 579–92.

Ricardo, D. (1951) 'On the principles of political economy and taxation', vol. 1, in P. Sraffa (ed.) *The Works and Correspondence of David Ricardo* (Cambridge: Cambridge University Press).

Richards, D. (1996) 'Elite Interviewing Approaches and Pitfalls', *Politics* Vol. 16, No. 3, pp. 199–204.

Ritzer, G. (1992) *Contemporary Sociological Theory,* 3rd Ed. (New York: McGraw-Hill, Inc.).

Robinson, W. and J. Harris (2000) 'Toward a Global Ruling Class?: Globalization and the Transnational Capitalist Class,' *Science and Society,* Vol. 64, No. 1, pp. 11–54.

Rose, R. (1992) 'Towards a Civil Economy', *Studies in Public Policy*, No. 200, (Glasgow: University of Strathclyde Centre for the Study of Public Policy).

Rosenberg, J. (1994) *The Empire of Civil Society. A Critique of the Realist Theory of International Relations* (London: Verso).

Rousseau, J. (tslt. M. Cranston) (1762/1987) *The Social Contract* (USA: Penguin).

———————— (1992) *Discourse on the Origin of Inequality* (Indianapolis: Hackett).

Rowley, C. and J. S. Bae (2002) 'Globalization and Transformation of human resource management in South Korea', *International Journal of Human Resource Management*, Vol. 13, No. 1, pp. 522–49.

———————— (eds.) (1998) *Korean Businesses: Internal and External Industrialization* (Frank Cass Studies in Asia Pacific Business).

Ruggie, J. (1982) 'International Regimes, Transactions and Change: embedded liberalism in the post-war economic order', *International Organisation*, Vol. 36, No. 2, pp. 379–415.

Rupert, M. (forthcoming) *Fordism*, in S. Burwood (ed.) *The Cold War: An Encyclopedia* (New York: Garland Publishers).

———————— (1995) *Producing hegemony: the politics of mass production and American global power* (Cambridge: Cambridge University Press).

———————— (2000) *Ideologies of Globalization: Contending Visions of a New World Order* (London: Routledge).

Rupert, M. and H. Smith (eds.) (2002) *Historical Materialism and Globalization* (London: Routledge).

Rutherford, M. (1994) *Institutions in Economics: The Old and the New Institutionalism* (Cambridge: Cambridge University Press).

Sakamoto, Y. (1997) 'Civil society and democratic world order', in S. Gill and J. Mittelman, *Innovation and Transformation in International Studies* (Cambridge: Cambridge University Press), pp. 203–19.

Salamini, L. (1981) *The sociology of political praxis: an introduction to Gramsci's theory* (London: Routledge & Kegan Paul).

Sanders, D. (2002) 'Behaviouralism', in D. Marsh and G. Stoker (eds.) *Theory and Methods in Political Science Second Edition* (New York: Palgrave Macmillan).

Say, J. B. (1953) 'Cours Complet', in *J. B. Say Textes choisis* (Paris: Dolloz).

Schechter, M. (2002) 'Critiques of Coxian theory: background to a conversation', in R. W. Cox and M. Schechter, *The Political Economy of a Plural World: Critical Reflections on Power, Morals, And Civilisation* (London: Routledge), pp. 1–25.

Schiller, D. (1988) 'How to Think about Information', in V. Mosco and J. Wasko (eds.) *The Political Economy of Information* (Madison: University of Wisconsin Press), pp. 27–44.

Schultz, T. (1971) 'Investment in Human Capital', in R. Wykstra (ed.), *Education and the Economics of Human Capital* (USA: Free Press), pp. 23–41.

Schwartz, H. (2000) *States versus Markets: The Emergence of a Global Economy* (London: St Martin's Press).

——————(1992) 'Hegemony, International Debt and International Economic Instability', in C. Polychroniu, (ed.), *Current Perspectives and Issues in International Political Economy* (New York: Praeger).

Scott, J. (ed.) (1990) *The Sociology of the Elites* (Aldershot: Edward Elgar) (3 volumes).

Shambaugh, D. (1993) *Beautiful Imperialist: China Perceives America 1972–1990* (Princeton: Princeton University Press).

Shaw, M. (1994) *Global society and international relations: sociological concepts and political perspectives* (Cambridge: Polity).

—————— (1999) 'Civil society', in L. Kurtz (ed.) *Encyclopaedia of Violence, Peace and Conflict* (San Diego: Academic Press) pp. 269–78.

Shin, D. C. (2000) 'The Evolution of Popular Support for Democracy During Kim Young Sam's Government', in L. Diamond and D. C. Shin (eds.) *Institutional Reform and Democratic Consolidation in Korea* (Stanford, California: Hoover Institution Press) pp. 233–56.

Showstack-Sassoon, A. (1982) *Approaches to Gramsci* (London: Writers and Readers).

—————— (1987) *Gramsci's Politics, Second Edition* (Minnesota: Minnesota University Press).

Shubik, M. (1975) *Games for Society, Business and War: Towards a Theory of Gaming* (Oxford: Elsevier).

Silverman, D. (2001) *Interpreting Qualitative Data: Methods for Analysing Talk, Text, and Interaction 2nd Edition* (London: Sage).

Simon, R. (1982) *Gramsci's Political Thought: An Introduction* (London: Lawrence and Wishart Ltd).

Sinclair, T. (1996) 'Beyond international relations theory: Robert W. Cox and approaches to world order', in R. Cox *Approaches to World Order* (Cambridge: Cambridge University Press) pp. 3–18.

Sklair, L. (1995) *Sociology of the global system* (London and Baltimore: Prentice-Hall and John Hopkins University Press).

──────── (1997) 'Social Movements for Global Capitalism: The Transnational Capitalist Class in Action', *Review of International Political Economy* Vol. 4, No. 3 Autumn, pp. 514–38.

──────── (2001a) *The Transnational Capitalist Class* (Oxford: Blackwell).

──────── (2001b) 'The Transnational Capitalist Class and the Discourse of Globalization' (Global Dimensions, LSE Centre for the Study of Global Governance), Online, Available at: http://www.globaldimensions.net/articles/sklair/LSklair.html.

──────── (2002) 'Globalization and Management: The Role of the Transnational Capitalist Class', in M. Warner, P. Joynt (eds.) *Managing Across Cultures* (Thomson Learning), pp. 269–80.

Smith, A. (1776/1991) *The wealth of nations* (London: Everyman's Library).

Smith, S. (1996) 'Positivism and Beyond', in S. Smith, K. Booth and M. Zalewski (eds.) *International Theory: Positivism and Beyond* (Cambridge: Cambridge University Press), pp. 11–44.

──────── (1995) 'The Self-Images of a Discipline: A Genealogy of International Relations Theory', in K. Booth and S. Smith *International Relations Theory Today* (Cambridge: Polity Press).

Smith, S., K. Booth and M. Zalewski (eds.) (1996) *International Theory: Positivism and Beyond* (Cambridge: Cambridge University Press).

Snidal, D. (1985) 'The Limits of Hegemonic Stability Theory', *International Organisation* Vol. 39, No. 4.

So, A. Y. (1990) *Social Change and Development: Modernisation, Dependency and World Systems Theories* (USA: Sage).

Sohn, C.-H. and J. Yang (1998) 'Korea's Economic Reform Measures under the IMF Program: Government Measures in the Critical First Six Months of the Korean Economic Crisis', *Korea Institute for International Economic Policy (KIEP)* Paper 98-01 (Seoul: KIEP).

Song, H. K. (1999) 'Labour Unions in the Republic of Korea: Challenge and Choice', *Labour and Society Programme Discussion Paper* (Geneva: International Institute for Labour Studies).

Staniland, M. (1987) *What Is Political Economy: A Study of Social Theory and Under Development* (Yale: Yale University Press).

Sterling, R. (1974) *Macropolitics: international relations in a global society* (New York: Knopf).

Strange, S. (1987) *States and Markets* (London: Pinter).

Strom, S. (1998) 'Labour Cutbacks Pose Problem for South Korean Economic Recovery', *New York Times*, 24 February.

——————— (1998b) 'Pitfalls in Cutting Korea's Lifetime Work Force', *New York Times*, 24 February.

Sunkel, D. (1972) 'Big Business and *Dependencia*' *Foreign Affairs* Vol. 50 (April) pp. 517–31.

Taylor, I. (2005) 'Globalisation Studies and the Developing World: making international political economy truly global' *Third World Quarterly* Vol. 26, No. 7, pp. 1025–42.

Tester, K. (1992) *Civil Society* (London: Routledge).

Thomas, P. (1994) *Alien Politics: Marxist State Theory Revisited* (New York, London: Routledge).

Thompson, E. P. (1963) *The Making of the English Working Class* (New York: Vintage).

Thompson, S. (1992) *An Introduction to the World Systems Perspective* (Colorado and Oxford: Westview Press).

Tilly, C. (1995) 'Globalization threatens labour's rights', *International labour and Working Class History*, no. 47 (Spring) pp. 1–23.

Tooze, R. (1990) 'Understanding the Global Political Economy: Applying Gramsci', *Millenium: Journal of International Studies*, Vol. 19, No. 2, pp. 273–80.

——————— (1999) 'International Political Economy in an Age of Globalization', in J. Baylis and S. Smith (ed.), *The Globalization of World Politics: an Introduction to International Relations* (Oxford: Oxford University Press), pp. 212–320.

Touraine, A. (1981) *The Voice and Eye: An Analysis of Social Movements* (Cambridge: Cambridge University Press).

Trevelyan, G. M. (1935) *Garibaldi and the Thousand* (London: Nelson).

Tripartite Commission (1999) 'The Tripartite Commission: surmounting confrontation and conflict, is opening up a new labour-management culture' (Seoul: KOILAF).

——————— 'The Third Tripartite Commission will open a new labour- management culture based on participation and cooperation', Online, Available at: http://www.lmg.go.kr/html/english.htm

Uh, S. B. (1999) 'Employment: Structure, Trends and New Issues' Labour Relations in Korea (Seoul: KOILAF).

United Nations Development Programme (UNDP) (1993) 'UNDP and Organisations of Civil Society: Building Sustainable Partnerships', Online, Available at: http://www.undp.org/csopp/CSO/NewFiles/toolboxsource.htm#Anchor-1.-20386

—————— (2000) 'Social Safety Net for the Most Vulnerable Groups in the Republic of Korea' (Seoul: UNDP).

—————— (2002) *Global CSOPP Programme*, Online, Available at: http://www.undp.org/csopp/CSO/NewFiles/toolboxsource.htm# Anchor-1-20386

United Nations Conference on Trade and Development (UNCTAD) (1993) World Investment Report 1993 (New York: United Nations).

United Nations Education and Science Organisation International Project on Technical and Vocational Education (UNEVOC) (2001) 'Knowledge and Skills', Online, Available at: http://www.unescobkk.org/education/aceid/unevoc.htm

United States Information Service (1999) Transcript: Secretary of State Albright on Labor Diplomacy, Official Text, #124/99 September 21 1999, Online, Available at: http://www.usa.or.th/news/press/1999/nrot124.htm

Van Apeldoorn, B. (2002) *Transnational Capitalism and the Struggles over European Integration* (London: Routledge).

Vanberg, V. (1994) *Rules and choice in economics* (London: Routledge).

Van der Pijl, K. (1984) *The making of an Atlantic ruling class* (London: Verso).

—————— (1997) 'Transnational class formation and state forms', in S. Gill and J. H. Mittelman, *Innovation and Transformation in International Studies* (Cambridge University Press, UK), pp. 118–33.

—————— (1998) *Transnational Classes and International Relations* (USA and Canada: Routledge).

—————— (2001–2) 'Globalisation or Class Society in Transition?' *Science and Society* Vol. 65, No. 4, Winter 2001–2, pp. 492–500.

—————— (2002) 'Historical materialism and the Emancipation of Labour', in M. Rupert and H. Smith (eds.), *Historical Materialism and Globalization* (London: Routledge).

Vigneswaran, D. and J. Quirk, 'International Relations' first Great Debate: Context and Tradition' Australia National University Working Paper 2004/1, Online, Available http://rspas.anu.edu.au/ir/working%20 papers/04-1.pdf.

Vogel, E. (1991) *The Four Dragons: The Spread of Industrialisation in East Asia* (Cambridge: Harvard University Press).

Von Thunen, J. H. (1875) (tnslt. B. F. Hoselitz) *Der Isolierte Staart*, 3rd edition, Vol. 2, Pt 2 (Chicago: University of Chicago).

Wade, R. (1990) Governing the Market: Economic Theory and the Role of Government in East Asian Industrialization (Princeton: Princeton University Press).

Wallerstein, I. (1974) The *Modern World-system: Capitalist Agriculture and the Origins of the European World-economy in the sixteenth century* (New York: Academic Press).

——————— (1984) *Patterns of Development and the Modern World System*, in T. Hopkins, I. Wallerstein and Associates (eds.) *World System Analysis, Theory and Methodology* (Beverley Hills, CA: Sage) pp. 41–82.

——————— (1996) *Historical capitalism; with Capitalist civilisation* (London: Verso).

Waltz, K. (1959) *Man, the State, and War* (New York: Columbia University Press).

——————— (1979) *Theory of International Politics: A Critical Review* (Reading, Massachusetts: Addison and Wesley).

——————— (1986) 'Reflections on Theory of International Politics: A Response to My Critics', in R. Keohane (ed.) (1986) *Neorealism and its Critics* (New York: Columbia University Press), pp. 322–46.

Waters, M. (2001) *Globalization* (London: Routledge).

Watson, I. (2001) 'Politics, Resistance to Neoliberalism and the Ambiguities of Globalisation' *Global Society*, Vol. 15, No. 2, pp. 201–18.

Wellington, J. (1987) 'Skills for the Future? Vocational education and new technology', Maurice Holt (ed.), *Skills and Vocationalism: The Easy Answer* (Milton Keynes: Open University Press), pp. 21–42.

Wendt, A. (1999) *Social Theory of International Politics* (Cambridge: Cambridge University Press).

——————— (2001) 'What is International Relations For? Notes toward a Postcritical View', W. Jones (ed.) *Critical theory and world politics* (Colorado, USA; London, UK: Lynne Rienner Publishers, Inc.), pp. 205–24.

Wells, K. (ed.) (1995) *Korea's Minjung Movement* (Honolulu: University of Hawaii).

Whitworth, S. (1994) *Feminism and International Relations: Towards a Political Economy of Gender in Interstate and Non-Governmental Institutions* (New York: St. Martin's Press).

Williams, G. A. (1960) 'The Concept of "Egemonia" in the Thought of Antonio Gramsci', *Journal of the History of Ideas*, Vol. 21, No. 4, pp. 586–99.

——————— (1975) *Proletarian order: Antonio Gramsci, factory councils and the origins of Italian Communism, 1911–1921* (London: Pluto Press).

Williams, R. (1980) 'Base and Superstructure in Marxist Cultural Theory', in *Problems in materialism and culture: selected essays* (London: Verso).

Williamson, J. (2000) 'Did the Washington Consensus Fail?', speech delivered at the Center for Strategic & International Studies, Washington, DC, 6 November 2002.

——————— 'What Should the World Bank Think About the Washington Consensus?' *World Bank Research Observer* (Washington, DC: The International Bank for Reconstruction and Development) Vol. 15, No. 2, pp. 251–64.

——————— 'What Washington Means by Policy Reform', in J. Williamson, (ed.), *Latin American Adjustment: How Much Has Happened?* (Washington: Institute for International Economics).

Wilson, J. (1973) *Introduction to Social Movements* (New York: Basic Books).

Wilson, P. (1998) 'The Myth of the First Great Debate' *Review of International Studies* Vol. 24, No. 5.

Woods, M. (1998) 'Rethinking elites: networks, space and local politics' *Environment and Planning A* Vol. 30, pp. 2101–19.

World Bank (1993) *The East Asian Miracle: Economic Growth and Public Policy* (New York: Oxford University Press).

——————— (1995) *World Bank Development Report: Workers in an integrating world* (New York: Oxford University Press).

——————— (1998/9) *World Development Report* (New York: Oxford University Press).

——————— (2002) *A Preliminary Strategy to Develop a Knowledge Economy in European Union Accession Countries, prepared for the Knowledge Economy Forum* (Paris, 20–22 February 2002) organised in co-ordination with the European Commission (EC) and the Organisation for Economic Co-operation and Development (OECD).

World Bank and OECD (2000) 'Korea and the Knowledge-Based Economy: Making the Transition' (World Bank and OECD).

Worth, O. (2004) *Hegemony, International Political Economy, and Post-Communist Russia* (Aldershot: Ashgate).

Wyn Jones, R. (ed.) (2001) *Critical theory and world politics* (Colorado, USA; London, UK: Lynne Rienner Publishers, Inc.).

Yoon, J. (1997) 'South Korean workers seen backing down pay claim' *Reuters's wire service*: March 1997.

Yusuf, S. and S. J. Evenett (2002) *Can East Asia Compete? Innovation for Global Markets* (World Bank).

Zang, X. and G. R. D. Underhill (2003) 'Private Capture, policy failures and financial crisis: Evidence and Lessons from South Korea and Thailand', in X. Zang and G. R. D. Underhill (eds.) *International Financial Governance under Stress: Global Structures versus National Imperatives* (Cambridge: Cambridge University Press), pp. 243–62.

INDEX

www.ingramcontent.com/pod-product-compliance
Lightning Source LLC
Chambersburg PA
CBHW050423280326
41932CB00013BA/1968